# Voice and Noise

Copyright © 2006 Per Kurowski
All rights reserved.
ISBN: 1-4196-2082-7

Library of Congress Control Number: 2006901828

To order additional copies, please contact us.
BookSurge, LLC
www.booksurge.com
1-866-308-6235
orders@booksurge.com

# Voice and Noise

Per Kurowski

2006

# CONTENTS

**Introduction** — xxiii
   **The World Bank Group? (WBG)** — xxvii
   **The Executive Directors? (EDs)** — xxix
   **The Nongovernmental Organizations? (NGOs)** — xxx
   **The Millennium Development Goals? (MDGs)** — xxxi
   **205 Development Topics!**
       —listed on the World Bank Web site. — xxxi

*My ED trips* — 1
   **Airport #1** — 1
   **Airport #2** — 1
   **The First Country** — 3
   **The Second Country** — 5
   **Airport #3** — 6
   **The Third Country** — 6
   **As far as you can go** — 8
   **The fourth country** — 10
   **A fifth country—while an ED but not as one.** — 14
   **Small memories from my Central America** — 15
   **The social contract of Teotihuacan** — 16
   **Small memories from my transitional hometown** — 17

*The Debt Sustainability Analysis* — 23
   **Why was it such an issue for me?** — 23
   **A word of caution about Financial Leverage** — 30
   **An Unsustainable Sustainability** — 31
   **Odious Debt** — 32
   **Odious Credit** — 34

*BASEL—Regulating for what?* — 37
   **Puritanism in banking** — 37

| | |
|---|---|
| A warning | 41 |
| About the Global Bank Insolvency Initiative | 43 |
| Some comments at a Risk Management Workshop for Regulators | 46 |
| Let the Bank Stand Up | 49 |
| BASEL and microfinance | 51 |
| The mutual admiration club of firefighters in Basel | 51 |
| Towards a counter cyclical Basel? | 52 |
| A new breed of systemic errors | 52 |
| *The debate about using Country Systems* | *55* |
| Why did I spend so much time on this issue? | 55 |
| Let them bike | 58 |
| About El Zamorano and the use of country systems | 59 |
| Lost in the water of globalization | 61 |
| *My very private fight for better privatizations* | *65* |
| Where do I come from? | 65 |
| Transmission and Distribution—T & D | 67 |
| Electricity for Brazil—and Isla de Margarita what? | 70 |
| Pay now and pray for the light | 72 |
| Hit in the head by the SENECA sale | 73 |
| The present value and short circuits | 76 |
| Reform fatigue opportunities | 78 |
| Fiscal Space—Public or Private | 79 |
| *About indexes and their disclosure* | *83* |
| The Riskiness of Country Risk | 84 |
| Disclosing the IDA Country-Performance Ratings | 85 |
| A first round of comments | 86 |
| About the Panel of Experts | 88 |
| Some follow up comments | 90 |
| US GAO Report | 93 |
| *A bit on some other indexes* | *95* |
| The through-the-eye-of-the-needle index | 95 |
| The index of perceived Corruption | 97 |
| Today, let us talk about the bribers | 100 |
| A dangerously failed index | 102 |
| How good or bad is your municipality? | 103 |

## *EIR & Environment* — 107
- My answer to the NGOs — 107
- The Amazon — 112
- Our quixotic windmills — 114
- Earth, the cooperative — 115
- A better alternative than a hybrid — 116

## *Oil* — 121
- About an Oil Market Update — 122
- It's an oil boom, stupid! — 123
- Kohlenweiss 1979 — 123
- The search for transparency in an oil-consuming world — 128
- We need the world price of gasoline (petrol) — 129
- Sovereignty — 130
- The Oil Referendum — 132
- Why do they point their finger only at us? — 133
- About accountability in energy planning — 133

## *Trade, agriculture, services, and growth* — 135
- On the road to Cancun...with new proposals — 135
- Place us next to something profitable... — 137
- Time to cover up? — 138
- An encore on nudism and WTO negotiations — 139
- Hosting the spirit of free trade — 140
- Time to scratch each other's backs — 142
- Of Mangos and Bananas — 143
- Local strawberries in season — 145

## *About remittances and immigration* — 147
- The nature of remittances — 147
- Remittance fees: The tip of the tip of the tip of the iceberg — 148
- What GDP? — 149
- Family Remittances — 150
- Some notes on the securitization of remittances — 151
- Safeguarding resources — 153
- Scaling up imagination about immigration — 155

| | |
|---|---|
| The Skin of the United States | 161 |
| A de-facto USA enlargement | 162 |
| *About cross-border services and emigration* | *165* |
| The prisoners, the old, and the sick | 165 |
| A wide spectrum of services for the elderly | 167 |
| The ethics of solving the shortage of caretakers | 168 |
| Are we truly a World Bank? | 169 |
| Get moving! | 171 |
| *Intermission…Out of the box tourism* | *173* |
| Lessons from Florence | 173 |
| A niche in crookedness? | 174 |
| Dead and Useful | 175 |
| Adventure tourism | 177 |
| Vanity tourism | 178 |
| Guaranteed boring | 179 |
| *On our own governance* | *181* |
| A real choir of voices | 181 |
| Voices, Board Effectiveness, and 60 Years | 181 |
| WB-IMF Collaboration on Public Expenditure issues | 182 |
| The Normal Distribution Function is missing | 183 |
| Board Effectiveness and the ticking clock | 184 |
| WBG's fight against corruption | 187 |
| The Annual Meetings Development Committee Communiqué | 189 |
| Hurrah for the Queen | 189 |
| Diversity | 190 |
| About the board and the staff | 191 |
| A very local World Bank or…the not in my backyard syndrome | 192 |
| *Budgets & Costs* | *193* |
| On the urgency and the inertia of our business | 193 |
| Medium Term Strategy and Finance Plan | 194 |
| Unbudgeted costs | 196 |
| Budget tools | 197 |

| | |
|---|---|
| The remuneration of our President | 198 |
| About our central travel agency | 200 |
| *Reshuffling our development portfolio* | *201* |
| Let us scale up the IFC | 201 |
| An encore on the BIG capital increase for IFC | 205 |
| The Multilateral Investment Guarantee Agency—MIGA | 205 |
| *On some varied homespun issues* | *209* |
| The Poverty Reduction Strategy | 209 |
| There should be life beyond 2015 | 210 |
| There should be new life beyond HIPC | 210 |
| We need to make more transparent our harmonization. | 211 |
| Transparently Understandable Debt Management | 211 |
| The Financial Sector Assessment Handbook—a postscript | 213 |
| Too sophisticated | 215 |
| About the addiction of guarantees to municipalities | 216 |
| About risks and the opportunities | 216 |
| Financial Outlook and Risks | 218 |
| *Some political incorrect Private-Sector Issues* | *219* |
| Is the private sector the same private sector everywhere? | 219 |
| Private vs. local investors | 221 |
| Some thoughts about financial good governance | 222 |
| What is lacking in the Sarbanes-Oxley Act. | 223 |
| Too well tuned? | 224 |
| Alternative Millennium Development Goals | 224 |
| *Communications* | *225* |
| Communications in a polarized world | 225 |
| Some other global communication issues | 232 |
| Red and blue, or, red or blue?—a postscript | 234 |
| *Some admittedly lite pieces* | *237* |
| The World Bank Special | 237 |
| Thou shall not PowerPoint | 238 |

| | |
|---|---|
| Deep pondering on labels | 238 |
| To write or not to write…by hand | 242 |
| Three bullets on punctuality | 244 |
| *On common goods and some global issues* | *247* |
| Towards World Laboratories | 247 |
| Daddy…the original or the copy? | 248 |
| The rights of intellectual property user | 250 |
| Who can enforce it better? | 252 |
| Moisés Naím's Illicit—a postscript | 253 |
| Global Tax | 254 |
| Labor standards and Unions | 257 |
| *A mixed bag of stand-alone issues* | *259* |
| My insecurities about the social security debate | 259 |
| About the SEC, the human factor, and laughing | 262 |
| Roping in the herd | 264 |
| A paradise of customs illegalities | 268 |
| Human genetics made inhuman | 270 |
| Justice needs to begin with just prisons | 272 |
| Real or virtual universities? | 274 |
| Brief thoughts on Europe | 276 |
| Some spins on the US economy | 278 |
| Is inflation really measuring inflation? | 281 |
| *My Venezuelan blend* | *283* |
| A Proposal for a New Way of Congressional Elections | 283 |
| Let's all whakapohane! | 285 |
| We enjoyed | 287 |
| Hugo, the Revolution, and I | 287 |
| April 11-13, 2002 | 289 |
| To the *opposition* | 291 |
| Synthesizing my current messages to my fellow countrymen | 293 |
| 167-to-0—a postscript | 295 |
| What is the financial world to do with Venezuela? | 295 |
| Massachusetts, please show some dignity! | 296 |
| Colombia & Venezuela | 297 |

| | |
|---|---|
| *My Farewell Speech on October 28, 2004* | *299* |
| *Did the Minister do right?* | *305* |
| *And now what?* | *307* |
| *The President's succession* | *309* |
|     My thoughts on the issue | 309 |
|     The OK Corral and the World Bank | 310 |
|     A letter to an another new American World Bank President | 311 |
| *On some current books, a movie, and a future book* | *315* |
|     *The World's Banker* by Sebastian Mallaby | 315 |
|     *The End of Poverty* by Jeffrey Sachs | 316 |
|     *The Elusive Quest for Growth* by William Russell Easterly | 317 |
|     *The World Is Flat* by Thomas L. Friedman | 318 |
|     *The Pentagon's New Map* by Thomas P. M. Barnett | 318 |
|     *And the Money kept Rolling In (and Out)* by Paul Blustein | 320 |
|     *Confessions of an Economic Hit Man* by John Perkins | 321 |
|     *The Constant Gardener* and the UN | 322 |
|     The future very last book about *Harry Potter* | 323 |
| *My book, Amazon's profits and the value of its shares* | *325* |
| *The last items in my outgoing tray* | *329* |
|     Pray for us, Karol | 329 |
|     We must aim higher! | 330 |
| *List of my fellow passengers who also dined at the captains table* | *333* |
| *A too long C.V. or a too short memoir, and acknowledgements* | *337* |
| *Some more blurring details about the MDGs* | *349* |
| *Shutting down* | *353* |
|     Keep in touch | 353 |
|     The Buck Stops Here | 353 |

# In search of a title

---

**1/24th**
By
One of twenty four Executive Directors of the World Bank Group
November 2002—October 2004

Some respectfully irreverent questions and suggestions about a great multilateral financial public-sector institution that the world needs more than ever to be a lean and mean poverty-fighting machine and that at sixty years of age should perhaps be renewing its vows in order to move up from "knowledge" into wisdom and instead of trying to advance impossible agenda like justice and social responsibility might do better settling for fights much easier to monitor against injustices and social irresponsibility...all made by a perhaps a somewhat naive but very well-intentioned former executive director equipped only with his long private-sector experience, and his willingness to speak out...sort of.
Or
**HAVE THINK-TANK, WILL TRAVEL**

Or
**ANOTHER MOUSE WHO TRIED TO ROAR**
Or
**Mr. KUROWSKI GOES TO WASHINGTON (My daughter's suggestion)**
Or
**VOICE AND NOISE**

That's it!

# VOICE AND NOISE

Having an opinion and voicing it is what Voice is all about. Putting together thousands of perfectly pure voices might synthesize into a harmonious symphony but, without some noise, it will never ring true and that is what Noise is all about.

The world I remember when I was young moved forward on carrots and hope in the belief that it was going to be a better place, while today's drivers are more the sticks and despairs of those looking only to hang onto what they've got.

To stand a chance of a better tomorrow, we need the Voice to recreate our dreams but also the Noise to make us want them come true.

A shrinking world that makes isolation impossible presents the human race with the challenge of really having to get along. If we resist facing this challenge, the world will be a much-saddened place: let me get off. However, if on the contrary we truly try to make it work, we will at least have some beautiful dreams again.

This book with all its simplicities and contradictions is but an effort to put my voice and noise on the table. All yours are needed too.

P.S. After having decided on the title I found on the Web an article by Ingo R. Titze, Ph.D., titled "Noise in the Voice" that originally appeared in the May/June issue of the Journal of Singing. It reassures me a lot, as it argues that "A little noise, turned on at the right time, can go a long way toward enlarging the interpretive tool.

To my father Tady, who passed away January 2003 and who all his life taught me that I can question a lot and still believe...a lot.

To my mother Inga, who taught me the immense worth of not taking myself all too seriously.

To my Mercedes, my beloved partner in the adventures of life.

And to my three daughters—Mercedes, Alexandra, and Adriana...it's for their world I am writing.

# Introduction

At this very moment, the night bridging from October to November 2004, they are busy destroying all those signs of my authority as an Executive Director at the World Bank Group, that they so gently put up exactly two years ago. On October 30, 2002, I was no one at the WBG, I could not get in without a special pass and nobody would take the slightest notice of me. Then, come the morning of November 1st, my name appeared everywhere, and I was really something—at least so they said. That nightly transition reminded me of Christmas, with all the dwarfs working overtime...not any longer.

To be an Executive Director at the Board of the WBG, or an ED, as they are known, could be described as being an astronaut suspended in space. Absolutely too far away to see the trees, but perhaps also too far away to get a good grasp of the forests. Now, forced back to earth after two years, I must get used to gravity again and what better way than putting together some of the notes I made there about some of the thousands of issues I encountered, and fought for, against, or sideways.

Before you run away from the clear and present danger

that the memoirs of just another nostalgic ED might pose, let me executive-summarize you about why you might hang on, at least for a while.

- I am multicultural, born in Venezuela, from a Swedish mother and a Polish father.
- I have much varied professional experience in the private sector.
- I have had no relation whatsoever with the public sector
- I classify myself as a "radical of the middle" or as "an extremist of the center," by which I mean that I do not belong to any of the two main political currents—without, however, being a bland third way.
- I was appointed as an ED through a process initiated by the Minister of Planning of Venezuela through a public announcement…on the WEB.
- I am opinionated and I arrived at the World Bank, with a license not to be silent.

For those who would like to know about who I am and how I got to the World Bank, I include a brief memoir as an appendix.

Here I will limit myself to writing about those issues where I felt that my opinion differed or deviated importantly from the correct World Bank Group and/or Nongovernmental Organizations NGOs consensus. I therefore run the risk that the reader might perceive me as a virulent critic of the Bank. Nothing could be further from the truth; the WBG is full of first-class people and of first-class initiatives—if anything, sometimes just a little too much first class.

In writing these notes I will shamelessly draw on articles I have written before and during my term, as that was just the way I tried to increase my voice, circulating comments and articles to my colleagues, trying to communicate more informally with them. The official Board proceedings are confidential, and I very much respect that, and agree with it as otherwise the procedures could turn into something even more surrealistic than now. I can just see WB-videoconferencing relaying the deliberations worldwide, competing with C-Span, and the EDs even having to take time out for powdering. By the way, I wish to make clear that while being an ED I never ever alluded to that fact in any of my articles or letters to the editors that were published—they all were just Kurowski's own voice.

Having said that, the EDs are free to voice their own opinions—and I will do exactly that. Anything written here is 100% based on my very own personal viewpoints and no one should infer any direct line of communication with any government.

Some government-inspired official statements were made by my chair, frequently prepared by my Alternate Director or Advisors, but none of those will be referred to here. That said I do believe I should say a word or two about my Constituency since its mixture of low-income, middle-income countries and a donor country, make up a little WB in itself. Costa Rica, El Salvador, Guatemala, Honduras, Nicaragua, Mexico, Spain, and Venezuela, all speak Spanish, but that's about all these proudly individual countries would claim to share.

Most of what I write about is part of an ongoing debate. My fellow colleagues were an extraordinary group of persons, and I deeply regret that I cannot reflect their many and intelligent consideration on these issues, but such is life: they have their voice, and I am trying to strengthen mine.

But if I just gave praise to my colleagues, sincerely and from my heart, so I feel I must do with respect to the management and staff, a really great group of dedicated professionals. I know that my continuous inquiries sometimes provoked their despair, rightfully so, excuse me, but let us remember that they had their job, and I had mine, or at least so I thought.

Since many of my comments will seem to be self-evident and as they cannot be contested in the book, there is a clear and present danger that I could be deemed to be what in German they call a "Besserwisser," meaning someone who is grandstanding and obnoxiously thinks he knows it all. Though it is said that there is always some truth in anything you wish to deny publicly, let me still assure my colleagues, management, and staff that this is really not the case. Please bear with me!

I am aware that this book will have no shape except perhaps that of a multicolored quilt sewn with many different and sometimes even repetitive patches, some more colorful than others, some more carefully sewn than others. As a patched quilt it does not have to be read in any special order, and so the reader can go ahead and choose whatever tickles his or her interest. But, even if it has no shape, it has a clear purpose.

Many of the current problems of the world lend support to doomsday prophecies and with all these scares flying around, there is a huge market in selling short-term solutions, insurance and shelters, to a developed world desperate to hang on to what it has. On the other hand, in much of the developing world there is also a growing and reality-based sense of desperation that, one way or another, they will never really be able to catch up or even get close. So there is also a booming market in shortcuts and magic potions, even when and where there is a suspicion that these could in fact be deathtraps or poison pills.

In these circumstances the last thing the world can afford is to have its intellectuals and leaders also smitten by distrust. The only possible way out of its many predicaments is to take on the challenges with aggressive optimism. My book, by looking to turn many issues on their head, in all its lack of humility, tries to introduce some fresh angles that could perhaps allow us to paint a couple of new and wide portals of opportunities for entering into a better future, instead of all the narrow escape doors through which to run, in panic.

Frequently we hear that the EDs' terms should be for a minimum of four years so that they can really apply the experiences they have gained. I believe that it is useful that the Board should arrive on the scene with a fair dose of old timers, who can put the procedures into some historical perspective, but it definitely also needs some newcomers who will dare to pose their innocent questions, without being hampered by the knowledge that most of these questions have been made before and will be made in the future, as part of the never-ending story of development and human betterment.

After two years, an ED might start losing some of that innocence and so, before that happens, let me hurry into my book. Before I begin, though, let me present some very general information concerning what the World Bank Group is all about; what an Executive Director is supposed to do; some words about the nongovernmental organizations, the NGOs; what are our current primary objectives, a.k.a. The Millennium Development Goals (MDGs); and, finally, an impressive listing, to say the least, of 204 Development Topics, a listing that appears on the current World Bank Web site—so as to help you all to get the feel for what it does...good luck!

**The World Bank Group? (WBG)**

WBG, the World Bank Group, consists of five closely associated institutions, all owned by member countries that carry ultimate decision-making power. As explained below, each institution plays a distinct role in the mission to fight poverty and improve living standards for people in the developing world. The term "World Bank Group" encompasses all five institutions. The term "World Bank," WB, refers specifically to two of the five, IBRD and IDA.

IBRD, the International Bank for Reconstruction and Development. Established in 1945, the IBRD aims to reduce poverty in middle-income and creditworthy poorer countries by promoting sustainable development through loans, guarantees, and (nonlending) analytical and advisory services. The income that IBRD has generated over the years has allowed it to fund several developmental activities and to ensure its financial strength, which enables it to borrow in capital markets at low cost and offer its clients good borrowing terms.

IDA, the International Development Association. Established in 1960, the contributions to the IDA enable the World Bank to provide approximately $6 billion to $9 billion a year in highly concessional financing (which means with such low interest and such long repayment terms that in relative terms it almost amounts to a giveaway...that is, of course, until your children or grandchildren have to repay it) to the world's 81 poorest countries (home to 2.5 billion people). IDA's interest-free credits and grants are vital because these countries have little or no capacity to borrow on market terms.

IFC, the International Finance Corporation. Established in 1956, the IFC promotes economic development through the private sector. Working with business partners, it invests in sustainable private enterprises in developing countries without requiring government guarantees. It provides equity, long-term loans, structured finance and risk management products, and advisory services to its clients. The IFC seeks to reach businesses in regions and countries that have limited access to capital, and it provides finance in markets deemed too risky by commercial investors in the absence of IFC participation.

MIGA, the Multilateral Investment Guarantee Agency. Established in 1988, the MIGA helps promote foreign direct investment in developing countries by providing guarantees to investors against noncommercial risks, such as expropriation, currency inconvertibility and transfer restrictions, war and civil disturbance, and breach of contract.

ICSID, the International Centre for Settlement of Investment Disputes. Established in 1966 the ICSID helps encourage foreign investment by providing international facilities for conciliation and arbitration of investment disputes, thereby helping foster an atmosphere of mutual confidence between states and foreign investors. Many international agreements concerning investment refer to ICSID's arbitration facilities.

### The Executive Directors? (EDs)

Who then are the Executive Directors in the WBG, and what are they supposed to do?

- *The EDs (24) are responsible for the conduct of the general operations of the Bank and exercise all the powers delegated to them by the Board of Governors. The EDs consider and decide on loan and credit proposals made by the President, and they decide policy issues that guide the general operations of the Bank.*
- *The EDs are responsible for presenting to the Board of Governors at the Bank's Annual Meeting an audit of accounts, an administrative budget and an annual report on the operations and policies of the Bank, as well as any other matters that, in their judgment, require submission to the Board of Governors.*

And, for that purpose:

- *Each ED shall appoint an Alternate ED with full power to act for him when he is not present.*
- *EDs function in continuous session at the Bank and meet as often as the Bank's business requires.*
- *EDs and Alternates are required to devote all the time and attention to the business of the Bank that its interests*

*require, and between them to be continuously available at the principal office of the Bank.*
- *In the event that both an ED and his Alternate are unable to be available, the ED may designate a Temporary Alternate to act for him.*

While considering that:
- *In the discharge of his duties, an ED or Alternate fulfills a dual function, as an official of the Bank and as a representative of the member country or countries that appointed or elected him.*
- *The ED owes his duty both to the Bank and to his constituency. The ED is not to act simply as an ambassador of the government or governments that appointed or elected him and is expected to exercise his individual judgment in the interest of the Bank and its members, as a whole.*
- *Neither the EDs nor their staff members actively participate in negotiations between borrowers and Bank staff.*

### The Nongovernmental Organizations? (NGOs)

Some words about the nongovernmental organizations. They include all those frequently opinionated groups from the civil society (whatever that now means) that participate intensively in the debates about development and other issues, expressing their many different concerns, for example, on the protection of the environment. The NGOs can be a one-man show, I for instance, or extremely well-organized and well-funded groups. In general terms, you could classify them into three types: the seriously concerned and truly interested, the bona fide NGOs; the self-interested NGOs (there are plenty of money and business or consultancy opportunities in development); and, finally the groupies, those who just get a kick in life out of hanging around. The NGOs and similar entities like the WBG fight a lot, but in fact their fights are normally more like husband-and-wife quarrels, as they need each other just as much. I have an immense respect for many of them and for the role they can play in modern society as our volunteer corps of ombudsmen, which is exactly why I am frequently critical of some of them. Many NGOs in the developing countries are frequently totally subordinated to sophisticated NGOs from developed countries, and I find this very sad. Also, from the very start, I decided not to name any single individual NGO in this book...If that makes me somewhat of a coward, so be it! I might be in enough trouble as is.

### The Millennium Development Goals? (MDGs)

Formally the WBG has accepted a series of tasks and responsibilities, known as MDGs, and these include eradicate extreme poverty and hunger; to achieve universal primary education; promote gender equality and empower women; reduce child mortality; improve maternal health; combat HIV/AIDS, malaria, and other diseases; ensure environmental sustainability and develop a global partnership for development. Each one of these goals has defined operational targets and at the end of the book, in an appendix, I list these, as well as the names of all the Millennium Development partners that are working towards the same objectives.

You could probably spend the rest of your life downloading information about all these entities from their respective sites. Don't do that! As you could also probably spend the rest of your life discussing the validity of the Millennium Development Goals and the Partners' commitment to them or lack of it, don't do that either. Whether you accept the MDGs or believe others are more appropriate, the important part is to do something! Anything! Soon!

### 205 Development Topics!—listed on the World Bank Web site.

Administrative & Civil Service Reform; Adult Literacy

and Non Formal Education; Agribusiness & Markets; Agricultural Knowledge & Information Systems; Agriculture & Rural Development; AIDS/HIV; AIDS Economics; AIDS in Africa; AIDS in South Asia; Air Pollution; Anti-Corruption; Asia Alternative Energy Program (ASTAE); Avian Flu; Banking Systems; Biodiversity; Biotechnology; Bond Offerings and Debt Securities; Capacity Enhancement; Child Labor; Children and Youth; City Development Strategies; Civic Engagement, Empowerment & Respect for Diversity (CEERD); Civil Society; Climate Change; Coal Sector Restructuring; Coastal and Marine Management; Community Based Rural Development; Community Risk Management; Community Driven Development; Community Contracting—Water & Sanitation; Corporate Governance; Corporate Social Responsibility; Culture & Poverty; Dams and Reservoirs; Debt Management, Public; Debt Issues: HIPC, Relief, Sustainability; Debt Securities; Debt Service Reports; Decentralization; Desertification; Development Communications; Disability; Disaster Management; Distance Learning; E-Government; Early Childhood Development; Economics of Education; Economics Growth Research; Education; Education Reform & Management; Education Technology; Effective Schools & Teachers; Empowerment; Energy; Environment; Environment and Energy Efficiency; Environment & International Law; Environmental Assessment; Environmental Economics & Indicators; Estimated Debt Service Reports (EDSR); EU Accession; Evaluation; Extractive Industries Review; Faiths and Development; Fast Track Initiative; Financial Markets; Finance, Specialized; Financial Products & Services; Financial Sector; Fisheries & Aquaculture; Food and Nutrition; Forests & Forestry; Foundation Partnerships; Fuel for Thought; Gender; Gender and Rural Development; GenderStats; Girls Education; Global Distance EducationNet; Global Education Reform; Global Environment Facility; Global Insolvency; Global Monitoring; Globalization; Harmonization; Hazard Risk Management; Health, Nutrition & Population; HNP Millennium Development Goals; Health Systems & Financing; Health Systems & Financing, Resource Allocation & Purchasing; Heavily Indebted Poor Countries (HIPC); HIV/AIDS; Human Rights; Impact Evaluation; Indigenous Peoples; Inequality & Poverty; Informatics; Information & Communication Technologies; Infrastructure; Insurance & Contractual Savings; International Economics & Trade; International Financial Architecture; International Trade & Development; Investment Climate; Involuntary Resettlement; Irrigation; Judicial Indicators; Knowledge Sharing; Labor Markets; Land Fill Gas Initiative for Latin America; Land and Real Estate; Land Resources Management; Land Policy; Law & Justice; Legal Institutions; Legal & Judicial Reform; Lifelong Learning; Local Economic Development; Low-Income Countries Under Stress (LICUS); Malaria; Mental Health; Millennium Development Goals; Mining; Montreal Protocol; Municipal Finance; National Health Accounts; New Ideas in Pollution Regulation; NGOs and Civil Society; Nutrition; Oil and Gas; Participation; Payment Systems; Pensions; Persistent Organic Pollutants; Pharmaceuticals; Policies; Pollution Management; Population and Reproductive Health; Ports & Logistics; Postal Systems; Poverty; Poverty and Health; Poverty and Social Impact Analysis; Poverty Reduction Strategy; Private Participation in Infrastructure; Private Sector Development; Private Sector Gender Initiative; Producer Organizations; Prospects for Development; Public Debt Management; Public Examination System; Public Expenditure; Public Sector Governance; Rapid Response; Railways; Resettlement; Roads & Highways; Rural and Renewable Energy; Rural Transport; Rural Urban Linkages; Rural Water & Sanitation; Safe Motherhood; Safeguard Policies; Safety Nets; Sanitation; School Health; Science, Technology and Innovation; Secondary Education and Training; Small Medium Enterprise Development; Small States; Social Analysis; Social Assessment; Social Capital; Social Development; Social Funds; Social Impact of Oil & Gas; Social Policy & Governance; Social Protection and Labor;

Sustainable Development; Tax Policy and Administration; Telecommunications; Tertiary Education; Tobacco; Transport; Transport Europe & Central Asia; Tuberculosis; Urban Development; Urban Housing & Land; Urban Services to the Poor; Urban Transport; Urban Waste Management; Urban Water & Sanitation; Utility Finance; Utility Operations & Maintenance; Vocational Education & Training; Water Resources Management; Water Supply & Sanitation; Water Sup & San, Economics; Water Sup & San, Monitoring & Evaluation; Water Sup & San, Pricing & Tariffs; Water Sup & San, Private Sector Providers; Water Sup & San, Partnerships in Hand washing; Water Sup & San, Regulation of Utilities; Water Sup & San, Serving the Urban Poor; Water Sup & San, Small Towns & Multi-Village Initiatives; Water Sup & San, Social Intermediation & Gender

**And, that's not all folks!**

# My ED trips

For an easy start, I include a series of reflections and mementos from those Executive Director's trips which I was lucky to take part in, and that are part of the efforts to make sure that the EDs get firsthand knowledge about the work of WBG, in different countries. I will also include some words about my temporary hometown, Washington. Since it could be uncomfortable for some governments in some countries, there was some talk about whether the EDs could take their wives on these trips, paying their traveling expenses on their own, of course. As my wife Mercedes was studying, she could not go but, had she, I am sure that I would have been able to observe and remember many more things.

### Airport #1
So close to the office and already I cannot get to the Web. Just because in this airport they were early starters, now they have to live with outdated technology.

### Airport #2
I am now on the other side of the globe, supposedly in the

disconnected part, but I just managed to connect easily to the Web.

## An encounter with NGOs

We met (yes in the airport) with an assorted group of NGOs that were all dead set against a big hydro project in a developing country. After debating the pros and cons of hydro, gas, and special environmentally friendly small energy sources such as wind and biomass, if not a truce, and most definitely not an agreement, I believe that there was at least a general consensus that most concerns and differences of opinion had been analyzed in a comprehensive way. Comprehensive? Forget it! Early next morning we all read an official announcement of a huge project to generate energy with coal. And I believe no one even mentioned coal the night before.

## Market driven visas?

Overstayed your visa? Concerned? "No problem, just pay 200 baths per day. We take credit cards." What a pragmatic approach! Others should learn. What if according to the size of their economy and population the countries would issue a substantial number of open working permits and give those to the World Bank to be auctioned out on a regular basis? Would this not provide a market-driven income-redistribution system to the world, one that could be used for taking care of our global problems such as environment protection in poor countries?

## Quality certifications!

Wow! Their immigration procedures have an ISO 9001 certification of quality issued by the International Standards Organization. What's next, the ISO9001 for the deliberations of Congress? In governance, should it not be the World Bank that certifies capacity instead of the ISO—or am I just being jealous?

From having witnessed this ISO9001 governmental application plus a couple that I read about in Mexico, came the idea of asking for a similar quality check of the procedures of my own ED office. I met with some ISO officers to discuss that possibility and I felt they were both intrigued and challenged by the prospect of writing an Executive Directors procedure manual. Unfortunately, I did not have the chance to do more about it—before it was all over. I hope some of my future colleagues further explore this idea.

### The First Country

### Gender

There I was listening to the pragmatic conversation between a grand lady colleague from the richest country in the world and a humble young farmer's wife from a truly poor country, and all I could think about was that, Boy! If gender were an issue here, we men could clearly be in trouble.

### A rural road to the town

Oh yes, we were helping out, providing a small school, some minor irrigation systems, hopefully some electricity and better roads. But wait! What on earth was this family producing 600 kilos (about 1,300 pounds) per year of rice going to live on, especially when this country's accession to the WTO—and indeed it is lurking around the corner—could put them out of a job? How come we do not work exclusively on job creation, so as to give them a chance to work themselves out of poverty and despair, instead of making their poverty and despair more livable and sustainable? Dear Colleagues, we should never invest in a rural road if it is only to facilitate the no-return-trip to the town.

### Motorbikes
- A hoard of motorbikes is coming at me. How on earth am I going to cross the street? At the end—

just like marrying—there comes a moment of truth when you just have to close your eyes and walk down that aisle to the altar with faith. I did just that, closed my eyes, and crossed the street. I did great! Just as in my marriage.
- There are too many motorbikes on this road so they should build a bike lane. Forget it! There are so many motorbikes that what we need here is a car lane. Boy, if they just went from bicycles to motorcycles, and last year over 1 million motorcycles were sold, which at only a thousand US dollars each means more than a billion in sales, just think what would happen if they went over to cars! With what would they power those cars? Has anyone considered this in the Country Assistance Strategy (CAS) of this country?
- But these motorbikes must be different from the motorbikes we used to know. We cannot even begin to fathom their significance in the local supply chain before we have witnessed the transport on a motorcycle of…FOUR FULL-GROWN PIGS!

## Are we few track-minded?

I listened for a presentation about how this big gas electricity-generation project matched the energy requirements of this growing country, but was instead served information on safety, environmental friendliness, and social participation during construction. I thought, if these are the only things that they think we want to hear about, then this might very well be what is wrong with us.

## Death penalty for corruption!

What does it really mean to have a death penalty for corruption—and still they tell you that corruption is rampant everywhere? In effectiveness, how does it compare to OECD's[1] recent huge step forward of not allowing tax deductibility of corruption payments any longer? Are there any anticorruption patches to be found that might make it easier to break the bribery habit? Or do you have to go cold turkey?

### A Luxurious Hospital

Here we are visiting a modern hospital that was built and is operated with the help of contributors from a developed country, on a let's try to cover the cost basis, and whose clientele must be the few wealthier in this country of poor. As our IFC is supporting this project with some loans and some equity, a big debate ensues as some of my fellow travelers question why the World Bank Group, in its fight against poverty, should get involved with a hospital for the rich. I feel a big divide. Coming from a developing country—one that has unfortunately been unable to find its road to the future yet—I put down my position by firmly stating: "You know that in real estate there is the mantra of location-location-location. Well, the same holds true in the fight against poverty; it is about location-location-location. I mean getting close to the rich, close to where the money is. There cannot be a better start for reaching good sustainable health services for the poor than making sure that the rich are willing to spend their health-related money in their own country. Not going this road makes us great charitable contributors, not promoters of sustainable development. Wanna help? Then stimulate some of our Washington staff to come down here and be treated at a fifth of the cost.

### The Second Country

### Hello Sir. Please GET UP! Five o'clock!

What a transparency! Here the authorities are very clearly ranked...from NUMERO UNO downwards.

### Gained in translation?

Have you seen *Lost in Translation?* Where Bill Murray is told five words by the translator after his Japanese director had babbled away at him for at least one minute? Well here, most probably someone found something in the five well-chosen words of our spokesman as it gave way to a full one-minute translation. Well as our translator was an extremely educated, amiable, and intelligent fellow, and the listeners seemed quite happy with *what had been said*, I guess no harm was done. Quite possibly it might have been just the opposite.

### Get them out of here!

NO WAY! I do not believe that we are doing right in resettling poor people in places where they will basically continue to do the same and most certainly continue to be poor. If any of the resettled fathers or mothers were to ask any of us EDs privately, "If you were in our situation, would you keep your children here?"—we would probably have to say, "No way! We would get them out!" And, if that is so, we are not doing our development work right. Sorry.

### Airport #3

It's 1 in the morning. It should be about 1 p.m. in Washington, but I am not really sure whether for my family I am in tomorrow or yesterday. The plane landed here for an hour, and we are shown into the duty-free hall where I buy myself a T-shirt as evidence that I have been in the Kingdom. Entering the duty-free shop, I see that a fifth of its available display shelving is filled with just one brand of tobacco for pipes. I sleepily conclude that in our next Country Assistance Strategy for them we should perhaps include something about modern supply-chain systems. But, then again, far away and on an island, this might just be an example of just-in-time inventories kept for a niche of pipe-smoking tourists.

### The Third Country

I hear the Prime Minister and the Deputy Prime Minister, and I sensed the following: This is not so much a place for facts and knowledge but more for intuition and wisdom. This is not a place that has been reached by the pressure of next quarter's bottom line, but this is a place where you plan your actions and discount your expected income giving due respect to past and future generations. And I like it, and I think perhaps we need these guys in the UN Security Council—or have I just been blinded by the beauty of the island?

### Support the *Small Are Beautiful* entrepreneurs

All is and probably will be and should remain on a small scale here, and we all know that small-scale activity needs much assistance in order to grow and survive:

- Here is this guy exporting traditional revitalizing essence in anonymous steel drums guaranteed never to be able to capture some big added value, condemned to search for his profit margin fighting the transport costs. No! He needs instead a product concept that has much added value, so that it can be shipped to the anxiously expecting world using expensive couriers. Let his local university take up the challenge and create a high value consumer product for him.
- Here is this guy that unknowingly has a great product concept but that, if not speedily protected, will be lost to generic competition. Let there be a place were small people can get effective and affordable assistance in matters such as copyright and intellectual-property rights. We all know that he cannot afford using the big-guy's law firms.
- Here are many small guys needing basic accounting, Web page design and just good advice that could perhaps be effectively provided by a One Stop Entrepreneurial Support Group financed on a continuous basis by the government, strictly monitored for results and client satisfaction.

\*\*\*

Here Jim, my editor, commented, "There was a fellow here in the Philadelphia area named Gil Engholm, a Swedish-American I believe, who lost his job about thirty years ago, started a business of his own and became successful, and then gave every Wednesday evening for the rest of his long life to running a career-counseling center at an Episcopal church. People he helped came back with their success stories to help the new people in trouble. I believe it was the best career center in the area, and it was open to everyone absolutely free. It was Gil's way of saying thanks for having overcome his own jobless situation". And though it's another era and another world I just felt I could not delete such comment.

***

### Another Private Hospital

This private hospital did not impress me. First, I felt that it was managed more to feed patients to some individual owner-doctors instead of maximizing the use of the hospital. However, my main objection was that in this hospital's case the location-location-location mantra was not really to be close to its potential patients, but to be close to those patients and only those patients whom the government would pay to send to them. This is pseudo-privatization that in my mind does not serve any real purpose. Perhaps developed countries can afford to consume some of their development in this kind of artificialities, developing countries cannot.

### As far as you can go

When I visited beautiful Samoa and had a chance to hear a bit about their tourism strategy, I sensed they were making too many efforts to minimize the cost of their remoteness, when they might benefit more from exploiting the worth of that very isolation. In a world where so much is brought so immediately close, there is a growing need to be able to get really away. For that, nothing is like Samoa...as far as you can go. When I hear of anyone wanting to write, compose, paint, sculpt, or just to regain a balance in life after an upsetting event or a batch of bad luck, I think of this island.

Is there a market in hermits? Of course! If only one of every thousand of the population has an artistic temperament or is in need of isolation-relaxation and Samoa manages to attract only one in every thousand of them, then just from the United States of America, Samoa would welcome about 300 each year. If each stays for an average of three months, that adds up to about 3,600 visitor-weeks. Not a bad thing for an island with a population of 177,714 (2004 estimate). But wait, that's not all.

Having attracted 300 bona-fide hermits (hopefully including a couple of modern-day Robert Louis Stevensons), Samoa could exploit the follow-the-hermits market. In this segment, it will find bona-fide hermit-followers, such as publishers with deadlines, girlfriends with broken hearts, and tax collectors with bills—but also those millions of groupies just wanting to rub shoulders with the hermits and let them rub something off on them.

Although I wish Samoa all the success in the world with its tourism industry, I also hope it never goes overboard and ends up finding that the world has gotten too close. Samoans seem to be very aware of these risks. In a round-table conversation with some private-sector representatives, I listened, amazed, as local entrepreneurs voiced their concerns that the 6 percent growth rate of their economy projected for next year was much too high to guarantee the harmonious development of their society—a first for me.

Having no interest whatsoever in space tourism, I knew very well that by going to Samoa I was traveling as far as I ever will. What surprised me, though, was seeing how as-far—you-could-go could grow so under-the-skin-close-to-you.

PS. The Minister got the idea right away: "Been the subject of a hostile takeover? Feeling bad after the divorce? Come to our wisdom island!"

## The fourth country

### Honorable Accountability

We sat down in some new and humble school installation, to listen to M/S Aisha Kimolo, the Head Teacher of Chamwino Primary School, giving us EDs a brief report on the implementation of a Primary Education Development Program.

Ten minutes later, after hearing Mr. Kimolo address his *Honorable Guests* in clear words and a firm voice, accounting for a Capitation Grant of TSHs (the currency in Tanzania) 7,614,873.60, (about 8.000 US dollars) down to the last cent, using clear indexes, and ending with a forward-looking description of how they intended to achieve sustainability, we knew that we had not heard just another project report, we had just witnessed a very rare and marvelous example of true accountability. We thanked him and regretted later not having been even warmer in our congratulations and not having had a group photo taken with such an honorable man.

\*\*\*

Here Jim, my editor, warned me about using "honorable" as it might remind people of Mark Antony's irony when he says "For Brutus is an honorable man; So are they all, all honorable men," (Shakespeare, *Julius Caesar*, Act 3, scene 2, lines 88—89). He suggests using "a man of such outstanding honor and wisdom" instead. Having traveled in Africa addressing all ministers as Honorable and also being always addressed as Honorable-ED, I ignore his suggestion, claiming, and shielding myself in, blissful ignorance.

\*\*\*

### Strategic Plan

Suppose the country was an island and that the only boat with which you could leave it for the next thirty years was scheduled for departure today. If you were an ambitious and hopeful 15-year-old who loved his country and that has just read the country's Strategic Development Plan, would you stay or would you take the boat?

When we read these plans, we are left with two lingering doubts:

What's in this plan that separates this country from all the rest? As it is obvious that all developing cannot occupy exactly the same place under the sun or find jobs in agriculture, what more is there to lead us—except for an "If it's Tuesday it's got to be Tanzania!"

Yes! All the basic necessary tools are included in the plan: macroeconomic stability, brushing your teeth, better governance, eating your breakfast. But, where are you really heading and where is that green valley that will motivate and inspire your efforts?

### Trains and privatizations

A functional modern two-track train is what they need in the long term, but somehow they can't seem to get it moving. Are they perhaps biting off more than they can chew? In countries with a lack of resources and high uncertainty, every single dollar requirement that you add on to a project will make it exponentially so much more difficult to complete, since when the investor expects high rates to make up for high risks, the lengthening of the duration of the concession offered is of little use as anything in a distant future is not really valued.

This is what I call the death-embrace of discounted cash flows. Normally a country gets into problems because of shortsightedness but, when it then is in a problem, the rates of return that investors demand shoot up, and so now it is forced to be even more shortsighted, as anything beyond the first couple of years is considered almost of no value.

So, forget the fringe on the top, go for a reasonable one single-lane restoration and, in the process, prepare yourself for more action a couple of years down the line. A clause that gives the government the right to repurchase a privatized project, in cash at a decent price a couple of years hence, does provide much flexibility without taking away too much from the general attractiveness of the project.

### Environmental disasters

There are about a million small miners whose uncontrolled activities are causing a lot of damage and there are also around 300.000 to 400.000 ha (750,000 to 1,000,000 acres) deforested each year. So what is to be done? The magnitude and urgency of the problem require some real out-of-the-box thinking. (Perhaps something like the suggestion that there might be better alternatives than hybrid cars, and that proposal I include in the chapter on environment)

### AIDS vs. Malaria

There we sat listening astonished to the Minister of Health describing that what she most needed was help in fighting the malaria that was killing more people in her country than the AIDS, but AIDS was what donors mostly prioritized. How sad! The high mortality rate of the malaria came as a surprise to me but from what I deducted the malaria strain in most of Africa is much worse that what we are accustomed to in South America. We were informed that the anti malaria drugs we have been supplied by the bank for the trip were not allowed in this country as they could create an even more drug resistant strain. Answering some nervous questions the Minister informed us EDs that the malaria mosquito attacked exclusively at night and only if the victim was still and that's why the protective nets are so important.

Malaria is a tragedy, and so you have to forgive me but I cannot refrain from telling you that after the minister's mosquito comments, I detected immediate incipient salsa-like movements in my colleague's limbs (mine as well) and that grew stronger as night approached.

## Giving away Bouncing Balls

During a previous trip I had learned from a grand lady colleague from the richest country to bring some bouncing balls to give away. I threw them at the dozen young kids standing there and only two of them moved. The rest did not even acknowledge it in their poverty and misery-filled glazed eyes. Per, what are you doing here? This is so far away from your realities that there is no way you could really add something useful. Yes. I know! But then again that is perhaps exactly what I needed to see...with my own tear-glazed eyes.

## Questions and answers

There I was in a meeting with several local NGOs and staff from other development organizations hearing about the "quiet time" that had been created in this country so as to permit the government to work without being continuously interrupted by the thousands of donors and officials that visited it. As the spokesman of the group, I innocently asked, "During what months of the year does the quiet time fall?"— only to realize in that same second that I should never have asked just that question! I remembered a movie where the senior defense lawyer counseled his younger partner never to ask a question to which you don't know the answer.

And talking about questions and answers, recently, when invited to a semiprivate screening of *The Fog of War: Eleven Lessons from the Life of Robert S. McNamara* (Errol Morris' 2003 Oscar-winning documentary about Secretary of Defense McNamara's role in the Vietnam War), Mr. McNamara himself answered some questions afterwards. When he was confronted with an especially difficult one, I heard him reply: "I learned never to answer the question that is asked of you but only to answer the question you wish had been asked of you." His answer opened up to me a huge window of understanding of all politicians, here, there, and everywhere.

## A fifth country—while an ED but not as one.

## The Chinese of China

I traveled to China and was mesmerized. I assure you that, as a leisure trip, if you manage to get a bargain-priced ticket, there is nothing like it. When visiting the Great Wall of China, I took a local bus with only Chinese passengers, who sang in Chinese with the help of a karaoke-style video that underscored each Chinese character. *But more than all these, for me everything was Chinese.*

Nowadays in China, the majority of families have just one child. What does this mean to society? Could Latin families retain their characteristic traits with families of just one offspring?

It is precisely when a country is getting out of poverty and seeks to position itself in an intermediate level that any improvement, such as going from a bicycle to a motorcycle and from a motorcycle to a car demands a tremendous amount of energy. Is there enough energy and oil in the world to satisfy China's growth?

China's current model for economic growth seems to be taking the country in record time from being a rural country to a country where its citizens are all sardine-like packed in gigantic cities, and we presume that such a move is not good or sustainable. When we observe that recent cutting-edge technological advances in the world allow even the most isolated countryman to be present, almost live, right in the center of the Empire's capital, we have to ask ourselves, are there really no other better and newer options?

China's present growth rate is colossal, and from what we can gather there will be great disparities among those who get on board today's developed consumerism and those who lag behind with no chance of having even a peek at this new millennium. Any progress entails risks and may even require leaving behind some victims in its passing, but if injustices turn out to be too vast then those passed by are sure to complain.

Could China achieve in some decades what previously took centuries to achieve, and still be China?

Please forgive my political indiscretion, but in the early morning just as the red flags were hoisted in Tiananmen Square and I saw how human masses were mobilized and kept in certain order only when instructed by the guards' blaring voices, I, discreetly, had to ask myself whether it could be possible to run China in the long run just like current à la mode democracies.

Finally, while climbing the Great Wall aboard a little yellow cart that looked just like an old and retired Disney theme park ride trying to make its way slowly through the crowds, I kept asking myself, will it withstand?

From *El Universal*, Caracas, February 12, 2004

## Small memories from my Central America

### Visas

When I used to have to renew my visa quite frequently for a Central American country, I hated the fact that I had to get a new visa every three months. I hated the fact that each visa ate up a complete page of my passport. I hated the fact that they, with bureaucratic inflexibility, required a new photo of me every six months, as if they were doing a Monet study of my graying hair, although at the end I must confess they were flexible enough to settle for just a fresh copy of the old photo. I hated their immigration form that was so impossible to decipher and fill out that it could easily substitute for the hardest of crosswords. Finally, I also hated the wait at the airport of at least one of those hours that multiply into three when one is tired. All that was true before I entered Europe—in less than twenty seconds—without anyone putting even the smallest stamp in my Venezuelan passport (years before, I had received my Polish passport and even more years before the European enlargement.) Hey, I thought to myself at least in Central America they recognize one as a human being, but here they just ignore you—and that is worse.

## Global info confusion

There I sat and listened, amazed, to the taxi driver in a small Central American country give me a perfectly accurate and up-to-date briefing on the political events in my Venezuela, only to end it by his asking me whether Venezuela lay north or south of Spain.

## The new frontiers of product development

I have just witnessed the most innovative product development. A mosquito repellent announced its extended protection with a "12 hour protection with 1 application every 6 hours". Beat that!

## The social contract of Teotihuacan

It is said that when the Aztecs in the early fourteenth century discovered Teotihuacan with all its pyramids, they were so impressed by the grandiosity of the place that they thought it had been built by giants. So they fostered the myth that the gods had gathered there to assure the world's existence. In fact, its most important constructions had occurred in the first two centuries of our era, carried out by human beings who might even have been the ancestors of the Aztecs. When I visited Teotihuacan, I understood those fourteenth-century Aztecs very well, because my first reaction was to wonder in awe about what social contract must have been in place so as to convince a population to dedicate themselves, over several generations, to building something like this. Since it is frequently difficult to convince even small communities about keeping the streets in front of their own houses clean, or, on a more mundane and personal level, so difficult for me to get anyone of my daughters to volunteer to do the dishes, I knew that if we could just lay our hands on a copy of the Teotihuacan social contract, then development work should be a breeze...and clearly WBG could be out of a job...and I would never have to wash plates again. It is surely a mystery how civilizations suddenly get the will to organize themselves to do the most amazing things. I am of course always on the lookout for that magic route, that I sometimes visualize a bit like Harry Potter's running into the wall at the train station and finding his parallel world. Anyhow, while leaving Teotihuacan, I was brought back to realities and reminded of the very fragility of civilizations. It seems that even though we find the magic potion for development, its effects are not necessarily long-lasting. In this sense, in the long run, WBG would still have a guaranteed clientele for its work as developed countries could implode into underdevelopment, and that one of my future descendants would also surely have to face a dirty pile on a Sunday morning a couple of centuries from now. Strangely, I sensed that this last reflection was not fatalistic at all, but, on the contrary, it aroused in me a great feeling of solidarity and appreciation for the daily grinding of forefathers and likewise of generations to come. It will never be over...and so as Dory says...Just Keep Swimming.

## Small memories from my transitional hometown

### Assaulted

Just barely 48 hours after coming to Washington, still not a full-fledged Executive Director, around seven in the evening of a dark October night, I stopped and looked up to admire the beautiful building of the National Geographic Society, especially its illumination, when suddenly I was thrown to the pavement by a third-rate version of *He-Who-Must-Not-Be-Named* who kept pushing a handgun into my belly while loudly demanding my watch and my wallet. The watchstrap had just broken, and so I had placed it in my pocket and had a hard time getting it out while being held down. After seconds turned into minutes, I was relieved of my wallet, with too much cash in it, although the watch, when I finally got it out, was scornfully rejected with a "Keep it!" Meanwhile my side of the street had of course emptied completely.

Shocked, I walked a block and entered a liquor store (I

don't know why) where they immediately called the police, who arrived in seconds. We started to discuss the incident. As it all had happened just blocks away from the World Bank building and the White House, I inquired whether this really could be considered a dangerous area of the city. The policeman told me no, it was a safe area, but, as people did not go any longer to the unsafe areas, all these small-time criminals had to come and search for their victims here. Although I strongly disagreed with reducing my assaulter to a "small-time criminal," as an economist I could identify with his looking for the appropriate market for his activity.

The policeman, very kindly, perhaps because he also had a Polish surname, presented his sincere excuse on behalf of Washington, with a "You know, this happens in all big cities." I, though grateful for his attitude, could just not resist letting out an "I know, but I come from Caracas, Venezuela, and we never see such incidents there." At that moment, I felt a lot better, so much so that I even left the liquor store empty-handed.

Days later, I found the incident reported by the police in "District Events," and that clipping became my first souvenir from Washington.

P.S. The last time I had been attacked, it was at knifepoint in the very shady port of Buenaventura, in Colombia, in 1966. At that time, the events featured the following incredible dialogue: "Give me your money!" "I don't have any money" "Come on, you must have hidden it—perhaps in your shoes?" "Well...perhaps?" "Well, if you care about the money enough to hide it in your shoes, then we don't take it." And that was it!

I always think back to this incident as the night I discovered some very particular ethics among Buenaventura's hoodlums.

## Washington and the GPS (Global Positioning System)

When I arrived in Washington I got to know the modern GPS systems that allow you to drive your car exactly where you want to go. Truly amazing although, as I probably said before somewhere, being able to lose yourself should still be a human right since otherwise how could you ever be able again to enjoy finding yourself. I still remember with much nostalgic enjoyment those many hours my wife and I spent, over and over again, just trying to get back into the City of London. That was true quality time together—the two of us against the world!

But let's not cry over times gone by. Let's look at it all from a more constructive and positive angle. As far as I see it, with GPS, you really don't need to have signs on poles display the street addresses any more. So, GPS opens up a world of new financial opportunities for governments. For instance: for how much could you auction away on e-Bay the rights for a corporation to have its name supplant that of Pennsylvania Avenue in Washington, for two months? Toyota Avenue? I am sure that would provide some politically correct fiscal income that could come in quite handy.

But then again, if there's ever a place you need a GPS, it has to be here. No matter how much this country has and says it thrives on diversity, it is amazing how its citizens then blend all the diversity together to come up with an absolute uniform product. I have seen the same suburb, the same mall, and the same street with the same stores, appearing at least under a thousand different GPS coordinates.

## Snowing in Washington

Yes, it had snowed a little, but never would I have imagined when I arrived for an early-morning conference at the World Bank that I would find the meeting had been suspended because of "inclement weather." Later I came to understand. Just a minimum amount of snow creates total havoc in Washington. The snow covers the streets for days and except for those few corners that are shoveled clean by some tropical Salvadorian saviors living up to their name, it will have to melt away either through warmth or tons of salt. The schools also shut down for any little flurry and although the news of this is received with great joy by all children, my daughter first among them, but nonetheless of course, not braving it will only make it harder for Washingtonians to conquer their weakness through Darwinian evolution. Indeed, Washington is a great and beautiful city and although it is the capital of the world's mightiest nation it has also its Achilles' heel. It could be completely shut down with just a couple of strategically located snowmakers.

### This would never have happened to John Wayne

About the same week as the United States Congress refused to renew some make-it-at-least-a-little-bit-difficult rules with respect to the purchase of automatic guns, a Colombian coffee shop duly named Juan Valdez was opened quite close to the WB in Washington. Mr. Juan Valdez himself attended the opening and stood there outside so that anyone who so wished could have a photograph taken with him. He was clad in his traditional white country suit, patting his traditional donkey—but with a machete holster that in the new traditions of some code-alert colors had been emptied. I felt so sorry for him having to stand there with no machete! What a shame! How come that in the land of Hollywood they were not able to come up with an innocuous substitute for his machete? Well, this would never have happened to John Wayne. Out of solidarity, I refused to have my photo taken with Juan Valdez. You have to respect a man when he needs to be alone.

### A monument to transparency.

I have no idea what is to come out of it and I have no idea whether it has anything to do with true accountability but, in my book at least, *The 9/11 Commission Report,* that in its 567 pages contains the Final Report of the National Commission on Terrorist Attacks upon the United States, and that can be bought in any supermarket for less than ten dollars is a true monument to transparency. I cannot imagine any other country being able to come out with so much information on a so sensitive a public issue in so short a time after the events. We, the rest of the world, should stand in awe in front of it! That, of course, does not imply not being critical of many other things going on in the United States, that land of contradictions.

***

### A photo album

At this point, I thought of including a series of photos from my ED trips but the cost of it would have increased the cost of the book to you, perhaps a bit too much, unless the photos were to be so small that you had to use a magnifying glass. So I decided instead to place these photos on file on my www.voiceandnoice.blogspot.com page. You are welcome to look at them.

And now, with the travel journal ready, it is time to get back to the daily grind and back to my issues. By the way if I use the word "issues" and other similar terms too much, please bear with me. I assure you, I wasn't such a bureaucrat previously.

# The Debt Sustainability Analysis

**Why was it such an issue for me?**

I come from a country that is living proof that public indebtedness does not necessarily produce growth or welfare. Therefore, having to discuss the issue of Sustainable Debt Levels (SDL) as a self-standing topic, came almost as a shock to me. I shouted out: "Just the idea of someone calculating a SDL with complex formulas is a scary thought, as it reminds me of a refined torturer calculating the pain tolerance for mediocre credits that might forever and ever tax one's economy."

Of course the whole SDL debate is based on some very good intentions, like not saddling the countries with excessive debts, and finding adequate means by which to allocate the IDA development resources between loans and grants. Nonetheless, when reading the many papers about "Debt Intolerance," most of them ridiculously obscured by complex econometrics, I felt that the WB was focusing on the issue from a totally wrong perspective.

Instead of analyzing the relevant issues such as the credit-absorption capacity of countries and of how their credits could better contribute to growth and repayment capacity, the WB now seemed to be appearing in the role of any investment bankers, worried about how much of their credit products they could push. In doing so I felt that the WB was, unwittingly and unwillingly, lending force to the belief that a debt was OK, as long as it was sustainable. In my mind, there cannot be a road more conducive to debt turning unsustainable, than to award credits just because they are sustainable.

My potpourri of sometimes somewhat repetitive and not always congruous objections included among others:

### Addiction

SDL analysis is somewhat similar to calculating a sustainable credit line for a compulsive gambler. What politician (anywhere) would resist the multiple temptations of not using an available "allotment" of sustainable credits? Worse, these levels would still be taken only as a minimum, with nothing to stop the rest of the markets pushing even more loans.

The debate on debt sustainability sometimes sounded to me like debating whether you can smoke one, two or three packages of cigarettes a day before smoking kills you. In my case, after not having smoked one single cigarette in more than ten years—and not one single week goes by without being seriously tempted—I am certain that my own "nonsmoking sustainability level" is an absolute zero cigarettes. With respect to public debt, we know there are governments really hooked on public debt and then perhaps their debt sustainability level should be an equally big zero. As it must be very difficult to free someone from a vice with as much addictive power as credits payable by future generations, it might be safer if the Bank and the Fund recommend cutting the habit altogether, cold-turkey, instead of suggesting a life on the border of sustainable (healthy?) levels of debt consumption.

There are cases were SDL calculations are clearly a very valid and needed starting point, as when they are made in relation to the restructuring of debts. Nonetheless, in those cases, attention needs to be focused more on issues such as the amortization profile of the debt, the lowering of interest costs, and the systems put in place to avoid contracting new general nonpurpose debt.

### The true purpose of credits

Let us never forget that if credits are correctly awarded and contracted, the whole concept of "debt sustainability" should be a moot issue. New mediocre credits awarded that have small chances to generate repayment capacity, might very well push a country into unsustainability but it is also very possible that new good credits to a country with excessive debt is the only alternative to get it out of unsustainability.

The WB should not be seen as lowering the bar by accepting the concept of unproductive credits as long as they are within certain limits. Instead, the real challenge is to go back to the basics, making effective use of scarce resources, assuring that new credits are productive and, one way or another, generate their own repayment. If this is not so, then the creditor, rightly, even the WB, should also stand to lose as a creditor.

We have been presented a framework for how these debt-sustainable levels are to be determined but in order to mean anything the framework needs to go much further than just determining whether a country can manage public debt of 40, 50, or 60% of its GNP, or of 100, 150, or 200% of its export earnings. Why is there so little analysis about the real causes of its current debt? And why is there so little effort made to ascertain that those causes are truly remedied?

Every dollar of debt that is not used adequately to advance development eats up a dollar of debt-servicing capacity that could be more productively used. In this respect, the use of available space calculated under this framework as a justification for an "increase in poverty-reducing expenditures" or "to meet their Millennium Development Goals" could perversely induce many low-income countries to fill up their credit space without generating the growth they so much need.

The framework, almost as an afterthought, on a case-by-case basis, even when there is no sustainability room left, contains some wording about the importance of accommodating loans designated for specific high-return projects. In fact, the WB should always be looking for those high-return projects that generate poverty-reducing growth.

## Moral hazards

One of the yet unsolved mysteries of the world of Public Finance is how politicians can delicately manage the contradiction that arises from declaring all outstanding old public debt to be evil, while simultaneously preaching the virtues of any new credits to their country.

Declaring a debt as "sustainable" (as opposed to self-repayable credit) implies that the debt will be repaid by those coming afterwards. So it would seem that perhaps those in real need of a voice speaking out on their behalf are the future generations.

There is a tough real-world question begging for an answer: What is better: to reach an unsustainable debt level, to have a crisis and get it out of your system, or to condemn yourself and future generations to living forever under the burden of technically correctly calculated sustainable debt levels?

Rewarding countries that have policies that development experts deem to be of poor quality with a higher proportion of concessionality (meaning more grants, fewer loans) screams out the presence of an immense moral hazard. Although reductions in the overall credit volume might in fact mitigate some of the problems caused by excessive debt, the framework has to be crystal clear about what it means, as there are always many parties interested in what it should not mean.

## On thresholds

The Bank cares a lot about keeping high standards in

procurement, but, out there, in the real world, there are many debt-pushers who just love the addictions they create. Much debt is contracted by nontransparent means, hidden, either in the darkness of smoky-room negotiations or in the technical financial sophistications that make it impossible for any mortal to understand what is going on, especially with so little intelligible data available to their mortal citizens. Odious debt? Yes, there is a lot, but let us not forget that for every penny of odious debt that exists, there is an almost penny by penny match of odious credit. I have written about Odious Debt and about Odious Credits; perhaps it is time for me to write about Odious Thresholds.

## Begging for humility

Most of the documents coming out from the Debt Sustainability Analysis (DSA) correctly state that the conclusions should at best serve as rough guidance and indicative guideposts. Nonetheless by including so many references to strong empirical evidence, robustness, and strong analytical underpinnings, they end up anyhow overstating its validity.

The case for more humility and lower expectations with respect to the reliability of the DSA is laid out with crude clarity by the United States General Accounting Office (GAO) in its study of the IMF's capacity to predict crisis, published in June 2003 (SecM2003-0306). In it, GAO states, among other things, that of 134 recessions occurring between 1991 and 2001, IMF was able to forecast correctly only 11 percent of them, and that it was similarly bad in forecasting current accounts results. Moreover, when using their Early Warning Systems Models (EWS), in 80 percent of the cases where a crisis over the next 24 months was predicted by IMF no crisis occurred. Furthermore, in about 9 percent of the cases where no crisis was predicted, there was a crisis.

## Domestic debt

Frequently, just because of the lack of adequate data,

there are proposals to disconnect the DSA from the analysis of the domestic debt, an idea which is just plain crazy. There is no way on earth that you can argue, or justify, that a debt-sustainability framework can be developed exclusively for the external public debt of a country, ignoring the domestic.

I guess the above is another prime example of what can happen when we allow the econometrists an excessive influence. Oh we cannot get data? Do not let that stop us! In their desperation, I even heard some of the number-masseurs put forward the weird argument that the assessment of, and the response to, domestic debt in low-income countries, although critical, did not lend itself to a threshold approach. Weird, because they did not seem to notice that, if true, this should cast doubts over the whole DSA framework itself.

### Crowding out the private sector:

Considering the importance given by the WB to the private sector as a development agent, I was always upset to find so few and sparse references in the DSA to the issue of how public debt crowds out of the private sector from the credit markets. From my point of view, one of the main determinants when calculating debt sustainability should be this factor and indeed if the DSA decrees as untenable any public credit that raises the cost of private debt more than x number of basis points, I might have reacted quite differently to the debate.

Currently defining a country's debt sustainability in terms of how much public debt it can have before risking default sounds to me like setting the bar unbearably high, since long before that happens, the private sector is probably already long gone.

As a sort of consolation I read somewhere that we Directors had agreed that private external debt was potentially less troublesome than public debt, but this is of course a far cry from declaring as an absolute development need that the private sector should have competitive access to external debt.

Of course there are traders and investors who do have a particular interest in the probability of sovereign risk defaults but, in fact, most ordinary citizens and entrepreneurs are much more interested in making sure that the public debt does not crowd out their own opportunities of accessing credits on reasonable terms and costs. Of course, the Bank and the Fund must know with whom they should team up.

Public debt could sometimes be described as financial emphysema inasmuch as it makes it harder for the private economy to breathe properly. In some cases the secondary hazards produced by public-sector debts, might be so large that they should perhaps be entirely prohibited.

### Credit Ratings?

Some of the data and conclusions coming out from the DSA are supposed to be made transparently public, as they indeed should be—to all the market. We have also been told that this information will not develop into a sort of credit-rating system but it is hard to understand why this would not happen. In this respect, the Bank needs to understand better the reactions of the market, because it might very well happen that when the Bank proposes more concessions in response to a low-debt sustainability, other market players might respond by asking for higher interest or shorter repayment terms, so as to make up for the higher risks announced by the Knowledge Bank.

### Why consensus?

While we appreciate the worth of a diversity of opinions, I cannot understand how at the same time we give such great importance to having a consensus of opinion between the Bank and the Fund. For instance, on the issue of banking regulations, I have frequently warned that the mentality of a Central Bank regulator who pursues with zealous fervor the avoidance of a crisis, at any cost may lead to the exclusion of other key objectives of a financial system, such as generating growth and distributing income. In this respect, we might on the contrary need the Bank to differ outspokenly from the Fund.

### Costs and efforts

Currently there is a lot of frantic activity analyzing debt sustainability, mainly in the Fund. If we add up all the resources used, we might come up with quite an impressive figure, and it would be a shame if all those efforts came to naught just because of a lack of focus. Whatever you do, please rein in all those econometricians who with little or no ideas about debt are having the time of their life, having been given a license to regress on whatever variable they can imagine.

### Development

Grants or loans? Neither! Just more open markets, let us trade, in all services as well, and let us do business.

### A word of caution about Financial Leverage

If a project is expected to produce 10% in returns and an investor can borrow half of the funds needed at 8% then, on his own investments, he will make 12%. That's why financial leverage is considered a good thing. Of course if the project then only makes 6% for the investor, as he still has to pay all the interest on the loans, he will see his return drop to 4% and that is why financial leverage has risks.

Mixing your capital and debts in such a way as to extract the highest possible profit for a certain level of risk is basically what finance is all about. As good and useful as financial leverage can be for the private sector, its application for the public sector though is far from that straightforward.

The main problem with financial leverage in the public sector is that there is a gap too wide between the immediate beneficiaries and the final payers of the risk. If a private investor does badly he will normally pay for it himself shortly, sometimes even before the investment has taken place, as there are stock markets that evaluate his investment decisions in a flash. However, if it is the public sector, the payee of any loss is an anonymous next generation of citizens or, at the earliest, the next government. When you can reap all the goodies today and have someone else pay for them tomorrow we must know that the stage is set for committing huge mistakes.

That is why I get so angry when financial professionals so haphazardly extol the virtues of debt and believe them applicable across the board.

\*\*\*

And here I follow up with three articles inspired by the discussions. I published them in my country while an ED

### An Unsustainable Sustainability

The latest fashion in the academic world of international finance is to calculate what is known as the Sustainable Debt Level (SDL). As you may have guessed, it has to do with the level of public debt a country can sustain without entering into a crisis. Normally the SDL is calculated based on the size of the economy (GNP) or on a country's exports.

Whatever scientific approach is given to the SDL issue, it sure seems somewhat obscene to the citizenry of countries where it is evident that public debt engenders low or even no productivity.

If a credit is granted properly, the credit is repaid and then debt levels never become a problem. It is only the bad or mediocre loans that accumulate—those that do not generate their own repayment. So it could be said that what is really being calculated with the SDL is the level of bad debt that a country can get saddled with. Quite frankly, a developing country with real needs cannot afford the luxury of canceling even one cent in interest on a debt level arising from a series of credits that are nonproductive on the average.

From this perspective and since what we really mean is sustaining something that is unsustainable, this question remains: wouldn't it be better to skip calculating this debt level and try to free ourselves once and for all from these mortgages, instead of condemning future generations to live forever under the weight of an SDL that has been perfectly calculated? How much torture can the torture victim take before passing out?

And who encouraged these countries to go into debt? Ask those who are well-acquainted with the temptation that credits pose to politicians. In China, they say that you wish for your enemies to live in interesting times. In Argentina, because of the suffering provoked by excessive debt, it would seem that what their enemies could have wished upon them was the trust and confidence of international markets.

On the day that our country Venezuela firmly and irrevocably sets upon the path of totally canceling its debt, on this day an enormous opportunity will open for all those private and collective initiatives that need financial oxygen. Unfortunately it will not be easy, since our politicians, while condemning past debts, have mastered the magic of simultaneously preaching the benefits of new credits.

From *El Universal*, Caracas, June 5, 2003

## Odious Debt

One of my recent articles, which focused on the need to protect the environment, concluded by recalling the ancient proverb, "We have not inherited the world from our parents; we have borrowed it from our children." On that occasion, as always, I thought about Venezuela and I knew that, as borrowers from our children, we have acted like veritable pigs. Not only have we extracted our country's oil without putting it to much good use, we've even mortgaged its future in the process.

Some countries may be in need of foreign loans to get on their feet, but here in Venezuela we ought to know by now that our foreign public debt, be it the debt of yesterday, today, or tomorrow, only serves to fasten us all the more securely to a sinking ship. Foreign public debt is a monstrous obstacle. It keeps our citizens from getting loans (or at least makes loans much more expensive) that could indeed lead to growth in the country and allow the government to satisfy social needs through taxation.

Our only salvation is to learn how to resist the lure of the eternal sirens' song, which goes "foreign debt taken on by the previous administrations is evil and good for nothing, but rest assured, with us, everything's going to be different." How do we—like the ancient Odysseus—tie ourselves to the mast?

There are those, in similar desperation, who argue that since our creditors were accomplices of those administrations, we shouldn't pay our debts to them. I accept the theory of complicity, at least on the part of the intermediaries, but I think we should punish them much more harshly, by canceling the entire debt and never again taking out another loan.

What can ordinary citizens do who want to and have to go about their daily lives and can't be continually overseeing the government? The same as any company: they can refuse to provide their management with authorization for contracting debts. Along these lines, a doctrine is now being discussed in the world according to which, if the debt was contracted by an illegitimate government, or for uses that were clearly of no benefit to the country said debt could be declared odious and, as such, would not be legally demandable.

Dear friends, if we are going to do right by our children, our grandchildren, and our great grandchildren, and return the country we borrowed from them in good shape, maybe we should take advantage of such a possibility and declare our foreign public debt eternally odious. Given that threat: Would creditors dare provide us with loans? What would the credit-rating agencies say? Or let us be even more clear about the message and amend our constitution to say that the government of Venezuela has no authority to borrow from foreign sources, that any attempt to do so is illegal, and hence that all such illegal debts will not be repaid. That should stop foreigners from lending us money!

From *El Universal*, Caracas, March 25, 2004

**Odious Credit**

I recently wrote about *odious foreign public debt*, that debt about which there is a current debate in the world as to whether it can be legally repudiated if it is taken on by illegitimate governments or for illegitimate ends. The other side of the coin is *odious credit*. Please don't think I'm against banks—quite the opposite. But I respect the role of the financial middlemen too highly to keep quiet when they are not doing their job right. In 1981, the representative of a foreign bank in Venezuela showed me a letter in which his boss instructed him to "give credit to the INAVI, Venezuela's National Housing Institute. It's the worst public institution, which means that it pays us the highest rate and, as you know, in the end it's just as public as the best of them and Venezuela will have to pay up just the same." Odious credit, isn't it?

The first thing a good banker should ask a client applying for a loan is *what is it for* and if the answer is not satisfactory he should reject the application, regardless of the guarantees offered. Simple *plain-vanilla* fraud of the Parmalat kind will always exist, but the asinine way all their creditors fell into the trap makes one suspect that this is only the first case of systemic risk in the banking system: tempted by the regulators in Basel, banks subordinate their own criteria to those dictated by auditors and credit raters. This development, bad in itself, is even more serious in the case of public credit, where the *what it's for* is being replaced by *how much can be carried*, perversely derived by calculating the level of sustainable public debt.

When I call for the total elimination of foreign public debt (which is feasible and would not require huge sacrifices in an oil rich land like Venezuela) my colleagues often argue that a certain level of debt is good and necessary for the country. This does not convince me, since it makes debt sound like electricity that must be kept at a certain voltage. Because public debt must always be paid back, regardless of whether anybody ever knew what or whom it was for, I'm fighting for the day when the private sector in Venezuela can return to the markets, freely, without having to carry that huge monkey—foreign public debt—on its back.

In my opinion, the *Benemérito* (the dictator Juan Vicente Gómez (1864—1935) who ruled the country between 1908 and 1935) deserved great credit for ridding Venezuela of her foreign debts He certainly knew that to shake off that vice more than patches or pieces of chewing gum are needed.

From *El Universal*, Caracas, April 22, 2004

# BASEL—Regulating for what?

I had witnessed from a very close range how an incipient bank crisis in my country was made a thousand times worse when some bank regulators, like kids with new toys, started to apply in a very sloppy way the first generation of Basel capital-requirement rules. I had also seen how perfectly good credits had later been deemed bad by regulators applying rules designed for economies without inflation without any adjustments to a country going through a significant inflation. From then on, I have voiced concerns about the risk of excessive banking regulations and, in fact, the following is the very first article I published in Venezuela.

### Puritanism in banking

In his book *Money: Whence it came, where it went"* (1975), John Kenneth Galbraith discusses banks and banking issues which I believe may be applicable to the Venezuela of today.

In one section, he addresses the function of banks in the creation of wealth. Galbraith speculates on the fact that one of the basic fundamentals of the accelerated growth experienced in the western and south-western parts of the

United States during the past century was the existence of an aggressive banking sector working in a relatively unregulated environment.

Banks opened and closed doors and bankruptcies were frequent, but as a consequence of agile and flexible credit policies, even the banks that failed left a wake of development in their passing.

In a second section, Galbraith refers to the banks' function of democratization of capital as they allow entities with initiative, ideas, and will to work although they initially lack the resources to participate in the region's economic activity. In this second case, Galbraith states that as the regulations affecting the activities of the banking sector are increased, the possibilities of this democratization of capital would decrease. There is obviously a risk in lending to the poor.

In Venezuela, the last few years [the 1990s] have seen a debate, almost puritan in its fervor, relative to banking activity and how, through the implementation of increased controls, we could avoid a repeat of a banking crisis like the one suffered in 1994 at a cost of almost 20% of GDP. Up to a certain point, this seems natural in light of the trauma created by this crisis.

However, in a country in which unemployment increases daily and critical poverty spreads like powder, I believe we have definitely lost the perspective of the true function of a bank when I read about the preoccupation of our Bank Regulating Agency that "the increase in credit activity could be accompanied by the risk that loans awarded to new clients are not backed up with necessary support (guarantees)" and that as a result we must consider new restrictions on the sector.

It is obvious that we must ensure that banks do not overstep their bounds while exercising their primary functions—a mistake which in turn would result in costly rescue operations. We cannot, however, in lieu of perfecting this control, lose sight of the fact that the banks' principal purpose should be to assist in the country's economic development and that it is precisely with this purpose in mind that they are allowed to operate.

I cannot believe that any of the Venezuelan banks were awarded their charters based purely and simply on a blanket promise to return deposits. Additionally, when we talk about not returning deposits, nobody can deny that—should we add up the costs caused by the poor administration, sins, and crimes perpetrated by the local private banking sector throughout its history—this would turn out to be only a fraction of the monetary value of the comparable costs caused by the public/government sector.

Regulatory Puritanism can affect the banking sector in many ways. Among others, we can mention the fact that it could obligate the banks to accelerate unduly the foreclosure and liquidation of a business client simply because the liquid value for the bank in the process of foreclosure is much higher than the value at which the bank is forced to carry the asset on its books. In the Venezuela of today, we do not have the social flexibility to be able to afford unnecessary foreclosures and liquidations.

In order to comprehend the process involved in the accounting of losses in a bank, one must understand that this does not necessarily have anything to do with actual and real losses, but rather with norms and regulations that require the creation of reserves. Obviously banks will be affected more or less depending on the severity of these norms. Currently, a comparative analysis would show that Venezuela has one of the most rigid and conservative sets of regulations in the world.

On top of this, we have arrived at this extreme situation from a base, extreme on the other end of the spectrum, in which not only was the regulatory framework unduly flexible, but in which, due to the absence of adequate supervision, the regulations were practically irrelevant.

Obviously, the process of going from one extreme to the

other in the establishment of banking regulations is one of the explanations for the severe contraction of our banking sector. Until only a few years ago, Venezuela's top banks were among the largest banks of Latin America. Today, they simply do not appear on the list.

It is evident that the financial health of the Venezuelan banking community requires an economic recovery and any Bank Superintendent complying with his mission should actively be supporting said recovery instead of, as sometimes seems evident, trying to receive distinctions for merit from Basel (home of the international bank regulatory agencies).

If we insist in maintaining a firm defeatist attitude which definitely does not represent a vision of growth for the future, we will most likely end up with the most reserved and solid banking sector in the world, adequately dressed in very conservative business suits, presiding over the funeral of the economy. I would much prefer their putting on some blue jeans and trying to get the economy moving.

From *The Daily Journal*, Caracas, June 1997

\*\*\*

Having had so many difficulties in finding the correct way of pronouncing "Basel," I just had to leave in my editor Jim's comment: Swiss names are a confusing mess because Switzerland has four official languages. Just imagine if a place name in Venezuela could be spelled in Spanish, Portuguese, English, or an Indian language! Well, Basel is mostly German-speaking, so Webster's prefers the German spelling "Basel." Modern French spells it "Bâle," with the circumflex accent hinting that a consonant has been dropped. "Basle" is the archaic French spelling, before the "s" was dropped. Basel is where Switzerland, Germany, and France meet. Some American dictionaries prefer "Basle," and I suspect that it was the spelling used in archaic French in a treaty recognizing the area as Swiss. I prefer Webster's "Basel," as you had earlier, but you must decide and then be consistent. My dear editor, ok, I have decided, but that's still no guarantee I will be able to manage consistency.

***

### A preliminary warning

My editor also tells me, "The upcoming paragraphs in italics are almost completely unintelligible to me. I would think that one would have to be a major in business, finance, banking, accounting, or economics to try to understand the jargon. Your writing is crystal clear in contrast with this bureaucratese. Why don't you get rid of this quotation, and sum it up in a few sentences of your own wording?" Well I can't do that, perhaps just the fact that they are unintelligible to most might be a part of the problem, and so…readers beware.

### A warning

Dear Colleagues,

An excess of Basel's banking regulations could be very harmful to your country's development.

Leaving the issue of prudent bank regulations exclusively in the hands of too prudish bank regulators might be dangerous for economic growth. It is not an unimportant issue, and I beg you to read the following extensive quote from the chapter about "Coping with Weak Private Debt Flows—Basel II" that appeared in the World Bank report "Global Development Finance 2003."

> The new method of assessing the minimum capital requirement is expected to have important implications for emerging-market economies, principally because capital charges for credit risk will be explicitly linked to indicators of credit quality, assessed either externally under the standardized approach or internally under the two ratings-based approaches. The implications include the likelihood

of increased costs of capital to emerging-market borrowers, both sovereign and corporate; more limited availability of syndicated project-finance loans to borrowers in infrastructure and related industries; and an "unleveling" of the playing field for domestic banks in favor of international banks active in developing countries.

If, as expected, most domestically owned banks in emerging-market economies adopt the standardized approach to credit risk, they will be at a comparative disadvantage vis-à-vis cross-border lending by international banks when attempting to lend to high-quality domestic borrowers. On the other hand, they will have a comparative advantage in lending to low-quality domestic borrowers (Fischer 2002, Hayes 2002).

Concerns over the increased cost of capital under Basel II relate to the cross-border lending of international banks, and the potentially higher capital charges associated with such lending, particularly under the internal, ratings-based approaches that international banks are expected to adopt. The regulatory capital requirements would be significantly higher in the case of non-investment-grade emerging-market borrowers than under Basel I. At the same time, borrowers with a higher credit rating would benefit from a lower cost of capital under Basel II. A quantitative assessment of such effects is not straightforward, as the results are sensitive to a number of factors, including banks' loan pricing policies and, in particular, the extent to which banks' economic capital, which derives loan pricing, may exceed the minimum capital charges under the IRB approach. A recent study by the OECD (Weder and Wedow 2002) estimates the cost in spreads for lower-rated emerging borrowers to be possibly 200 basis points.

Finally, the prospects for capital flows for infrastructure projects from the market in syndicated commercial-bank loans depends on how the BCBA ultimately elects to treat structured credit products, including project finance. The current proposal places project loans in higher risk category than corporate loans, leading the BCBS to recommend higher capital requirements that could reduce the availability of syndicated project-finance loans and possibly increase their cost to borrowers in infrastructure and other sectors. But according to evidence provided by the private sector in response to the BCBS´s recommendation, project-finance loans outperform unsecured corporate loans, both in default rates and recovery performance, thus requiring lower capital charges, not more (Berner and others 2002). The BCBS is reportedly considering this evidence.

After having seen the World Bank Group capable of expressing such serious warnings as those quoted above, its continuous silence about the issue truly astonished me. Frankly our wish to harmonize with the International Monetary Fund cannot, and should not, mean we silence our voice.

Per

Now, I certainly did not keep silent, and the following are just some examples of my voiced observations.

### About the Global Bank Insolvency Initiative

Dear Friends,

We recently had a technical briefing about the Global Bank Insolvency Initiative. Having had a special interest in this subject for some years, I wish to make some comments.

As I have always seen it, the costs related to a bank crisis are the following three:

- The actual direct losses of the banks at the outbreak of the crisis. These are represented by all those existing loans that are irrevocably bad loans and therefore losses without a doubt.
- The losses derived from mismanaging the interventions (workout costs). These include, for example, losses derived from not allowing some of the existing bad loans the time to work themselves out of their problems. They also include all the extraordinary legal expenses generated by any bank intervention in which regulators in charge want to make sure that they themselves are not exposed to any risk at all.
- The long-term losses to the economy resulting from the "Financial Regulatory Puritanism," that tend to follow in the wake of a bank crisis as thousands of growth opportunities are not financed because of the attitude "we need to avoid a new bank crisis at any cost."

For the sake of the argument, I have hypothesized that each of these individual costs represents approximately a third of the total cost. Actually, having experienced a bank crisis at very close range, I am convinced that the first of the three above costs is the smallest...but I guess that might be just too politically incorrect to pursue further at this moment.

In this respect, it is clear that any initiative that aims to reduce the workout costs of bank insolvency is always welcome and in fact the current draft contains many well-argued and interesting comments, which bodes well for its final findings and suggestions.

That said, the scope of the initiative might be somewhat limited and outdated, making it difficult to realize its full potential benefits. There is also the danger that an excessive regulatory bias will taint its findings.

Traditional financial systems, represented by many small local banks dedicated to very basic and standard commercial credits, and subject to normally quite lax local regulation and supervision, are mostly extinct. They are being replaced by a system with fewer and bigger global bank conglomerates governed by a global Basel-inspired regulatory framework and they operate frequently by transforming the economic realities of their portfolios through mechanisms and instruments (derivatives) that are hard to understand even for savvy financial experts.

In this respect I believe that instead of dedicating scarce resources to what in some ways could be deemed to be financial archaeology, we should confront the new market realities head on, making them an explicit objective of this global initiative. For instance, what on earth is a small country to do if an international bank that has 30% of the local bank deposits goes belly up?

We all know that the financial sector, besides having to provide security for its depositors, needs also to contribute toward economic growth and social justice, by providing efficient financial intermediation and equal opportunities of access to capital. Unfortunately, both these last two objectives seem to have been relegated to a very distant plane, as the whole debate has been captured by regulators that seem only to worry about avoiding a bank crisis. Unfortunately, it seems that the initiative, by relying exclusively on professionals related to banking supervision, does little to break out from this incestuous trap. By the way if you want to see about conflict of interest, then read the section "Legal protection of banking authorities and their staff." It relates exactly to those wide blanket indemnities that we so much criticize elsewhere.

And so, friends, I see this Global Bank Insolvency Initiative as a splendid opportunity to broaden the debate about the world's financial systems and create the much needed checks and balances to Basel. However, nothing will come out of it if we just delegate everything to the hands of the usual suspects.

By the way, and I will say it over and over again, in terms of this debate, we, the World Bank, should constitute the de facto check and balance on the International Monetary Fund. That is a role we should not be allowed to ignore—especially in the name of harmonization.

Per

### Some comments at a Risk Management Workshop for Regulators

Dear Friends,

As I know that some of my comments could expose me to clear and present dangers in the presence of so many regulators, let me start by sincerely congratulating everyone for the quality of this seminar. It has been a very formative and stimulating exercise, and we can already begin to see how Basel II is forcing bank regulators to make a real professional quantum leap. As I see it, you will have a lot of homework in the next years, brushing up on your calculus—almost a career change.

But, my friends, there is so much more to banking than reducing its vulnerability—and that's where I will start my devil's advocate intrusion of today.

**Regulations and development.** The other side of the coin of a credit that was never granted, in order to reduce the vulnerability of the financial system, could very well be the loss of a unique opportunity for growth. In this sense, I put forward the possibility that the developed countries might not have developed as fast, or even at all, had they been regulated by a Basel.

**A wider participation.** In my country, Venezuela, we refer to a complicated issue as a *dry hide*: when you try to put down one corner, up goes the other. And so, when looking for ways of avoiding a bank crisis, you could be inadvertently slowing development.

As developing sounds to me much more important than avoiding bank failures, I would favor a more balanced approach to regulation. Talleyrand is quoted as saying, "War is much too serious to leave to the generals." Well, let me stick my head out, proposing that banking regulations are much too important to be left in the hands of regulators and bankers.

Friends, I have been sitting here for most of these five days without being able to detect a single formula or word indicating that growth and credits are also a function of bank regulations. But then again, it could not be any other way. Sorry! There just are no incentives for regulators to think in terms of development, and then the presence of the bankers in the process has, naturally, more to do with their own development. I believe that if something better is going to come out of Basel, a much wider representation of interests is needed.

**A wider Scope.** I am convinced that the direct cost of a bank crisis can be exceeded by the costs of an inadequate workout process and the costs coming from the regulatory Puritanism that frequently hits the financial system—as an aftershock.

In this respect, I have the impression that the scope of the regulatory framework is not sufficiently wide, since the final objective of limiting the social costs cannot focus only on the accident itself, but has also to cover the hospitalization and the rehabilitation of the economy. From this perspective, an aggressive bank, always living on the edge of a crisis, would once again perhaps not be that bad, as long as the aggressive bank is adequately foreclosed and any criminal misbehavior adequately punished.

**On risks** In *Against the Gods* Peter L. Bernstein (John Wiley & Sons, 1996) writes that the boundary between the modern times and the past is the mastery of risk, since for those who believe that everything was in God's hands, risk management, probability, and statistics, must have seemed quite irrelevant. Today, when seeing so much risk managing, I cannot but speculate on whether we are not leaving out God's hand, just a little bit too much.

If the path to development is littered with bankruptcies, losses, tears, and tragedies, all framed within the human seesaw of one little step forward, and 0.99 steps back, why do we insist so much on excluding banking systems from capitalizing on the Darwinian benefits to be expected?

There is a thesis that holds that the old agricultural traditions of burning a little each year, thereby getting rid of some of the combustible materials, was much wiser than today's *no burning at all*, that only allows for the buildup of more incendiary materials, thereby guaranteeing disaster and scorched earth, when fire finally breaks out, as it does, sooner or later.

Therefore a regulation that regulates less, but is more active and *trigger-happy*, and treats a bank failure as something normal, as it should be, could be a much more effective regulation. The avoidance of a crisis, by any means, might strangely lead us to the *one and only bank*, therefore setting us up for the mother of all moral hazards—just to proceed later to the mother of all bank crises.

Knowing that "the larger they are, the harder they fall," if I were regulator, I would be thinking about a progressive tax on size. But, then again, I am not a regulator, I am just a developer.

**Conspiracy?** When we observe that large banks will benefit the most with Basel II, through many risk-mitigation methods not available to the smaller banks which will need to live on with Basel I, and that even the World Bank's "Global Development Finance 2003" speaks about an *"unleveling" of the playing field for domestic banks in favor of international banks active in developing countries*, I believe we have the right to ask ourselves about who were the real negotiators in Basel?

Naturally, I assume that the way the small domestic banks in the developing countries will have to deal with these *new artificial comparative disadvantages* is the way one deals with these issues in the World Trade Organization, namely by requesting safeguards.

**Credit Ratings** Finally, just some words about the role

of the Credit Rating Agencies. I simply cannot understand how a world that preaches the value of the invisible hand of millions of market agents can then go out and delegate so much regulatory power to a limited number of human and very fallible credit-rating agencies. This sure must be setting us up for the *mother* of all systemic errors.

**The Board** As for Executive Directors (such as myself), it would seem that we need to start worrying about the risk of Risk Managers doing a de facto takeover of Boards—here, there, and everywhere. Of course we also have a lot of homework to do, most especially since the devil is in the details, and risk management, as you well know, has a lot of details.

Thank you.

## Let the Bank Stand Up

Dear Friends and Colleagues,

After having identified in our Review of the Financial Sector Assessment Program the problems of: "(i) weak credit culture with the prevalence of non-payments mechanism that undermine the development of the formal financial sector; (ii) limited access to formal, affordable financing by small and medium enterprises, a typical development trap in transition economies; and (iii) the slow pace of banking sector consolidation," it is shameful to observe that the only recommendations we put forward are "(i) enhancement of the central bank's ability to deal with insolvent banks, (ii) strengthening of penalty provisions, and (iii) increasing minimum capital requirements." Come on!

We all know that risk aversion comes at a cost, a cost that might be acceptable for developed and industrialized countries, but that might be too high for poor and developing ones and, in this respect the Bank has the responsibility of helping developing countries to strike a right balance between risks and growth possibilities. Please, let us never forget that the other side of the Basel coin might be many unique developing opportunities (credits) forgone.

Why do I make these comments with such candor? Besides having been alerted during many years about the consequences of a Financial Puritanism that seems to be invading the world—and that does not get the real culprits either—in the specific case of my country, the combined portfolio of credits in commercial banks fell in real terms from about US$ 16,000 million in 1982, to only about US$ 4,000 by 1997. In such scenario, to then hear about Basel and its prudence regulations reminds me of the makeup of a corpse already in rigor mortis although I should perhaps note that in the case of this particular corpse, even almost *six feet under*, it has anyhow been able to generate surprisingly large profits, for itself.

In the area of risk management in finance, it might be an appropriate time to remember what Franklin Delano Roosevelt said in his First Inaugural Address, March 4, 1933, namely that "the only thing we have to fear is fear itself" and so in this respect we very much need the Knowledge Bank to evolve more into a Wisdom Bank or at least a more humble Common Sense Bank.

In a seminar on housing finance we heard that "Basel is getting to be a big rule book," and, to tell you the truth, the sole chance the world has of avoiding the risk that Bank Regulators in Basel, accounting standard boards, and credit-rating agencies will introduce serious and fatal systemic risks into the world is by having an entity like the World Bank stand up to them—instead of rather fatalistically accepting their dictates and duly harmonizing with the International Monetary Fund.

As a small example, let me remind you that the World Bank has for some time and to no avail argued with respect to its own accounting that were it to follow strictly the current accounting rules, its financial reports would not reflect reality. Well, if the Bank has difficulties, imagine the rest of the world.

Per

## BASEL and microfinance

Most of our old banks were doing microfinancing through their small local branches where the local bank manager knew everyone and could even call up the borrower's mother to remind her of the importance of her son's commitment. Those loans never caused any bank crisis but were nonetheless almost prohibited by the work of Basel regulators that required that all loans should be such that they could be monitored by bank officials' continents away—without access to mothers. In this sense, our efforts to develop new micro-financing entities are just reconstructing what Basel helped to demolish.

## The mutual admiration club of firefighters in Basel
(A letter *Financial Times* did publish)

Sir, if a citizen from a developed country wishes to obtain finance from his local bank to buy a pricey retirement home in his local overheated market, then Basel poses no problem.

But should he want to buy a much more affordable home in a developing country and have his bank there finance him, then Basel slaps such capital-reserve requirements on the bank as to make it an impossibly onerous proposition.

This is just one way by which our bank supervisors in Basel are unwittingly controlling the capital flows in the world.

We also wonder how many Basel propositions it will take before they start realizing the damage they are doing by favoring so much bank lending to the public sector. In some developing countries, access to credit for the private sector is all but gone, and the banks are up to the hilt in public credits.

Please, help us get some diversity of thinking to Basel urgently; at the moment it is just a mutual admiration club of firefighters trying to avoid bank crisis at any cost—even at the cost of growth.

*Financial Times*, Letters, November 2004

## Towards a counter cyclical Basel?
(A letter *FT* did not publish)

Sir, the financial system is there to safeguard savings, to generate economic growth by channeling investments, and to promote equality by providing full and free access to capital and opportunities. Currently, our bank regulators headquartered in Basel are primarily concerned with the first goal, that of avoiding bank collapses, and how could it be otherwise, if you have only firemen on the board that regulates building permits.

Now, one of these days, the financial system, neatly combed and dressed in a tuxedo, but lying more than seven feet under in the coffin of financial de-intermediation (Jim, my editor: "Is there really such a word?" I: "If not, there is now!"), is going to wake up to the fact that it needs the presence of others in Basel. At that moment, perhaps we might start hearing about flexible capital requirements, moving up to 8.2 % or down to 7.8% by region, in response to countercyclical needs.

Meanwhile it's a shame that even their first goal might turn out to be elusive, since although the individual risks have fallen with Basel regulations, the stakes have increased, as those same regulations accelerate the tendency towards fewer and fewer banks.

## A new breed of systemic errors
(A letter *Financial Times* did publish)

Sir, except for regulations relative to money laundering, the developing countries have been told to keep the capital markets open and to give free access to all investors, no matter what their intentions are, and no matter for how long or short they intend to stay.

Simultaneously the developed countries have, through the use of credit-rating agencies, imposed restrictions as to what developing countries are allowed to be visited by their banks and investors.

That two-faced Janus syndrome, "you must trust the market

while we must distrust it," has created serious problems, not the least by leveraging the rate differentials between those liked and those rejected by our financial censors. Today, whenever a country loses its investment-grade rating, many investors are prohibited from investing in its debt, effectively curtailing demand for those debt instruments, just when that country might need it the most, just when that country can afford it the least.

Everyone knows that, sooner or later, the ratings issued by the credit agencies are just a new breed of systemic errors, about to be propagated at modern speeds. Friends, as it is, the world is tough enough.

*Financial Times*, Letters, January 2003

# The debate about using Country Systems

**Why did I spend so much time on this issue?**
Whether to let the countries learn and develop on their own in their own way and assisting them by freely giving some of the very scarce resources or whether to impose some conditions on how they are to manage these resources is one of the most difficult balancing acts of any development policy.

There must be thousands of examples of how development funds have been squandered to no avail by bad governments and crooked politicians, and certainly there are thousand of examples of how good-intentioned agencies have, in a quite similar and yet opposite way, squandered these scarce funds by imposing absolutely misplaced rules and conditions.

As I never believed that you could create good artists by having students practice painting by numbers, this little spot number 17 blue, and as those wanting to impose more and ever stricter conditions on the borrower were in the clear majority, my devil's advocate instincts and my normal tendency of siding with the weaker inspired me to take a very strong position in favor of allowing for a more frequent use of the countries' own systems.

**Ownership yes, but of what?**

In the many debates that followed it seemed that some minimum agreement had been reached, as everyone played at least lip service to the importance of "ownership" by which was meant, I think, that the countries really had to feel that they were enacting their own plans and policies. What never became really clear to me was whether there was any agreement on what it was that was supposed to be owned.

Was it about the ownership feeling that came out of having to struggle on their own to come up and enact a plan, or was it just about being able to feel as their own a plan suggested by others. If the later, it always seemed more a marketing problem to me and, in the corridors, I sometimes a bit irreverently wondered why we did not make more use of famous personalities to market our more difficult and less popular conditions.

\*\*\*

I here let Jim, my editor, express his doubts, expansively. (NGOs beware of Latin and Greek teachers!) The Philadelphia public-school system in the 1960s started a plan to introduce Latin and Greek studies into the elementary schools, so the Inner City kids would feel pride that they were getting a good education like kids in expensive private prep schools. They asked me to help develop textbooks. I liked the idea. I had started studying Latin in 1945 at the age of eleven, and I knew that even younger kids could do so if they studied hard. But the other committee members started screaming that we couldn't use any grammatical terms because it would make these kids feel dumb since they didn't know any English grammar. We couldn't do anything that threatened their little egos. I quit when I discovered that their idea of teaching Latin was to wave a picture of a dog biting a boy, and have the "Latin" class shout "Canis mordat puerum." I learned later that when their graduates with good grades in this program tried to take a beginning real Latin course in high school, there was no transfer effect, meaning they did no better than kids who didn't take elementary Latin. The city had thousands of these kids, and bragged that it was one of the most academic school systems in the country when the whole thing was a mockery, a silly game, a worthless waste of time except for teaching a little English vocabulary such as "canine" and "puerile," which could have been taught better in an English class. They wanted the "feel" of doing Latin and Greek on their own without the reality of doing so. Could your giving countries the feel of designing their own projects if they have nobody competent to do so turn into a similar charade? I don't know one way or the other.

Jim, let us hope not but, now back to my voice.

\*\*\*

### Participation, but of whom?

A parallel theme was that of participation, which meant that everyone in the country should be able to participate in the developing of the plans and policies of their country and also in their enactment. Without such broad participation, it would be impossible to foster a broad sense of ownership. Of course, I and everyone else agreed 100% with the statements of ownership and participation—which only made it more embarrassing when reality pointed out that the broad participation that we endorsed and applauded was normally just the participation of the same NGOs over and over again, as in the Groundhog Day movie.

To illustrate my various points of view during the debate without risking boredom, I hope, I will include just one personal statement, "Let them bike," one travel report to my colleagues, "Zamorano," and one article that I published some years ago in Venezuela—the three of them showing you where I am coming from.

## Let them bike

Friends, listening to your exhaustive list of concerns, I was reminded of the moments when I had to teach my daughters how to ride their bikes: I heard their mother's anxious calls in the background; I felt my own nervousness; nonetheless, I just knew I had to let them go.

One could find and read thousands of manuals about how to put a bike together safely; about all the safety implements a kid should wear, such as helmet and wrist-guards; about all the precautions he or she needs to take, not going downhill or out on the main road; but nowhere can you find even a single manual that clearly and exactly instructs you how to learn to ride a bike. Left leg up, right leg down! Or was it right leg up first?

We need to understand that development is a bit like learning how to ride a bike and, at the end of the day it is something that must be done on one's own. In fact, no matter how much we could help in the preparations, we will not stand a chance to achieve lasting results if we are not willing or do not know how to let them go.

It is not easy to let go, I probably even closed my eyes for fractions of seconds after letting my girls roll away on their bikes, but I let them go and they know how to ride a bike now.

So, my colleagues, in these discussions, not as caring parents but as caring development partners, let us try to act accordingly, letting them go, always remembering that, at the end of the day, countries need to do it on their own. What else could ownership mean?

Of course, anyone might fall trying, but that is exactly the risk we need to be able to take if they are going to achieve real sustainable development results and, if they fall, there is probably nothing more to do than to help them rebuild their confidence so that they can just have another go at it.

Moreover, if you try to hold the bike while they ride it, the bike might not really behave like a bike, and so they might never get the hang of it. What we really should be concerned about is that they have what is most needed at the time of trying: sufficient confidence in themselves. In fact, what unwillingly might be the first victim of all our other secondary concerns is precisely that, their confidence.

So, my colleagues, let them go, again and again and again, learning to ride their bike, and as they believe a bike should be ridden.

P.S. I know it is not as easy as it sounds and in fact I would only give someone the freedom to try it on their own whenever he or she convinces me she or he is ready for it and is sufficiently confident.

### About El Zamorano and the use of country systems
Dear colleagues,

Traveling in Honduras recently, I heard on the radio the old rock band *Enanitos Verdes* singing about having to run the risk of getting up, in order to keep on falling, and it reminded me of our recent discussions about "use-of-country-systems" where I gave you my mumbo jumbo about having to let them go, since this is the only way they could learn how to ride a bike.

I was on my way to visit the agricultural school *El Zamorano*, cajoled (with no major effort needed) by one of its graduates—a friend of ours, Jorge Wong, and little did I know I was heading into true learning-how-to-bike land. The motto of this most amazing school is "learning while doing" and...Boy, do they! Boy, do they learn!

In *El Zamorano*, kids have a school year of 11 months and are rigorously awakened every morning at 5 am—hellish but I tell you that it has been a long time since I've seen such a group of enthusiastic, happy, and feeling-good-about-the-future young faces. There are about eight hundred boarding students, of whom more than two hundred are girls. They come from many Latin American countries, from all backgrounds, and any differences are neutralized with education, companionship, and uniforms.

Along with their formal academic classroom studies, the kids, from seventeen to twenty-three, are taught about every imaginable (and also some you-do-not-want-to-imagine) agricultural and farm chore there is, by being handled full responsibility for doing them. They grow crops, milk cows and in the industrial installations where they produce cheeses, juices, marmalades, sausages, and much more that they sell in Honduran supermarkets, the managers are the students from senior grades and the workers their younger friends.

And *El Zamorano* goes way beyond teaching knowledge. When I heard some kids explain to me about the biologic pesticides they develop and market all over Central America, could it be to make it the "Green Subcontinent"? It became clear that besides algebra, they must have gotten lectures on confidence building, communication skills, and character formation too.

Although I was told that in the dry season the landscape changes somewhat, *El Zamorano* as I saw it lay snuggled in a beautiful valley, where it has about 10,000 acres of land and great and functional facilities. This *El Zamorano* seed effort is more than ready for some heavy-duty scaling-up, and they have already started doing so with some interesting and substantial extension programs, reaching out to their neighboring communities. Envying their tremendous educational expertise, I am already on my knees, begging them to branch out into my favorite Central American growth program—you bet, those who know me: educating doctors specialized in geriatric ailments and bilingual nurses, certified by schools and health authorities of developed nations.

In the last couple of weeks we have been reminded of some of Ronald Reagan's "one-liners" (slogans), among them, "trust but verify." It is clear that we face serious challenges when monitoring or verifying the results of our projects, but, frankly, after having been in *El Zamorano*, I am convinced that it is exactly in the trusting department where we really are in the backwaters. We need not worry, though. *El Zamorano* was founded three years before the World Bank, and so we still have a chance to catch up.

Back in D.C., on my radio, Joan Manuel Serrat was singing about Africa—something about the world not letting it go, yet not holding onto it.

### Lost in the water of globalization

I have just returned from a trip to Central America (October 2000) during which I noted that an important issue in the debate on how to improve public services like water and power was the awarding of concessions to international water companies. I thought at that moment, not without some sadness, how some cultures that hundreds of years ago were expert at building and managing their aqueducts have today simply given up even trying.

Having three daughters of different ages, I have several times had to watch a movie aimed at adolescents called *Clueless* (in fact, it's a great movie, and I might be using my daughters just as an excuse). In this movie a young girl tries to pass the exam for her driver's license. After being severely reprimanded by her instructor for not knowing how to park her vehicle, she curtly answers back with the excuse that valet parking could be had everywhere. I feel that today many of us react in the same way to the difficulty of improving our public services and making them more efficient: "why try so hard when foreign investors can do it?"

Evidently it is very often necessary to invest a considerable amount of resources or advanced technological know-how in order to offer an efficient and economically viable public service to the end user. In these cases a country may not have any alternative but to call on international investors and offer them a deal. However, in those cases where the only thing that is required to make a project go forward is good administration and a sound strategy for creating and maintaining relationships with users, specifically addressing issues such as quality and tariffs, it is difficult to condone the lack of desire to find a local solution to a local problem. One asks simply where we stand on our ambitions as a nation.

You may ask what, for example, the administration of water systems or the distribution of power has to do with being a nation. The answer is probably "directly—nothing." However, building a nation is not easy and requires at a minimum that its society learn how to resolve certain problems on its own. Taking the easy way out and simply calling in foreign assistance in order to solve problems in the water or power sectors could be compared to parents doing their child's homework to insure a good grade while at the same time not allowing the child to learn how to do things on his or her own.

Much of the pressure that creates the conditions for the sale of concessions of public services to multinational companies comes from multilateral agencies. You know the saying, "Do not give a man a fish, but teach him instead how to fish"? On occasion I ask myself whether these agencies "are not really asking developing countries to sell their fish-rods and their oceans.

In Venezuela, we are close to renewing our efforts to privatize certain public services. In this sense, I feel it is important to ask ourselves without any inferiority complex, whether international investors should or should not have access to these services at all. I make reference to complexes simply because I feel many of us suffer from a "globalization insufficiency" complex that now exceeds that of the ardent nationalism that affected us a few decades ago.

What should we do then, in order to insure that national interests are always present in the privatizations that loom in the future? Above everything else, it is important to recognize that the way the privatization process is designed will either attract or scare away national investors. For example, if in the case of the privatization of a power distribution network the state wishes to obtain a large price for selling the utility which it has owned, a price which must then be passed on to the customers of the network itself, the total costs involved will be so high that they will automatically disqualify or discourage any local investor. If on the contrary, use of the power-generation assets were awarded on the basis of who offers to charge the end user the lowest possible rate, local investors would have a better chance of participating.

Finally as no one is prophet in his own land, looking for foreign support I wish to make reference to a declaration I heard by David Montgomery, Viscount of Alamein, son of Field Marshall Montgomery (Monty) and the new British Ambassador to Mexico. He maintained that he simply could not understand why Argentina had sold all its public utilities to foreign investors. I do not understand it either, but what I am sure of is that unless we wish to lose our country in the waters of globalization, we must define with utmost clarity some strategic borders, and I don't mean just our geographical ones.

How depressing! With so much to be gained from globalization, why do they have to do it the wrong way, and why do they have to start doing it wrong just here and now?

From *El Universal*, Caracas, October 27, 2000

# My very private fight for better privatizations

To me, good privatizations can only be implemented by those who believe in the public sector and want to see it strengthened, and never by those who because of an ideological indigestion want to see the public sector weakened...or, worse, just want to exploit its weaknesses.

### Where do I come from?

I worked all my life in the private sector. I have assisted local and foreign bidders in privatization processes. I am an absolute believer that the public sector can derive a lot of strength by endorsing as much as possible to the private sector. That said, by sheer accident, I suddenly found myself aligned with many vociferous NGOs fighting against privatizations. How come?

In my country, more specifically on that beautiful Island of Margarita, in the Caribbean, that I urge you to visit, the privatization of its electrical distribution company was announced in 1997. Of course it was quite welcome news but, early in the process, I discovered that the central government (in Caracas on the mainland; Isla de Margarita has a capital of its own, La Asunción) aspired to collect a very large sum from whatever private company was to have the right to supply the service. Since to get the highest possible price they had to offer the investor the highest possible rates this meant that its effect would be felt in the pockets of private consumers, like me. Simultaneously, while the island was suffering severe scarcity of electricity the government also announced that it would sell hydro electricity to Brazil, going right through our national parks, the most beautiful there are, instead of sending it to our own Island. This also got me involved in some environmental issues.

As a one-man NGO (bona-fide and not organized), I wrote many warning articles to no avail. They privatized it, got a lot of money for it, and we islanders got stuck with the bill. Given that the WBG was very closely involved in similar processes, to the extent that I once even heard a Bank consultant suggest that the increases in the rates needed to be postponed until two years after the privatization, "so that the consumer does not identify the causality," you can very well see why this issue was on my personal agenda.

To me, the money received by governments for the concession rights to a public-utility monopoly should always be regarded as part of the public debt. It has to be canceled—not by taxes but by bills paid by customers. I always wondered how IMF did not see this happening, for instance, in Argentina.

If, for instance, a public utility such as electricity distribution is privatized against a payment of 100 million, and the buyer has to make 50 million in new investments, currently we register it as a 150 million investment in infrastructure. This is not right or transparent as the real investment in infrastructure is only 50 million, and the other 100 million is just fresh public-sector lending to be paid through higher tariffs. If our "Knowledge Bank" wants to understand what has really happened in this sector, it has to be able to call a spade a spade.

I really do not know what I managed to achieve on this

during my two years, perhaps not much, most especially since the issue of privatization has escaped the world of rationalities and entered the world of faiths and magic—black or white.

To give some examples of my advocacy, I include here a brief informal memo I wrote to my colleagues when we were discussing the Private Sector Development in the Electric Power Sector, plus two of my early warning articles, dating from way back.

### Transmission and Distribution—T & D

Dear Colleagues.

Until future fuel-cell availability frees electricity from the need of cables, transmission and distribution will be natural monopolies and, as such, they have to be regulated Among the many aspects of regulations, there is little doubt that setting the rates charged the customer is the most important and controversial issue. Whatever "reform" might mean, it is expected that in order for it to be successful, it needs to get the rates right, or at least reasonably right.

I strongly believe that the setting of rates in privatizations of public services that are in effect monopolies has not been sufficiently discussed in the WBG. I think that much more understanding of some mistakes made is necessary, not only to avoid repeating them, but also because the Bank might have an important role in assisting to correct the mistakes.

To make my point better, let me use the following example.

The balance sheet of a government owned electrical distribution company founded many years ago, and after the government has cleaned up their balance sheet paying off debt for the umpteenth time, has 1.000 in Total Assets represented by 100 in Cash and Accounts Receivables plus 900 in Net Electrical Fixed Asset, these last made up by a Gross of 2.000 less a depreciation of 900. The company has been very poorly managed and has accumulated urgent investment needs of 400. Privatization is therefore an option.

Basically there are three very different alternatives for how to privatize this company, based on how the electrical assets are valued. Each alternative will result in significantly different rates for customers and investment requirements.

- Alternative 1. The priority is given to the urgent investment needs. The government is willing to give up the headache, just to have someone run the company and supply the 400 needed. The investor would only have to put up initially 400 and the electricity rates could be set at the lowest reasonable level that also takes into accounts future investment needs. The transfer of the current electrical assets would probably be in terms of a concession to operate the assets for a fairly long period of time, conditioned on performance.
- Alternative 2. If instead the assets are going to be sold and there is a need to accommodate for either legal or political requirements, or both, the overall investment would add up to 1.400 (400 in new investments plus the current book value of 1.000) and the final structure of electricity rates offered to the investor would obviously be that much higher.
- Alternative 3. The priority is to maximize fiscal income. The government would like to sell at maximum value and so therefore it needs to justify maximum rate structures. An energy "reformer" would then perhaps suggest that the adequate value of assets, for the purpose of calculating rates, should be the "current replacement costs of an effective distribution net," for example assessed to be 2.200. A rate structure built around 2.200—if all other components such as having to pay adequate investment returns that cover both business risk and country risk are duly considered—would, self-fulfilling, most probably generate an offer of 2.200 for this monopoly. This offer, deducting the 400

in new investments, would then *release* 1.800 to the government…and perhaps help it to recover what it previously has lost due to its own inefficiencies.

I have seen privatizations structured along the third alternative, leading to unnecessarily high rates for the poor customers and consequently giving privatization an unnecessarily bad name.

I have personally conversed with local regulatory authorities in developed countries, even some of them here in Washington and when I showed them examples of the formulas for calculating rates for electricity that were part of the reforms WB sponsored during the last 15 years, their reactions were almost always the same: "If we would have applied those formulas here, we would have been out of a job." Why? Because the rates would have been so high that politicians would need to fire the regulators in order to get themselves reelected. And friends, that's even in places where there are no major country risk spreads to be taken into account for the discount rate.

I believe that The Knowledge Bank, in relation to privatizations and the setting of rates, sided either with the hopes for profits of the private investors or with the hopes of governments to receive as much up front as possible—all against the interests of the consumer.

Considering that competitively priced public services are a must for any development, it is amazing to see how poor developing countries are forced to offer 15 to 20 percent rates of return for the safest, or sometimes the only, feasible investments in their country. A poor country that needs to pay a 20 percent return to the investors who distribute its electricity is almost mortgaging its future, since how much would you then have to offer for riskier ventures?

I do not pretend to have the answer to all these issues, but I have no doubt that something has gone haywire. Evidence that we might not be playing fair is the absence of efforts to measure the real returns paid to the investors in the privatizations.

The squeeze produced by the high returns expected by the investors and the high prices asked by the governments has frequently resulted in unsustainable rates for the poor customers. The WBG could play an important role in making these more manageable since providing some long-term funding at reasonable rates, could perform wonders to achieve negotiated rate reductions.

Colleagues, this is a very difficult topic, and just to make an example let me pose the following question: If a country a priori requires a very high rate, 20%, because it is deemed to be very risky, does the investor really require 20% or would he afterwards be happy to ascertain that it was not that risky and that he is making a very acceptable 12%?

Do I hear any answer?

### Electricity for Brazil—and Isla de Margarita what?

We have been reading (1998) during the past few months about the development of a project which will supply electricity to Brazil and which involves construction of extensive distribution systems.

I must admit that my first reaction upon hearing about the project was sheer envy. This sentiment comes from my conviction that if we are to invest in transmission lines, the Island of Margarita for one is probably more deserving in relation to Venezuelans than Brazil. I simply don't understand how and why an important pole of development for the country such as Margarita is being forced into more expensive energy systems such as, for example, the timeworn idea of a gas pipeline from the mainline to the island, while we are simultaneously developing mega-projects in order to export power to Brazil.

You don't have to be an expert in environmental affairs to suspect that a 217-km (135-mile) suspended power line which must be supported by 512 towers, each of them 36 meters (over 100 feet) high, spread out through environmentally sensitive areas such as the Canaima National Park, the Imataca Forest

Reserve and the Southern Protection Zone of the State of Bolívar, must have serious implications. It is not enough to assert that there will be special care taken to camouflage the towers in order to reduce contrast with the horizon.

I propose that we study a swap. Hydroelectricity to Margarita, through airborne lines or submarine cables and a gas pipeline (underground) to Brazil. The latter can then build own power plants, wherever and whenever it sees fit.

I may be accused of being Brazil's enemy; I certainly am not! But Venezuela has yet to develop a coherent border policy. A power line aimed at developing an area where we still do not have effective representation seems more like a humanitarian-aid shipment of medicine, blankets and food parachuted into an unknown neighboring foreign territory, strengthening the latter's hand, without insuring that our own side of the border is equally populated, developed, and supplied.

How can a simple columnist dare comment on matters completely outside his direct scope of expertise? I believe the answer lies in the fact that it is not necessary to have technical know-how when the objective is to try to put projects into social perspective in such a way as to be able to analyze their priority for the country. We obtain proof on a daily basis that the country lacks a central entity whose responsibility is the adequate allocation of priorities to the many important projects. In this sense, it could be that the Brazilian project is valid, but would it not behoove us to analyze whether it is better and more important than others?

One more comment. Frequent mention is made about an environmental-impact study undertaken by a "specialized firm." I sure hope that these studies are entrusted to serious professionals with names and surnames rather than to an anonymous company. If we had their names, data on their identity cards, and addresses, we could conceivably exact some future accountability from them; if anything, for the honor or shame of their descendants.

By the way, forty years ago, this responsibility would have been assumed by politicians personally. They would not be hiding behind the skirts of a political organization. If dictatorship in any way could show something superior to democracy, it is because, at least in our country, Venezuela, dictators are held historically and directly more responsible for both good and bad; much more so than today's executives of Political Party, Inc.

From *The Daily Journal*, Caracas, February 20, 1998

### Pay now and pray for the light

The government has announced the sale of Nueva Esparta's electrical distribution company SENECA. The company's value, as a concession, is based more on the cash flows that are derived from the rates it charges customers, than from the value of its very old electrical assets.

As a consequence FIV (Venezuela Investment Fund), in its role as seller, might be tempted to offer the potential buyers the possibility of charging very high prices for its electricity. If we add to this the new investments that are required to improve the service, then we might face a truly horrifyingly high electricity bill.

Any privatization of a public service should be aimed at insuring that a continuous and acceptable service is made available to its users, at a reasonable cost. On the contrary, the SENECA privatization looks like one in which the sale is used cover up other fiscal necessities. This is made evident by the fact that the monopoly will be handed over to that bidder who "offers the highest price, on strictly cash terms and without any financing from the Venezuelan State."

On the FIV's Web page, the agency declares the following: "As far as the supply of primary energy to the before mentioned Island is concerned, the Economic Cabinet has decided that the winning bidder must present the National Executive, after the public bid, and no later than six months after the same, with an investment plan detailing the minimum cost associated with the delivery of the service, which must in turn reflect the tariffs to be applied."

The above declaration could in the layman's terms be interpreted as saying "Pay us now and let us know within six months what you are going to do with regards to the Island's needs." As such it would confirm the existing fiscal voracity and the general indifference of authorities to Margarita's well being. I am one of the most arduous defenders of privatization around, and therefore I hereby express my most vehement protest.

Everyone is well aware that the energy problems on the Island must be solved, and quickly. I have been one of the victims of burned-out compressors causing rotten food in my refrigerator, and so on, and therefore am among the first to assert that the most costly service is the bad one or, worse, the one you don't receive at all. However, I do believe that celerity is not incompatible with intelligence.

Before allowing the Venezuelan state to get rid of SENECA, we should request the authorities to lay a new submarine cable that would allow us to purchase cheap hydroelectric power from the national company Edelca. This is done in most other parts of our country, even in areas much more distant from the hydroelectric dams. We have also heard about plans to export hydro to Brazil and Colombia. Why, then, not our own Margarita?

As a minimum, the Island should insure that all the income from the sale of SENECA is deposited in an escrow account, to finance other sorely needed investments on the Island.

From *The Daily Journal*, Caracas, June 18, 1998

### Hit in the head by the SENECA sale

On Tuesday, September 14th, the power system of the Island of Margarita, SENECA, was finally privatized. The Venezuelan Investment Fund (FIV) had established a minimum price of 35 million dollars. The price finally paid by the winning bidder was 90 million dollars, thus awarding the sellers 55 million dollars more than they dreamed of or had originally thought would be fair.

There is no doubt that, in general terms, this is a great achievement and it would be very selfish not to congratulate those involved in this transaction for having concluded their job. Evidently, this privatization bodes well for the supply of electricity for the State and in this sense its population can celebrate the happening.

I have, however, time after time maintained the thesis that the privatization of a public service company should aim at improving the service while minimizing the cost for its users, and not at maximizing the central government's income. It is in this sense, then, that I express the following reservations with regards to this particular transaction. I am not criticizing the privatization SENECA per se, but I am raising the flag with regards to the "morning after" effects of doing so.

Evidently, should the SENECA have been sold for one dollar, the charges for electricity required in order to recover the investment would have been much lower. Today's financial community has awarded the Republic of Venezuela's long-term debt a tax and project risk-free return of over 20% per annum. In this sense, it would not be exaggerated to say that SENECA's buyers will expect a return of at least 20% on their own investment.

This implies that Margarita will have to come up with 18 million dollars (i.e. 20% of 90 million dollars) every year, and that this flow must come from the electric bills paid by the end users of the service. In tourism terms, this is like paying for a small brand new five-star hotel every year. To this amount, we must also add the outlays represented by salaries, new investment, purchase of electricity, and taxes.

It could very well be that this annual toll of 18 million dollars for the right to liberate itself from Cadafe's management is actually a great deal for Margarita. However, since Cadafe and the FIV obtained 90 million dollars for the privatized entity while projecting rates on a minimum price of 35 million dollars, there is room for the following questions:

First: Who, if anyone, went overboard when promising potential investors what future rate levels were to be paid by Margarita's population? Who calculated these rates? Did they make a mistake? If so, was it made on purpose, or was it simply incompetence? It is obvious that if the rates offered in the bid documents had been lower, the investors would not have put an extra 55 million dollars on the table.

It bothers me to no end to be treated as a moron by public officials. When they maintain that they obtained this premium simply because of the excellence of their management of the transaction, I feel they are sticking their tongues out at all of us. Why then didn't they establish a minimum bid of 25 million dollars? The premium would then have been 65 million dollars instead of 55 million dollars. Why didn't they offer an even higher rate structure and obtain, say, 120 million dollars instead of 90 million dollars?

We obviously understand the laughter and back slapping by state officials. We can almost hear them say "Marvelous. We have gotten rid of the responsibility for the supply of power to the island. On top of this, we have received an initial income of 90 million dollars plus all the other taxes we will be able to charge in the future! Nobody was the wiser for it! What a deal! Let's do the next one!"

Second: If FIV says it would have been happy with their asking price of 35 million dollars, why then will they take the 55-million-dollar premium away from the island? We must remember that the entire 90 million dollars, and specially the premium of 55 million dollars, will ultimately be footed by Margarita's population.

Immediately after the sale, one official celebrated the event by saying he felt like Sammy Sosa of the Chicago Cubs baseball team when he hit home run No. 61. As a user of the electrical system in Margarita, I felt more as if I had been hit in the head by the very same baseball bat.

I suggest we analyze the possibility that the 55-million-dollar premium be retained by the island. This would at least assuage some of the pain caused by the swinging bat. Some direct benefit for the island could then be gleaned from the affair, for example, another pipeline for potable water. Evident, if all the 90 million dollars were left on the island, so much the better.

In summary, there is no doubt that as Venezuelans we should all be applauding the success of the privatization of SENECA in the face of current tough times. However, as an assimilated Margariteño, I find it difficult to celebrate since its cost, a mortgage of 90 million dollars, has been placed directly on the island's shoulders.

From *The Daily Journal*, Caracas, September 19, 1998

## The present value and short circuits

The "present value" is an important financial concept that we should know about in order to understand many of the problems of development. As in my experience I have seen that not many are too clear about it, even though they affirmatively shake their heads, let me try to explain it a bit.

The easiest way I have heard the present-value concept explained is by asking a teenager for how much he would settle if he could receive a million-dollar inheritance today, instead of waiting until his grandmother passes away. The more the deal is urged on him, the more needed the money is, or the more wishful for the money the kid is, whether rightfully or not, the smaller amount he would be willing to accept as full payment now instead. The longer the kid believes his grandmother will live (time), the smaller amount he would be willing to accept now instead. The more the kid knows or has access to other productive things to do with this money, (opportunity costs), the smaller amount he would be willing to accept. The more he believes his grandmother could change her mind (risks), the smaller amount he would be willing to settle for now.

Another extreme way to look at it is by asking ourselves what would be the present value of a dollar received tomorrow, for someone who does not have the dollar he needs for him and his family to eat today.

But as we are talking "sophisticated finances," let's put some figures to it. If you wish to make a 10-year investment of 100 dollars in a fairly low-risk activity in a land that is deemed to have almost no country risk and if you are willing to settle for a 7 percent return, then, at the end of the first year your investment should be worth 107, after the second year with 7% more calculated on 107 it should be 114.5, and so on, until it reaches 197 dollars in year 10, thus averaging a return of 7% a year. Now, going back in our own tracks we can then establish that the present value of 197 in year 10 at 7% interest is 100, which is also the same as saying that each dollar received in year 10 is worth only 51 cents to day (100 divided by 197). (Jim, my editor's Q: "Are you assuming no inflation?" My A.: "Jim, it is imbedded in the 7%. You can look at it as 3% inflation plus the real 4% rate which the investment should provide.")

Now, if the country is deemed to be a quite high-risk country and should therefore command an additional 10 % for a total of 17%, then similar calculations would lead to expecting to receive 481 dollars instead in the 10th year, and in this case the present value of each dollar received in year 10 is therefore only 21 cents (100 divided by 481). (Jim: "Or you may receive zero in the tenth year because the country has expropriated private savings and investments." I: "Yes but that is exactly why you expect higher returns so as to reward you for higher risks. What I refer to in this case has more to do with the possibility that the risks you believed were there actually were not for real? I refer to something like an ex-ante and an ex-post rate")

And so if for instance there is a need to invest in the distribution of electricity we could say that the consumers of a high-risk country would have to cough up with 481 dollars over time while those in a low-risk country only need to pay 197. If this were all, then most probably a high-risk country would be doomed forever. Luckily this is not all. Not only because a country can reduce the perceived risk by behaving better, or at least being perceived as behaving better, but it can also try to reduce the cost of the project itself. For instance, if they took some measures that could induce investors to require 14% instead of 17% like putting in place a decent regulatory framework; and they could reduce the needed up-front investment from 100 to 80; and they could get a grant to pay for 20 so that the initial investment would only be 60, then the consumers, instead of having to pay 481 would have to pay 222, and that now is livable, indeed close to the 197 of the low-risk country.

But, what happened in many privatizations? Well, governments frequently did not put in place credible regulatory frameworks or, when they did, not early enough for the required rates of return to drop before the privatization; the participants were frequently foreigners who did not realize you could actually do it locally for 80; and finally the government, instead of looking for how to give the project a grant piled up instead its own cash-flow aspirations, and added 50. The final results: 150 at 17%. No wonder consumers are up in arms having to pay 721 over ten years.

## Reform fatigue opportunities

I hear so much about reform fatigue in the developing countries because of some of the disappointing results. Mostly I hear it blamed on the lack of follow-up reforms and on some economic exogenous shocks. Who knows? I for myself blame it much on the bad implementation of many reforms. For instance, privatizations that could have brought so much better results in their wake have been dragged into disrepute by some absolutely inept implementation. The World Bank Group has uttered some mea culpa in the process but by allowing the analysis of the results still to include some bias, it has not done enough to discover, acknowledge, and correct the mistakes. Now I can hear everyone shouting, "Per, give us proof of what you are saying!"

Well, go to any evaluation of privatization results and you will find thousands of tables indicating the proceeds of investment funds that benefited those countries that privatized. Now, try to find any data about the resulting outgoing cost flows. You found any? You need any more proof? How can you do a cost-benefit analysis leaving the costs out?

In many cases foreign investors acquired electrical, telecommunication, and other public quasi-monopoly services and milked them for all they were worth, as is normal and perfectly expected that they should. Why should they behave differently from other investors? Through dividends, through the purchase of goods and services from affiliates at inflated prices, and through the leveraging of the privatized companies to their tilt, they frequently managed to recover in quite a short time all their investment cash-flows, which thereafter left them to earn freely, without risks, from whatever high-country-risk tariffs they had been able to negotiate. I frequently ask my colleagues from the developed world, "If this had happened to your local utilities, what would you have said?" They respond with silence—but I can see them shudder.

When I arrived at Washington my phone calls to Venezuela cost me ten times more than my calls to Sweden, and that was about ten years after the telephone company in Venezuela had been *successfully* privatized...Hah!

Let's get out of the Bad Reform Fatigue with truths and creativity! For instance, let's fix some bad privatizations!

### Fiscal Space—Public or Private

Dear Colleagues,

Last Thursday we had a technical meeting to discuss investment in infrastructure in the context of two IMF papers: "Public Investment and Fiscal Policy" and "Public-Private Partnerships," and I must confess I found it somewhat confusing.

Suppose that we at the World Bank are analyzing

an investment proposal of 100 million dollars for the construction of electrical transmission lines presented by one of our shareholders. Then, if the project is to be executed by the public sector we are told that we might have a problem if there is not sufficient "fiscal space" (room for fiscal spending) available, while, if the project is private, the fiscal space is not even an issue. I simply do not get it. If it is the same project, with the same transmission lines, to be paid, or not paid, by the same users and with exactly the same monetary effects for the country, why on earth should it be deemed, a priori, good or bad, depending on the verdict of what basically just sounds like a sloppy accounting standard.

We could generalize that the public sector would normally have access to loans at lower interest but would also suffer from more inefficiencies, and that its private-sector counterpart, being more efficient, would also have higher expectancies in terms of financial returns. How the final balance turns out is indeed important and should be carefully considered in the project design but, whether a country can afford or not to execute a project in these normally non-contestable monopoly-prone infrastructure markets, cannot and should not be based on whether it is public or private.

Of course general debt sustainability is an issue but, if this were to be a limiting factor, it should apply equally to projects in private and public sectors, since the provision of indispensable public services through well-established regulatory systems creates exactly the same final obligations as a formal public debt.

More so, analyzing the fact that through the privatization of infrastructure projects there has frequently been a release of funds to the public sector, one could make a case that this only amounts to contracting expensive public debt off balance sheet that is to be served not by taxes but through higher user fees. In this respect it would be enlightening if, when furnished historical figures on infrastructure investments, there is a clearly quantified distinction between new fresh investments and the release of funds to the public sector. If a state company is bought by a private firm for five-hundred million dollars but only 100 million dollars is for new projects and 400 million dollars is paid to the government for the right to provide these public services, then in fact, a true accounting tale should have 400 million dollars accounted as new public-sector debt and only 100 million in infrastructure. Not having adequate information makes our development task so much harder.

\*\*\*

My Editor's Q: Per, you have said several times that when a government robs a foreign investor of hundreds of millions of dollars more than a utility is worth, these hundreds of millions should be thought as debt of the government. I would imagine that the hundreds of millions are a profit of the government, which should help reduce its debt if it was in debt at the time of the sale. Explain this paradox to your readers. If you pay me a million dollars for editing, it reduces my few debts to zero and leaves me a profit. Why should my accountant say it adds to my debt? Some of what you economist take for granted seems very counterintuitive to us lay persons.

My answer: Jim, of course if governments would take all this money and repay their debts, nothing would have happened. Unfortunately the way they normally behave they will consider this money as windfall-profits, spend it, and saddle their constituencies with higher rates. It is a bit like you taking the million for editing, going out and spending it, and thereafter having your wife Zaida having to do the editing so as to defend the honor of the McDonough family. But also, besides being just similar to public debt, it can also turn out to be very expensive public debt. For instance, on July 26, 2005, The Washington Post reported that "A consortium...said it plans to offer Virginia a lump sum of more than $1 billion in return for revenue generated by the Dulles Toll Road for the next 50 years..." I do not know where this offer is going to end but, at least in this case, someone seems to be aware of the implications, since the paper also reports, "Others said Virginia should raise the money it needs by selling bonds and keeping control of the cash generated by the toll road."

# About indexes and their disclosure

I remember that a few years ago I argued the thesis that lack of information actually could be valuable as a promoter of development. On some occasions, ignorance of certain matters kept alive the dreams of finding the greener valley. These dreams are the ones that drove Americans to invest in Italy, Italians to move to Venezuela and Venezuelans to find work in the United States. This generated economic growth all around.

The increasing speed of today's information flow raises some doubts. Although it is certainly advantageous to insure that correct and relevant information as well as good news is transmitted rapidly, it is also certain that this same speed is usually applied when propagating incorrect and irrelevant information as well as increasing volumes of bad news. For some not totally identified reasons, I feel that the magnifying effect of speed upon bad information is somehow greater that on good information. Making peace, for example, requires much time that is often not available. Provoking war is often a matter of seconds.

Some of the previous concerns plus the fact that we

continuously observe how media can make so much of so little have made this whole evolution of jumping from blissful ignorance into urgent pseudo certainties a quite important issue to me.

## The Riskiness of Country Risk

How horrible it must be to work as an air-traffic controller! Any slight error can provoke an unimaginable human tragedy. No wonder these professionals burn out so rapidly. I "suppose" the same must happen with the country-risk assessors, those people who carefully pass judgment as to what the country risk is for any given nation.

The all important mission of these risk evaluators is twofold. The first, that for which they are actually paid, consists of analyzing whether or not the debtor nation will ultimately be able to honor its obligations. This determines whether or not pension funds, banks, and insurance companies will be willing, or even allowed, to invest in that country's sovereign debt instruments. The second, even more important than the first, is to send subtle signals to the governments of these nations in order to help them improve their performance.

What a difficult job this is! If they overdo it and underestimate the risk of a given country, the latter will most assuredly be inundated with fresh loans and will be leveraged to the hilt. The result will be a serious wave of adjustments sometime down the line. If on the contrary, they exaggerate the country's risk level, it can only result in a reduction in the market value of the national debt, increasing interest expense and making access to international financial markets difficult. The initial mistake will unfortunately turn out to be true, a self-fulfilling prophecy. Any which way, either extreme will cause hunger and human misery.

What a nightmare it must be to be risk evaluator! Imagine trying to get some shuteye while lying awake in bed thinking that any moment one of those judges, those with the global reach that have a say in anything and everything, determinates that a country has become essentially bankrupt due to your mistake, and then drags you kicking and screaming before an International Court, accused of violating human rights. If I were to be in the position of evaluating country risk, I would ensure that the process is totally transparent, even though this takes away some of the shine of the profession and obligates me to sacrifice some of my personal market value.

How lucky we are that we are neither air-traffic controllers nor sovereign-risk evaluators! However, since we can easily become victims of their missteps, it behooves us, if only because of our survival instinct, to make sure that both do their jobs correctly.

We have seen in recent *Country Reports* how, after having introduced a myriad of information into the black box of methodology, as if by magic, a credit qualification is produced. Many of these reports seem to me like the pronouncements of film critics. It would seem that, more often than not, the individual evaluator is determining more how much he likes the ways or forms the *Directors* of a nation try to honor its obligations than on producing an honest and profound financial analysis of the country's capacity for servicing its debt correctly.

In his book *The Future of Ideas: The Fate of the Commons in a Connected World* (New York: Random House, 2001), Lawrence Lessig maintains that an era is identified not so much by what is debated, but by what is actually accepted as true and so is not debated at all. In this sense, given the risk that the *perceived country risk* actually becomes the real country risk, it is best not to assign an AAA rating *blithely* to the risk qualifiers—perhaps not even *a two-thumbs-up*.

From *The Daily Journal*, Caracas, September 27, 2002

## Disclosing the IDA Country-Performance Ratings

The World Bank manages a very large pool of donated development resources from the International Development Agency, IDA. To allocate these resources among the countries and also to decide whether these resources should be given out as loans or grants, they use a methodology that reviews many different variables and ends up in a product known as CPIA. These Country Performance Index Assessments had previously been disclosed in a sort of fussy way (with countries being classified in quintiles), but now there was strong pressure from most of the donors that these Country Performance Index figures should be disclosed in much more detail—I guess to reward the good countries and shame the others.

Nothing wrong with that, except if you thought that those performance indexes, though probably a good approximation of the reality, did not reflect all the difficult aspects of development and could also, if taken on their own and erroneously interpreted, make development more difficult.

I had had enough with organizations publishing indexes that were later appropriated by the selfish interests of others, making them mean more than they really do, without the originator responding clearly enough—as it was honored just by the attention given to its index and did not want to hurt a member of its fan club. And so the table was set to ignite my devil's advocate genes.

### A first round of comments

As so many of us invest much of our hopes for a better tomorrow in achieving a more transparent society, it is important that we always remind ourselves that there is nothing so nontransparent as a half-truth, said at the wrong time, at the wrong place, and not in a fully comprehensible way.

But, in a world that frequently demands that information be transmitted through easily digestible means, such as oversimplified rankings, we would rather have the World Bank (WB) doing it than any of the many not-accountable-to-anyone rating agents that frequently pursue undisclosed agenda. That said, it is not an easy decision for the WB to get into the rating game, and much care is needed.

It is by definition an impossible task to compress in an adequate way all the very complex realities of a country into a simple index or rating, and in doing so it is absolutely certain that many mistakes will be made. On the other hand, one also needs a simple, comprehensive and understandable tool to be able to convey results powerfully, and a simple index or rating can do just that. The balancing of all the various elements and contradictions needs to be done with much concerned carefulness. If a minor agent such as an NGO would go wrong, there might not be much to it but if it is the *Knowledge* Bank that puts forward the impreciseness, this could be leveraged into extremely negative consequences.

If we were to use only the term of an "IDA Resource Allocation Index" this would make the whole disclosure more transparent and honest, as this would indicate that when monitoring results and performance, it takes two to tango, the evaluated and the evaluator, and anyone—or both—could make mistakes. We should ban, forever, the use of the very arrogant and error-prone term "Country Performance Ratings."

Friends, it is just because we believe in disclosure that we should strive to find the right disclosure.

## Development alchemy

Somewhere in the documentation the "Weighting Procedure" is described as taking four parts of CPIA and one part of ARPP (I don't remember what ARPP stands for but I guess that is not so important either) and multiplying this by a "governance factor that is calculated by dividing the average rating of these seven criteria by 3.5 (the midpoint of the 1—6 rating scale) and applying an exponent of 1.5 to this ratio." Friends, whatever it means, this sounds just too much like a "Potteresque" development alchemy that even a studious Hermione would find difficult to understand.

Excuse the jest, my colleagues, but we could encounter some serious risks to our reputation. For instance, the Credit-

Rating Agencies—at least with respect to sovereign credits—refuse to describe their methodology in too much detail, and they officially justify this refusal by stating that they do not wish the countries to know about how to get a great rating—although I truly suspect that they just don't want to be called on their bluff. In our case we might be expected to come up with a more substantial explanation than the mixing of the potion above—and what if we can't?

## Confusion

I have heard that "ratings should depend on actual policies, rather than intentions," which sounds quite right, especially remembering that the road to hell is paved with good intentions. However, I have also heard that "the criteria are focused on policies and institutional arrangements, the key elements that are within the country's control, rather than on actual outcomes." Simplifying arithmetically both possibilities, it would seem to me that we could end up with a rating system that depends on policies rather than results. This, although perhaps quite acceptable to a private charity, seems a bit out of place for the World Bank. But then again, I might just be confused.

### About the Panel of Experts

Dear Colleagues,

With respect to the Terms of Reference (TR) for the Panel of Experts—I would like to make the following brief comments.

To begin with, I believe we should avoid qualifying the panel as a "Panel of Experts," as clearly the whole issue of rating, in this case of development adequacy, is governed by subjectivities and not by that kind of know-how that permits anyone to represent himself or herself as an "expert" without being deemed presumptuous. A reference to "experts" may also convey an unearned sense of precision that might backfire.

Reading through our methodology manual, we understand that if the Panel is to review whether the criteria used in the ranking provide an adequate basis to asses the quality of policies and institutions and, at the same time, the quality referred to means the degree to which a country's framework is conducive to growth and poverty reduction, then, in all logic, it would seem that the Panel is supposed to review the whole effectiveness of the current development strategy of IDA. Although this could perhaps be a welcome exercise we find it hard, if not again presumptuous, to believe that it could be done during just 48 hours in March, unless of course the Panel is just called to apply freely any preconceptions of their own.

Frankly, when I thought about a panel in this matter, I never visualized a team able to reconstruct or even evaluate a methodology and a ranking that have been developed over many years, and I believe that for that purpose we already have other more appropriate procedures that we are already paying for and that work fulltime.

No, I thought we were talking of a Panel that could advise us on how to design and communicate and control the interpretations of the rankings, so as to maximize their potential benefits and minimize the risks, for all, of this extremely hazardous activity.

The questions for such a panel are almost infinite; for instance, how do we make sure that the ratings are not used for any wrong purpose, which could even conspire against our development mission? Is the ranking a proprietary good to be controlled and marketed? Do we allow any media to report on the ratings out of context, or perhaps even redesign their presentation, for instance by cutting the axis and thus seeming to have the WB endorsing erroneous interpretations? What are the market implications of putting the whole credibility of the WB behind a rating? Will the other raters only follow us? Will this only reinforce the cyclical nature of capital flows creating "the Mother of all systemic risks"? If it does not work, can we pull out?

With respect to the list of the named "experts" not knowing them, I cannot endorse or object. Nonetheless, I sincerely hope that the list does not include any ranking fanatics, but includes more the well-intentioned healthy ranking skeptics who, aware of the needs for rankings, are also conscious of the risks. In other words, I hope the panel does not end up being a panel of "formula builders" but a panel of people who know why, when, and how to use the ranking formulas.

## Some follow up comments

It is symptomatic of the many difficulties with rating that the request by the Panel for more analytic work in relation to the weighting system was answered by the Bank with a very basic equal weighting, backed by some correlation analysis. Equal weighting could very well be the best answer, at least in simplicity, but it is also a very normal and transparent way of admitting to not-having-a-clue. In the area of the CPIA ratings, we are indeed walking on very loose sand, and we need to be very careful, come disclosure time.

When thinking about all the suggested CPIA criteria, I would have many fewer problems with fully disclosing the exact information on each of these fifteen criteria, than with having them all stirred into a murky and totally nontransparent cocktail.

I saw that some Panel members noted that once the disclosures occur, "The Bank should closely monitor any potentially adverse impacts on borrowers, such as misinterpretation of ratings by financial markets, any impact on foreign direct investment, and/or the abuse of ratings for political gains." This is all well said but, in today's world of rapid and active communication, those are the things you analyze before you communicate and not after. We wonder whether now is not the appropriate time to leave out the economists, and call in some experts on communication.

Let us never forget that the rankings, unfortunately, say almost as much about the one doing the ranking as they do about the one being ranked.

Just as an example of rankings gone haywire, let me refer to the Globalization Index published some months ago by A. T. Kearney and Foreign Policy. Their ranking method assigns globalization points to countries by measuring the number of internet users, hosts, and secure servers, without even bothering about what contents are transmitted over them and similar media. Who is more global, a family of a rich country with ten televisions for ten local sitcoms, or a family of a poor country with only one TV, but who mostly have to watch foreign programming, and many of whose family members are working abroad?

Let me again illustrate three risks that I believe have not been sufficiently considered.

- When discussing Argentina we heard comments as to how it changed (almost overnight) from being A Golden Poster Boy into an Ugly Duckling. This begs the question of what could have happened to the reputation of the Bank if our ratings had officially indicated very good results over a long period and then, suddenly, something went wrong. Would creditors sue us? Would credit rating agencies sue us?
- There is always a risk present when good ratings are thrown in the face of crude realities of poverty, since the hope of food for today is not easily appeased by the promise of food in a year or a decade.
- The risk that bad ratings could in fact be turned against the interests of furthering development, for instance when bad ratings are brought forward by bad governments as an evidence of their ability to defend their "true" sovereignty.

In the very little which our Panel of Experts (mercifully not eminent persons) mentions about disclosure, it urges for the preparation of adequate information to help the public interpret the ratings. This recommendation stands, at least in terms of transparency, in stark contrast with the other recommendation "that the write-ups that accompany the ratings should not be disclosed—as this might discourage candid assessment by staff." We do not believe that in this respect you should be able to have your cake and eat it too, and so, if you are prepared to disclose a rating, you must be willing to disclose fully how you got it.

### About our own accountability

Of course I agree with the recommendation that the disclosures of any results should always include a statement indicating that the ratings are the product of "staff judgment." That said, and given the importance of checks and balances, and accountability, we would like to know a little about the foreseen consequences to staff. This is no minor issue as their judgments, if wrong, and even if right, could foreseeable bring down governments and also stoke anti—World Bank sentiments. I need to bring this up, as the debate reminded me of the note I wrote about the US GAO Report on the IMF.

### What if they rank us?

Finally, as we see in the documents on the IDA disclosure policy that this exercise generates a normal distribution curve where we can point out the best and the worst performers, I cannot but reflect on the fact that within the Bank, for its own internal evaluation purposes, it seems impossible to gain acceptance for this sort of useful ranking tool. In fact, in most internal evaluations that are presented to the Board, we have not even reached a name disclosure by quintiles and have been basically limited to a binary grading (satisfactory or not), mostly without really even knowing who belongs to any of those groups. Just think about our reactions if some NGO would start to rank the performance of our own country teams and to disclose the results on the *www*, with three-decimal precision, and arguing that, given the utmost importance of the WB's poverty-fighting mission, this should be quite helpful

## US GAO Report

Dear Colleagues,

Last week, our Corporate Secretariat sent us a document dated June 26 titled U. S. General Accounting Office: International Financial Crisis...Challenges Remain in IMF's ability to Anticipate, Prevent, and Resolve Financial Crises.

It is an extraordinary document, as within the context of "According to World Bank estimates, the financial costs to countries that experienced crisis in the 1980s and 1990s exceeded $1 trillion—greater than the total amount of all donors' assistance to developing countries," it puts forward statements such as:

"During the 1991—2001 forecast periods, 134 recessions occurred in all 87 emerging market countries. We found that the WEO (World Economic Outlook) correctly forecasted only 15, or 11 percent, of those recessions, while predicting an increase in GDP in the other 119 actual recessions."

"Our analysis for the 87 emerging countries shows that, for more than 75 percent of the countries, the WEO current account forecasts were less accurate than if the Fund had simply assumed that the next year's current account would be the same as this year's. The results are even more dramatic for G7 countries: a forecast of no change was a better predictor than the WEO forecast for six of the seven countries. This demonstrates that, even in stable economies with excellent data, the WEO has done a poor job of forecasting this key crisis anticipation variable."

"Internal assessment of the Fund's EWS (Early Warning System) models shows that they are weak predictors of actual crisis. The models' most significant limitation is that they have high false-alarm rates. In about 80 percent of the cases where a crisis was predicted over the next 24 months, no crisis occurred. Furthermore, in about 9 percent of the cases where no crisis was predicted, there was a crisis."

I find that the document, presented not by any unknown NGO but by an important official entity of the United States, raises some very serious questions that we cannot, and should not, ignore.

In any normal private environment, unless the forecasters were sons of the founders, they would have been fired. In institutions such as the IMF that predicate accountability, has this ever occurred?

With such an amazingly lousy track record, would the Bank be better served by assuming a contrarian strategy in terms of getting in when IMF announces crisis?

Does IMF's lackluster performance suggest the need for reviewing the risks of delegating so much authority in today's financial markets to perhaps equally fallible credit-rating agencies?

Yesterday, we had a Steering Committee and, to my surprise, I did not see even a small informal session planned for the discussion of this document. I can perfectly understand the need of solidarity with institutions such as IMF, but it has to have its boundaries especially as our solidarity with the countries and the poor has to be in the forefront.

The world will take this document in its hand and, once it really comprehends that it is reading what it is reading, suddenly very serious questions could be asked.

Finally, the report includes on its cover the legend: "This document has a restricted distribution and may be used by recipients only in the performance of their official duties. Its contents may not otherwise be disclosed without World Bank Group authorization." As its whole contents, and much more, can easily be found on the GAO's Web page, I wonder whether we are not better served by including the confidentiality clause only when it is truly confidential, at least in these times of transparency.

Per

# A bit on some other indexes

**The through-the-eye-of-the-needle index**
"It is easier for a camel to pass through the eye of a needle than for a rich man to enter the Kingdom of God" (Matthew 19:24), and recently the Center for Global Development and *Foreign Policy* gave us their impression as to how 21 rich nations are wiggling along, according to their annual *Commitment to Development Index* (CDI) which grades rich nations on how much they help or hurt poor nations.

The CDI effort is truly welcomed as it tries to rate the other side of the coin of development, just as Transparency International does when it publishes a Bribe Payers Survey to balance (or ask for forgiveness) for their much more famous Corruption Perception Index, where the blame is squarely laid on the shoulders of the weak party.

CDI is a young index and probably needs a couple of years before developing into a strong and coherent index (I am too fed up with the use of *robust*) and so the many changes in the ranks of this year's CDI, are mostly consequences of changes in the methodology. Trying to nudge the future of the index into an even better direction, I dare to make following comments.

What I like least about the CDI is that, in the long term, it can become too good for its own sake, or so developed, so to say, that it risks becoming a goal in itself that may lead everyone to work toward a good rating in the index instead of toward true development. As development is a very difficult and serious matter where diversity of opinion is much needed, there is always the risk that by standardizing its arguments, one could introduce fatal systemic errors. Neither do I like its current scale, from 1 to 10, as it could perhaps give the impression that, although in different degrees, all rich countries help, and so a scale from minus 5 to plus 5 would perhaps tell the story better.

It is said that the different categories are equally weighted, since the average point of each is five, but the fact that within each category the distribution of the points is uneven—with standard deviations ranging from 1.11 points in investment to 3.54 points in aid, and skew factors as high as 2.82 for trade—results anyhow in a not so transparent weighting, whether intended or not.

At the end of the day, commitments to development need to translate themselves, one way or another, into real financial flows, unless we want to settle for a hybrid Intentions to Help Development Index. In this respect trade, migration, investment, and aid are quite plausibly more important and easier to measure in an objective way, than environmental security and technology, and so perhaps the different categories should be unevenly weighted. Let me comment on the more difficult categories:

Technology, currently measured as R & D as a percentage of GDP, seems to ignore what the R & D is used for. Clearly the development of global goods must, at least in the short term, have quite different implications for poor nations than R & D investments that are going to translate themselves into new ways to extract intellectual property rents, to be paid for by developing nations.

Security, a category that includes peacekeeping and forcible humanitarian interventions (approved by international bodies such as the United Nations), might somewhat cloud the issue as it is hard to differentiate between proactive assistance in preventing disasters and reactive response, once the disaster is unfortunately taking place.

Environment is clearly of utmost importance for all countries, especially the poor ones, but, until we can ascertain for a fact that environment investments are made according to criteria of economic efficiency, measuring may only introduce unintended bias. For instance, the investments in windmills instead of compensating Brazil for the opportunity cost of not developing the Amazon do not make much global sense and seem more directed to satisfy the interests of some individual countries.

What I most like about this index is that it should help to remind its developers from the rich nations about how difficult this art is, and also remind the rich countries themselves how it hurts when any of its unfairness gets to be marketed as if it were the result of an exact science Although a good start—the CDI needs a lot of improvements before it can show the rich nations the route to their eye of the needle. Whether they later want to and can make it through it that is altogether a much more difficult question.

P.S. Colleagues, I tried to get this one published…no such luck.

## The index of perceived Corruption

Transparency International (TI) has developed an index by means of which it ranks countries around the world according to their perceived levels of internal corruption. I have a Danish friend who recently came to me for the umpteenth time with this list clutched firmly in his fist, proudly crowing over the fact that Denmark once again tops the list as the least corrupt country while Venezuela once again comes in toward the bottom, beaten out for the basement spot by only seven countries among which we find Colombia and Nigeria.

As a Venezuelan, I immediately went into a defensive mode. I argued that since the index is based on the perception of corruption, it could be that the results merely indicate a serious problem of exactly that, the perception, not the reality. Additionally, should this actually be true (evidently not the case), I told him that although I did lament the fact that Venezuela was not mentioned in the top half of the list, I was at least satisfied that we were definitely not occupying any "not too human" first place.

My good friend, observing my discomfort, realizing that I have some Swedish blood in my veins, and in a sincere effort to console me, blurted out that in reality he also did not understand why Denmark had been ranked first while Sweden was ranked third. My immediate reply was "Chico, Denmark must simply have paid more for it."

Jest aside, the index is the result of a serious effort on the part of professionals of diverse backgrounds who, using the few tools available, have managed to develop a system of evaluation which is useful and of great support for every citizen wishing to combat this age-old plague.

Its importance is of even greater significance when we hear that Transparency International suggests that we don't attribute more accuracy than necessary to its index. Venezuela's ranking on this list of 85 countries is such that it is evident, to say the least, that the country's level of corruption is far greater than average. This is bad enough!

Any debate over whether Venezuela should be ranked higher could be perceived simply as a strategy aimed at discrediting the index. Only the beneficiaries of corruption could possibly have an interest in doing this. A true patriot would not waste one single second of his or her valuable time in debating why people speak poorly of our country. On the contrary, he would dedicate all his time and energy to correct the reality instead of objecting to the perception.

This debate on corruption is truly difficult and complicated. Even though we should be pleased that such an index exists,

I am worried that the mere fact that we are trying to reduce corruption to terms of a measurable dimension may lead us to oversimplify the problem dangerously.

The index, in principle, only measures the perception of corruption in general terms. This is defined in ample terms as "the abuse of public office for private gain." In this sense, and because of the nature of the problem, I am sure that when using the term "gain" we are referring mostly to a monetary benefit. This avoids measuring other aspects of corruption that could be just as important or more.

For instance, I believe that the appointment of someone to public office for reasons other than his or her capacity or professional integrity is a corruption that is even more pernicious and costly to the country than the sum of all monetary corruption put together.

An example of this is our recent banking-sector crisis. The costs caused by the poor administration of this crisis are far and above the costs attributable directly to the bankers involved. It's not that the bankers are free of guilt. They did undoubtedly start the fire. But whose fault is it that the financial firemen were caught napping and did not hear the alarms, and that once they finally got to the scene of the disaster they tried to douse the flames with gasoline instead of water?

I make these comments to remind all that the monster of corruption has a thousand heads. It would be sad if all the result of the efforts to slay this monster would simply be the elimination of the traditional offers of discounts for prompt payment, right then and there, and that we frequently receive when fined for a traffic violation.

Let me make one last comment on this quite tortuous subject. In Venezuela, perhaps more than in any other country, there is more than sufficient evidence of the total administrative ineptitude of the state, and all of our governments have absolutely no results to show, considering all of their income. Nonetheless multilateral agencies, such as the International Monetary Fund, frequently come to the country and recommend an action that could only mean allowing the state to squander even more resources. For whom then is the IMF working? For the politicians? Could we then be staring at another unknown dimension of this monster called Corruption?

From *The Daily Journal*, Caracas, November 4 1998

### Today, let us talk about the bribers

On the 26th of October, Transparency International, TI, published its annual index ranking the Perception of Corruption that exists in various nations. As usual, Venezuela was somewhere down at the bottom of the list. However, for the first time, TI also published an index related to the Bribe Payers (BPI).

This index ranks the 19 countries with the most exports and is based on the perception of how corporations from those countries use bribes to generate business.

A professional firm interviewed 770 high-level executives in 14 emerging markets with geographically diversified imports. Venezuela was not included among the interviewed parties, since most of its imports come from only one country, the United States.

The executives interviewed belonged to large firms, banks, chambers of commerce, auditing firms, and law firms. A result of 10 points means no bribes are used while 0 means, naturally, that bribing is used as a norm. The countries with the highest ranking were Sweden (8.3), Australia and Canada (8.1) and those at the bottom of the ranking were China (3.1), South Korea (3.4) and Taiwan (3.5). The ranking of some of our main trading partners were England (7.2), Germany and the United States tied at (6.2), Spain (5.3), France (5.2) and Italy (3.7).

Just like the Corruption Index, the Briber's Index will create much argument and rebuttal, especially from those that were not favored by their ranking within the index.

Among the traditional arguments, we are sure to find that many will maintain that the index is not really objective, but is really all about perception and that therefore, before being an ethical problem it is really more an image problem.

We will perhaps also hear technologically inspired arguments, such as accusing the better-positioned countries of using advanced versions of corruption, something like the stealth planes that do not appear on the radar. Sometimes when I read about the lobbying in the United States, I can't avoid a nagging feeling that corruption has just been institutionalized.

I have often seen how citizens of many developed countries shed their shackles and truly enjoy as tourists the perhaps humanizing experience of trying to avoid a traffic ticket by negotiating avidly with the particular foreign public servant who has accosted them.

On the other hand I have also seen people who behave better away than at home. We see it over and over again when Venezuelans, who, although notorious tax evaders at home, become exemplary citizens when overseas—to the extreme of not using readily available and popular loopholes.

Because of those contradictions it could be interesting to compare the two indexes side by side, and find out whether there are some significant inconsistencies. It does not look that way as with the exception of 5 countries, all those that have been ranked in both indexes, are basically in the same relative position. As it were, Sweden is first in both indexes while China is last.

The two main exceptions to this rule are Singapore which, in this group of 19, appears as 3rd in terms of the least corrupt nations but as number 11 in the Bribers Index and Belgium which, contrary to Singapore, ranks as number 15 of the least corrupt nations, but comes out somewhat better as number 8 among the Briber's. Let us speculate a bit about the meaning of these results.

On Singapore the results would indicate that it behaves very well at home, but goes haywire and is a menace when abroad. Without a doubt, a country like this must be a formidable competitor in foreign trade and one would entreat the OECD to insure that it is also enrolled among those countries that have recently signed the OECD Anti-Bribery Convention.

But what about those Belgians? Surprisingly they seem to behave better abroad than at home. Could this be some kind of special "stealth" technology at work? Could it be that they on purpose wish to be perceived as corrupt at home, in order to enhance belief in their human nature? Or could it be that they simply have decided to invest in a change of their image abroad, and that this was ultimately successful?

We shall see what gives next year when new investigative technologies tackle the inexplicable.

From *The Daily Journal*, Caracas, November 4 1999

### A dangerously failed index

Quite recently another index was published in the July/August 2005 issue of *Foreign Policy*. It is called the Failed States Index, and it is obnoxious. Even though the owner of the index (the methodology is copyrighted, and the software has a patent pending), the Fund for Peace, tells us that its mission is "to prevent war and alleviate the conditions that cause war," we cannot fathom any crazy way this index could help to do that. Expecting such beneficial results from this index is like expecting that any common, scandalous, and frivolous magazine that gorges on gossip about failed marriages will help save a troubled marriage. The very existence of this index itself is a clear indication that something is going really haywire, and the world could do without it.

On top of it all, even though the creators state that the methodology has been "tested over the last ten years," it seems intellectually to be a very weak index, built solely around the concept of scanning thousands of articles about disasters and tragedies (you get a patent on that?), and then producing a listing, something like an index of the most failed marriages in Hollywood according to the tabloid press.

As to results, well, even though they are really not worthy of a comment, let me just tell you that, as I see it, the resilience and fighting spirit shown by Colombia in trying to overcome the most difficult circumstances while embraced by the corrupting world demand for narcotic drugs, evidence anything but a failed state. Nonetheless in this index, among 72 countries Colombia occupies number 14, squeezed in between North Korea, slightly more failed, and Zimbabwe, slightly less failed. Come on!

About a decade ago, while doing a location study for a brewery in Colombia, in a small public-information office, I was able to find the most updated socioeconomic data, which they sold for peanuts on small diskettes. I was impressed with the discipline and sense of long-term vision that, almost in the middle of a battle, still prevailed in that country. Since the index now includes Colombia, I think it should at least be renamed the Struggling Countries Index, and Colombia should then, honorably, be ranked among the first, as doing their very best.

Of course there is nothing wrong—and plenty of potential good—that could come from finding a valid methodology to understand better what "failed states" are all about. However, from there to presume, as the Fund for Peace does, that by publishing this index one "presents a more precise picture of the scope and implications of the problem," is to me more of a sign of failing minds of the authors.

Friends, even while acknowledging that these indexes might provide some fun reading, as magazines like *Hola* and *People* also do, I believe it is high time to put a stop to the belief that "you ain't nothing if you don't have an index."

(And finally an Index I would love)
## How good or bad is your municipality?
I recently had the opportunity to travel to a Central American country. I was impressed by the fact that many professionals, both from the public as well as the private

sector, both local and foreign, were basically in agreement as to which municipalities were well governed and which were not.

Evidently, there are a great number of subjective factors that may influence or "color" opinions from municipality to municipality. Some of these we have seen before, such as the mayor's looks and/or congeniality or how big a share of the nation's global resources he has been allotted to manage. Certain variables can, however, be objectively evaluated in order to allow a reasonable ranking of municipalities as far as effective government is concerned.

In many parts of the world, including Venezuela, we have seen that expectations of improvements in public services are based on decentralization of power. As a result, it would seem positive to be able to develop a methodology which would help the population measure the results and efficiency of its local government(s).

Bad results are immediately evident; their causes are not. An inefficient municipality can easily justify its unsatisfactory performance by alluding to a lack of resources. On the other hand, a below-par result can also be hidden behind a surplus of resources. Having to take care of his day-to-day duties, how is a simple voter to know which is which?

The absence of knowledge or of access to information based on very certain and objective data about municipal government, as well as the normal dislike of changes, attempts against a healthy renovation of the latter's authorities. This lack of benchmarks and standards of measurement may also mean that results which may seem poor in the short run but that are designed by provide meaningful long-term improvements are not suitably rewarded.

Just imagine the chaos and confusion if our system of education all of a sudden decides to do away with the report card. How would parents evaluate the scholastic capacity of their children, especially when many parents nowadays haven't even heard about the existence of some of the subjects that are taught. This is very similar to the confusion of most voters when the time comes to choose their local authorities for the next period.

We have about three hundred municipalities that hold official elections in Venezuela. Few voters, so much so that I personally don't know of one, have even the remotest idea whether their municipal government is better or worse that his neighbor's. A ranking such as that mentioned above would help us comply with our obligations as voters.

Evidently, nobody can say that the measurement of results, however objective, will result in the correct analysis of any particular administration. However, just a reasonable ranking could go a long way toward becoming a valuable tool to identify extreme situations. It would certainly identify those governments which one should hang on to for dear life and flag those that should go as quickly as possible.

At a time when the country is betting the farm on decentralization, even in the face of certain risks such as runaway federalism, I am under the impression that one of the best possible investments we could make would be the creation of an evaluation committee whose task it would be to review efficiency at municipal levels. This committee or group, in addition to having solid methodological knowledge and ample resources with which to insure that the job is done, must be totally independent of all political movement and of all people who could aspire to posts in municipal governments.

*Perfection is the enemy of good.* We don't have to be overly precise. I don't doubt for one minute that the 50 municipalities that are ranked at the top of the list would realistically belong at least in the top 150 and that the bottom 50 would really belong in the bottom 150.

A country of this composition that manages through elections to keep 50 good ones and trash 50 bad ones is certainly on the road to a better future than a country that bases its choice primarily on election-period jingles. This means taking firm command of our future based on realistic information.

By saying all this, I'm not saying that I want our rights to vote reduced. By having declared myself incapable of saying with reasonable certainty whether things in my municipality are going well or not (in terms of what can be done and what can't), I don't wish to disqualify myself as an electoral illiterate. I simply wish someone would give me some glasses with which to see the municipalities clearer.

From *The Daily Journal*, Caracas, February 12, 1998

# EIR & Environment

---

**My answer to the NGOs**
**The EIR discussions...a missed opportunity**

Friends,

I am one of the executive directors of the World Bank who recently were bombarded with your mostly similar and spam-like messages urging us to approve word by word all the recommendations that the so-called "eminent person" made in conclusion of the Extractive Industries Review (EIR).

Most of what is said in the EIR is logical and already has been considered and applied by the World Bank. Nonetheless, there were some issues and recommendations that carried more than a hint of radicalism. These extremist suggestions blind the world from finding the pragmatic solutions it so urgently needs to solve the problems of environmental degradation and adequate energy availability.

In his book, *The Future of Ideas: The Fate of the Commons in a Connected World*, Random House, 2001, Lawrence Lessig writes that "a time is marked not so much by ideas that are argued about as by ideas that are taken for granted." In this respect, I had big hopes that the discussions on the EIR would help us unlock the current debate, which seems to be suffering from another bout of failure of imagination.

Unfortunately that was not to happen, since many of the really significant problems and solutions were just ignored, while minor issues were highlighted. Even the Bank management's final response, although technically quite adequate, in using an excuse-us-NGOs-for-daring-to-disagree tone, does not put forward the differences of opinions with sufficient strength and clarity.

In this and all other respects, the real challenges still lie ahead of us. Therefore, I wish to send you herewith my thoughts on some of the issues covered by the EIR, hoping this will help to focus our energy and concerns in more productive directions. By the way, what follows are strictly personal opinions and they do not reflect any formal statement made during the discussions of the Board, as these need to be confidential to guarantee that they are never taken out of their overall procedural context. And so, in a nutshell, here is what I think of the EIR.

The high growth rates of some countries, which are undergoing the highly energy-demanding transition from bicycles to cars, are forcing the world to face two very important constraints more than ever: general energy availability, and the capacity of an already overstretched environment to absorb the carbon impact of such growth.

Instead of discussing issues such as whether the world needs to find a way to tax excessive energy consumption to promote fairer global distribution of energy use or how to compensate for the quickly growing opportunity cost of not developing environmentally sensitive areas such as the Amazon Jungle, some very parochial NGO perspectives captured the EIR, and most of the participants just played along.

Yes, we all want clean energy, but given the urgency and magnitude of the problem, it must be clear that the world cannot afford to waste resources on unaffordable solutions. The money not spent on early prototypes of hybrid cars, or on subsidizing wind or solar-power generation plants that are not yet economically justifiable, could be much better spent on research for truly sustainable renewable energy sources, fighting poverty, or even directly paying for environmental priorities, such as keeping the Amazon intact.

\*\*\*

Jim my editor: "A rare case where I disagree with you. We need to develop hydro power (especially of slow-moving tides as well as fast waterfalls), solar, geothermal, wind, and other energy sources that do not burn fossil fuels, or nonfossilized soybeans for that matter."

I: "Except for the nonfossilized soybeans that I never heard of, we do agree, 100%. What I am emphasizing though is that we should spend the money developing economically feasible energy alternatives, and not waste that money in using alternatives that are still uneconomic.

Back to my answer:

\*\*\*

Yes, the world should move away from coal and oil, especially as oil is too valuable just to produce energy. But as the price of gas has reached the unaffordable level of US $6 per Mcf (one thousand cubic feet) and is generating billions of dollars in losses for electricity generators, realities are driving the world back to coal. In this respect in particular, the recommendation of the so-called "eminent person" for the Bank to withdraw fully from coal, gas, and oil is so completely out of synch with current realities that perhaps the Bank should have done best by just ignoring it.

\*\*\*

Jim, my editor again: "Perfecting clean energy sources now is probably not as impossible as building an atom bomb seemed to be in 1941 or building a moon rocket seemed in

1961, yet each of these was accomplished in fewer than ten years."

I: "Dear Jim, yes I hear you, you could be right, let us hope so…but this is my voice, and this was my answer to the EIR."

Back again.

***

Although countries with annual incomes of US $30,000 per capita might survive using uneconomic environmental approaches, those with US $3,000 or less will certainly not. In this respect, the Bank should have reiterated more firmly that under no circumstances can it be allowed to cut the umbilical cord that needs to run between its efforts aiming at poverty-reduction on the one hand and economic rationality on the other.

Yes, human-rights issues are of extreme importance, and the Bank, by nature and through the quality of its people, does always give them due consideration. But to tie up the Bank and its extractive-industries (EI) operations with additional sector-specific formal rulings will only hinder reaching the acceptable balance between individual human rights and collective human rights.

Yes, the interests of indigenous groups should always be considered respectfully, but assigning special and near-veto rights to them will clearly infringe on the rights of the rest of us, who all are indigenous to this planet.

Yes, if we all agree that a holistic approach is needed, why is then the analysis of the demand side for the resources produced by the extractive industries missing? It is clear that in most cases, the share of revenues among local participants has not been adequate. But to ignore the fact that the slice of the pie to be shared locally might be too small—as many nonrenewable resources are sold at a price equal to their marginal extraction cost and therefore don't leave much room for earnings—is not really an objective approach.

Yes, initiatives such as the Revenue Transparency Initiative might not be perfect, but they are a step in the right direction, and the Bank should pursue them always, not only in the EIR. For instance, the use of the economic surpluses created when granting patents, presumably to pay for research, should also be more transparent so as to better measure the prohibitively high prices of vital medicines. Since the treasury of most industrialized countries perceive through their gasoline taxes more fiscal income from a barrel of oil than the producer, this not only begs the question of who might really be cursed, but also whether those flows could also benefit from more transparency. Taxes collected on gasoline in the name of the environment (more than $100 billion a year on unleaded gasoline in Europe alone) of which basically nothing really goes to the environment and much of which has even been used to subsidize the coal industry could be the foundation for a real environmental global fund or, better yet a global tax program. By the way, if we are to have a global tax based on a gasoline tax, then I am of the opinion that ALL countries should pay an amount per liter consumed, albeit at rates that are adjusted for their national income per capita. (Even the poorest have the right to feel they are contributing toward a shared world cause)

Yes, there is always a need for better practices, as in gender issues, but for EIR to go to such an extreme as to single out the sector and specifically link it with issues such as rape and prostitution is unacceptable, both on moral and intellectual grounds.

Friedrich List[2] wrote that free trade was the means through which an already industrialized country "kicks away the ladder by which it has climbed up, in order to deprive others of the means of climbing up after it." If we were to paraphrase List, the way the "eminent person" wanted the EIR to conclude would have kicked away the ladder for many undeveloped countries, preventing their use of their natural resources.

In conclusion, it is unfortunate that these EIR discussions

did not advance a more rational agenda, especially since the World Bank is one of the few worldwide institutions that could really establish a leadership role in environmental and energy issues. Nonetheless, let us not cry over spilled milk. There are so many urgent challenges and opportunities for the Bank and all of you to play a truly creative and proactive role.

For instance, in one African country, millions of small and unorganized miners who need their jobs in order to survive create severe environmental damage. The same country also suffers yearly deforestation of hundreds of thousands of acres of forest. In such a case, wouldn't perhaps a "Forest-Growing Miner Cooperative" be a quite sensible program for the world to sponsor? Would not this make more sense as an investment vehicle for all those environmentally sensitive dollars that the rich nation's consumers are currently willing to spend on much less worthy proposals, such as building windmills in their gardens or driving around in their hybrids?

Let us not be busybodies blocking the world from going forward. Let us instead be very busy bodies helping it to go forward…in the right direction.

Regards,
Per

Sent by e-mail in October 2004, to each of over 900 persons who had previously e-mailed me

## The Amazon

Dear Friends and Colleagues:

Today we approved a US$505 million *Programmatic Reform Loan for Environmental Sustainability* to Brazil. Frankly, how could it be otherwise, when in fact we should be on our knees thanking a country like Brazil that with so many other problems commits to repaying 100% of principal plus interest of an environmental-sustainability loan that will benefit the whole world and all of us.

Honestly, I do believe the World Bank should occupy a stronger leadership in these matters from the very beginning, advocating for the cooperation of the rest of the world. If silly windmill projects can have access to carbon credits, the Brazilian environmental program should too.

For instance, if 20% of a loan like this were to be repaid by some international-support mechanism, this would not only motivate the Brazilian government to sell environmental protection locally, but it would also be a clear sign that in these matters, Brazil does not stand alone. Of course any external assistance would have to come with the clear understanding that it does not impose additional conditions on the country, as this is the best and perhaps only way to guarantee true sustainability and ownership of such programs.

This morning we had a two-hour discussion about the Development Committee agenda. Frankly, however, the issue of how the world can help in crucial global matters, as in the case of the Amazon—where the need of avoiding the very negative externalities of large deforestation have to compete with so many other urgent local needs, as well as with the rising opportunity costs of not exploiting the forests—should be a foremost issue. If it already is there—for instance hidden in a global taxation initiative—I very much welcome it but, if not, we should strive to put it there.

Last year at least 25,000 hectares were deforested in the Amazon. At a low carbon value of US$20 per hectare/year, this would indicate a value of about US$50 million a year if the program were successful at stopping deforestation. Add ten years of stopped deforestation, and the value of this would be—in approximate Kyoto terms—about US$500 million a year for the rest of the world. If this is so, how come we can spend so much time and money on expensive initiatives such as the *Extractive Industry Review*, and not come up with something more reasonable for the Amazon, than to have the Brazilians pay for it, 100%?

Per

## Our quixotic windmills

It has been a hard year for the promoters of wind energy. Though the economic viability of the windmills has improved considerably as oil has become more expensive, they have had to fight many battles on the environmental front which must have been somewhat surprising for these valiant champions of the green. Besides the aesthetics, where people still cannot make up their mind whether they are impressive or horrendous, over the last year we have read a lot about the problems of their causing death of birds and bats. But if they thought that was it, they had better prepare themselves since there is an ongoing study that seeks to measure the impact of the windmills when and if there would be enough of them to produce 5% of the world's electrical needs. That would signify, worldwide, hundreds of thousands of them.

From the initial results that have been privately circulated, the study has identified some new threats never even thought of before but that could become insurmountable hurdles. The first is whether the friction produced by the wind will in itself increase global warming. Second, as the windmills are located in windy areas and therefore not equally distributed over the world, there is the possibility that the world could turn some degrees over its axle, a bit like the effect of the recent mega earthquake that produced the tsunami. The final threat identified is that the windmills, by acting like some big sails, could accelerate the rotation of our planet. Luckily this final concern has already been eliminated as the calculations showed that this effect was to be neutralized by less wind impacting mountains and other places. Nonetheless, by just posing the argument it has also opened problems of a legal nature. For example, neighboring countries might complain that the windmills are literarily taking the wind out of their sails. The final problem identified but that lies outside the scope of the current study is related to what will happen to the ecology of previously windy area when the winds are gone.

As this year we celebrate Cervantes' Don Quixote we

cannot but reflect on how the modern windmills are fighting a quixotic war on their own.

P.S. Early one morning I met with some WB staff who wanted to tell me about the details of an alternative-energy project—windmills. Coming from an oil-producing country, in jest I improvised the above have-you-heard-the news-about-windmills story, and to my delight, some fell for it. Later for April Fool's Day I sent it out to some of my knowledgeable friends. To my surprise instead of laughter, many of the answers were of a yes-this-needs-to-be-better-researched nature. Could it really be that my joke contains some truths?

## Earth, the cooperative

Even if there is still confusion over the path the world is taking on environmental pollution, there is consensus at least on the following. The developed countries are doing the most polluting, the developing countries are suffering the most from this contamination, and, in the world today, there does not seem to be enough environmental space to allow the undeveloped world to catch up to the developed world.

The above statements should be enough to fuel a spirit of cooperation within this cooperative we call the Earth, and of which, like it or not, we are all members. Unfortunately, little or nothing has been done as of this date to correct the imbalance.

Some years ago we saw (or we imagined) small points of light when a series of environmental limitations were imposed through the Kyoto Protocol. There was talk of a market of "compliance with environmental standards bonds" which contemplated the possibility of transferring environmental funds from the developed world to the rest of the world.

A tree captures carbon. And thus hypothetically, a polluter in New York should plant a tree in his/her city in order to avoid a fine. However, to plant a tree in New York would be very costly, so the polluter in New York could also utilize the option of asking a Venezuelan investor to plant this tree in

Venezuela instead. The investor and the polluter would then share the net cost savings. This is the essence of the idea.

There are obvious difficulties with this proposal. The assurance that the tree is actually planted in Venezuela, and that it grows and captures carbon and does not later become burning firewood, are just some of the technical challenges that need to be resolved. However, we know that if the demand for these bonds is high enough, we can be certain that the creativity of technicians would be sufficiently stimulated.

There have been some initial successes with these bonds. But to tell the truth, the main buyers have been well-intentioned institutions, and today it is difficult to envision how this market could become self-sufficient in terms of volume, without assistance. Particularly when we see how there has been a relaxing of will or an increase of laziness in terms of applying Kyoto standards—unless...

Today we are conscious of the very high taxes on gasoline and other petroleum derivatives in many parts of the world. In Europe, at a price of 26 dollars per barrel of oil, these taxes amount to more than 400% of the oil's value. In 1998, when oil was 10 dollars a barrel, taxes amounted to over 700%.

These taxes, categorized as "environmental" since they reduce the demand for oil, have a direct negative impact on an oil-producing country such as Venezuela. However, what really bugs us is that the majority of these taxes are not at all used for environmental purposes and even when they are, adding insult to injury, it is only as a subsidy for other energy sources, furthering the discrimination of oil.

I challenge all of our rich fellow cooperative members in the developed world to set aside at least 10% of taxes collected on oil for the purchase of true Environmental Bonds.

Published in *El Universal* (Website), December 2002

## A better alternative than a hybrid

Currently, some of the car makers are being criticized for not doing enough developing environmental friendly hybrid vehicles. But, before they commit large amounts to it, they might look at alternatives such as the following "as-good-as-it-gets forest mining carbon sink".

We burn oil and coal and foul up the environment and thereafter we hope to make up for it by planting forests that recapture the emitted carbons. We won't, but at least it is better than doing nothing, especially if we do it right.

The Web site of a car maker announces that their best-selling hybrid vehicle costs around 4.000 dollars more than the comparably equipped standard version. In compensation the hybrid car will, by given 14 more miles per gallon of gas and if driven 20.000 miles per year, save the owner over ten years about 3.000 gallons of gas and thereby save the environment from having about 7.3 tons of carbon converted into $CO_2$. The technology used in these hybrids is quite creative as it harness the energy obtained when braking in a battery and uses it thereafter as much possible.

If we assume no new-technology surprises, for instance battery problems down the line, this environmental conscientious investment proposal seems reasonable for the individual US motorist in the US at current $2.20 per gallon and indeed splendid in Europe with their over $7 per gallon gas, although there it clearly has more to do with saving taxes paid on gas, than with the value of the gas itself saved. Nonetheless in terms of the environment, the results are not that impressive and the world could do much better in terms of the social and environmental impact.

For instance there is Tanzania, an extremely poor country, with a per capita income of about 300 dollars per year, with not enough prospects to get it out of its predicaments and where much of its land is slowly but surely turning into desert, at a pace of more than 300.000 ha per year. Although there are some major mining companies operating in Tanzania and that we hope are doing their extraction in the right way, their environment is also suffering at the hands of about one million unofficial freelance miners that roam the country trying desperately to make a living.

Putting it then all together it would seem like a good idea to set up cooperatives for these miners and turn them into reforesters, the whole project financed by buyers of cars. Is it feasible and sustainable? Absolutely!

If our car buyer, instead of buying a hybrid, saved four thousand dollars by buying a standard car and then would pay just 2.000 dollars to a cooperative, this amount could, after reasonable promotional and administration costs, cover the initial reforestation of about 5 ha and the carbon thereby captured would be at least 200 tons, 27 times more than the hybrid-car savings. Yes we all know that a ton of carbon saved by not converting a stable sink like petrol that has been there for millions of years is much better than a ton saved in an unstable forest that can burn or rot, but never 27 times better. The reforested area could be maintained with the income obtained from selling the emission-savings certificates based on the Kyoto protocol.

We do not wish to demean the efforts of any car company that invests in the research of more energy efficient cars but that does not necessarily mean it needs to sell their hybrid cars before they are as-good-as-they can get. At this moment of scarce resources and urgent environmental needs perhaps we would all be better of if the car industry offered their consumers, instead of hybrid cars, to drive away in standard cars that carry on their windows bright emblems that certifies each one of them as proud financiers of 5 ha of reforestation in Tanzania, and that could be observed live at the Web site of The First Forest Mining Cooperative of Tanzania.

P.S. Besides the fact that in real environmental terms we could spend our resources much better than buying hybrid cars there is also another reason why I don't find them so convincing. By taking us down the route of delivering more miles per gallon, we might give less emphasis to the real problem of improving our general transport systems. Just think of how much resources we could save if someone were to develop a car-key system that allowed multiple users to record their individual use of a car, in time and mileage, so that instead of each household having a second car, each little street had some easily available shopping cars that any neighbor could use. And what about the nonhybrid public-transport systems?

\*\*\*

Here Jim my editor takes off, and I'm not the one to hold him back. "When I was a kid in Boston, each mass-transit vehicle had at least two employees of the transportation company at work in the vehicle: a driver who did nothing but drive (sometimes closed off like the pilot in a plane) and a conductor who made change, collected fares, gave transfers to other vehicles, answered questions, especially about directions (they had little books listing every location in Greater Boston and the public transport that went there), and maintaining law and order in the vehicle. During World War II, we were told that the driver would temporarily perform all these functions while driving (not the best idea), since almost twenty million Americans were in the armed forces. The promise was that when the war ended we would go back to a separate driver who did nothing but drive, and a conductor in the middle of the vehicle who did everything else, serving the interest and convenience of the passengers. They even helped old ladies get heavy packages on and off the vehicles. The war has been over sixty years, but, the last time I visited Boston, the driver was still trying to do everything.

We need to train the conductors in the police academy, give them weapons, uniforms, badges, handcuffs, and powers of arrest. Then we should put one such transit police officer in the middle of each vehicle. Then people would feel safe to go back to riding streetcars and busses the way they did during the Great Depression when most people, including my parents, didn't own even one car, and when we couldn't imagine the reality of a "two-car family." Vandalism to public-transit vehicles would be almost nonexistent. The atmosphere in the vehicles would be quiet and friendly with the conductor preventing anyone from playing loud radios or otherwise disturbing the peace. And hiring and training all these new transit police would put a sizeable dent in our unemployment figures.

Getting the masses back into mass transportation would free a lot of parking space, making finding an available parking space much easier when one really needed to use one's car. It would cut down on pollution. It would conserve fossil fuel. It would speed up rush-hour traffic. It would make life less hectic for pedestrians. In short, BRING BACK CONDUCTORS!"

# Oil

I come from an oil-exporting country and so you could not expect me to shut up about it. In fact, in Venezuela I have written around eighty articles related one way or another to oil, although I wish to make it clear that I have never ever collected one single dollar as a professional from anything or anyone related to oil, whether private or public. I have always analyzed the oil situation from the perspective of the totally ignored shareholder that we all Venezuelan citizens indeed are.

Also, as a citizen of the world it is not that I am not concerned about the environmental effects of oil, just the opposite, but I do flare up when I see how consuming countries place exorbitant taxes on gasoline, with which they sometimes subsidize coal. And I also flare up when I hear environmentalists advocating using very scarce resources for uneconomic solutions such as hybrid cars and windmills, when those same resources could do so much better for the environment if only used otherwise.

That said I will limit my flaring here to a brief comment I made on one of those ever recurring Oil Market Updates plus including an article I wrote long before ever having to think about the World Bank...and geopolitical diplomacy. For good measure, I also include some brief pieces about transparency, curses, and sovereignty.

### About an Oil Market Update

A while ago at a seminar the facilitator asked the group to look at a video and try to keep count of how many times a group of persons passed a white ball among themselves. After one minute he asked around, getting answers like 13, 14, and 15. He then asked whether someone had noticed something strange. I, who had as it seems been distracted from looking at the ball (through luck or genes), had noticed the presence of a gorilla coming into the scene, pounding his chest and then leaving. No one else did. Today it would seem to me that the price of oil itself has become the white ball the World Bank keeps its eye on to such an extent that it might be losing the whole picture.

It has been absolutely clear for quite a while that there was not enough energy to accommodate the current growth rates of several major countries and so, in this context, it is clearly out of place even to mention the existence of an oil shock, and even less a supply-driven one. We have been urging the Bank for a long time to include energy planning as a fundamental part of any economic forecast and any Country Assistance Strategy.

The real oil shock occurred in 1998 and 1999, when prices fell so low that it scared away all investments.

It is now high time, long overdue, for the Bank to be much more forthright about oil and other sources of energy. For instance, in Laos—the number-one country mentioned in the chart about the import burden of oil—perhaps a lot of the pressures could have been alleviated by a more forceful and effective assistance in the construction of the Nam Theun 2 Hydropower Project.

The fact is that only a few months ago we sat down to

discuss an EIR where all the current energy problems were so gallantly ignored. To lend our credibility once again at this time to these "oil update" notes could mean increasing an already serious reputation risk.

We do not agree with the current list of "Advocacy Messages," as they seem to imply not only that the oil-producing countries are at fault, but also that they represent the solution, and that the only solution lies in producing more oil and selling it at a lower price. Why should oil-producing countries develop costly extra production capacity which, when demand slows, only forces them into a suicidal price competition? If extra capacity is needed, why do not consumers also help to finance it? Let me remind you that at this very moment, the taxman of most European countries is still receiving about four times the income per barrel of oil as the oil-producing country gets.

Oil is a nonrenewable resource, and this has to be taken into account, which may mean that some important depletion allowance should be charged by oil-producing countries. If push comes to shove then, as ideas are renewable, why do we not, on behalf of all poor countries, request instead a reduction of all those monopolistic rents that are collected on patents (like those in medicines)?

## It's an oil boom, stupid!

Sir, In March 1999, in "The next shock?", *The Economist* wrote that "in today's conditions the price [of oil] would head down towards $5 [per barrel]." Now again, for the umpteenth time, *The Economist*, so serious and clearheaded on most issues, loses it all when it comes to oil. In "Counting the Cost" of August 27, 2005, and even while assisted by a clear chart of the real prices of oil in 1980 terms, your editorial staff insist on labeling an oil crisis when the index is getting close to 100 and not when that index in 1998 dropped to only 20. That was the real oil crisis, and that is what the world is paying for today! To top it off, *The Economist* seems also to be preparing the terrain to blame oil for the collapse of the high real estate property prices that they duly classify as a "boom", instead of looking at much more plausible culprits. Come on, we expect more from you.

These were some of the arguments presented in March 1999 by *The Economist* in its article "The next shock?": "$10 might actually be too optimistic. We may be heading for $5. Thanks to new technology and productivity gains, you might expect the price of oil, like that of most other commodities, to fall slowly over the years. Judging by the oil market in the pre-OPEC era, a 'normal' market price might now be in the $5-10 range.... Nor is there much chance of prices rebounding. If they started to, Venezuela, which breaks even at $7 a barrel, would expand production; at $10, the Gulf of Mexico would join in; at $11, the North Sea, and so on. This will limit any price increase in the unlikely event that OPEC rises from the dead. Even in the North Sea, the bare-bottom operating costs have fallen to $4 a barrel. For the lifetime of such fields firms will continue to crank out oil, even though they are not recouping the sunk costs of exploration and financing. And basket-cases such as Russia and Nigeria are so hopelessly dependent on oil that they may go on producing for some time whatever the price."..."the Saudis may now do what once would have been unthinkable: throw open the taps. That, according to McKinsey, a management consultancy, would certainly herald an era of $5 oil." What was clearly left out of the analysis was the demand. For instance, about China, only the following was said: "In places like China, most power now comes from plants using inexpensive, but filthy, coal...a $5 per barrel of oil world might encourage a shift to oil-fired plants or, better still, to cleaner ones using natural gas.

By the way, let me assure my readers that I still consider *The Economist* one of the best journals around, and I remain a vivid reader of it, even though on the subject of oil they have been bewilderingly lost. One reason for this lapse might be that they have gotten too befuddled by Sheikh Zaki Yamani, an ex—Saudi Arabian who served as his country's oil minister for some decades. He is famous for his much-repeated saying that "The Stone Age did not end for lack of stone, and the Oil Age will end long before the world runs out of oil."

One thing that frequently crosses my mind these days is what would have happened if my country, Venezuela, had privatized all its state oil industry in 1998 when prices hovered around eight dollars per barrel when and if, like now, these prices start heading to a hundred dollars? You tell me!

### Kohlenweiss 1979
It's been twenty years, and the deadline established to keep the minutes of the European Union (EU) Inter-Ministerial meeting secret has elapsed. At last, we can read what was agreed to in the small German town of Kohlenweiss during a rainy autumn weekend in 1979, when EU Energy Ministers met in conclave to draw up a strategy on "how to defend oneself from the crude rent aspirations on crude of OPEC countries."

One debate registered in the minutes seems particularly horrible with all its prejudices against oil-exporting countries. However, because of lack of space, I will limit myself to summing up the approved plan, as originally presented by German minister Grüngelde, a plan that allegedly hinged on the following five key actions.

The first measure (the most innocuous) was to strengthen the relations between European governments and the environmental organizations to such a degree that the latter could be used to apply pressure in favor of diminishing oil consumption without its affecting the more contaminating coal, which Europe happened to possess.

Secondly, a program of continued hikes in taxes on oil and its derivatives, especially gasoline, was established to ensure not only a drop in demand but also that day after day the oil producers would receive a lesser and lesser proportion of oil's real value in the final market, namely, the price paid by the consumer. In this respect, the countries pledged themselves not to allow a lowering of gas prices to the consumer so, each fall in the price of crude should set off an immediate increase in taxes.

The third course of action was aimed at weakening OPEC's internal cohesion and in that sense, using Cold War tactics (the Berlin Wall hadn't tumbled yet), disinformation was one of the recommended instruments, aimed principally at sowing doubts and suspicions inside OPEC itself regarding such things as compliance with quotas set by the organization.

The fourth element agreed to was the "Community's prior interest to promote and support efforts that would lead to the privatization of the oil industry in OPEC countries." The reasons are understandable, when among the arguments, is that "as long as the oil industry belongs to the states, they will have the possibility of brandishing the weapon of geopolitical bargaining." The report established that "to achieve the goal of privatization, the ensuing competition among the partners would guarantee greater volumes of production and lower prices, in view of the fact that they all have a common interest in increasing profit and cash flow in the short term."

The Fifth...? Why continue?

I admit the above is pure fiction and that, as far as I know, it doesn't exist except in my imagination. There's no Kohlenweiss or Grüngelde. I have no knowledge of any such meeting and I definitely don't believe that the European Union fixed a period of only twenty years to make documents of this kind public.

However, since reality is stronger than fiction, I trust the reader will pardon my cheek. Let's see:

Since 1980 all taxes on oil and derivative have been hiked. For example, in the United Kingdom they went from

85% added value in 1980 to a confiscatory 456% in 1998. Obviously, during the same period oil products price index on the consumer level increased in the UK in constant terms from 100% to 247%, while, as if it were planned, the crude oil price index fell from 100% to a miserable 18%.

A barrel of oil contains around 160 liters of oil products broken down into gasoline (84), jet fuel (12), gas oil (36), lubricants (16) and heavy residuals (12). Today, when oil in Europe sells at a minimum $1.20 per liter, we see that this component represents more than $100—adding the other derivatives we come to a market value, that is, the price the consumer is prepared to pay, of more than $150 per barrel. If we start from the fact that refining, transport, and distribution costs aren't high, let's say around $20 per barrel, we can conclude that the European Treasury retains a minimum of $100 per barrel, while the producer, who actually sells an asset and sacrifices a nonrenewable resource, has to be satisfied with $30—scarcely 20% of its European value.

As for cooperation with environmental movements, there's no doubt it's been a complete success, since oil has been punished with all kinds of possible taxes, thus diminishing its consumption, while coal hasn't been touched even with a feather, arriving at the absurd situation where it's even being subsidized in some countries by taxes on oil. The consequence of such disparity in treatment can be seen in International Energy Agency statistics, which indicate that in 1973 oil accounted for 44.9% of world fuel consumption compared to 35.3% in 1996. Coal consumption in 1973 represented 24.8% and had maintained the same percentage in 1996.

Despite the fact that the figures mentioned above show clearly that only through geopolitical instruments like OPEC can existing injustice can be reversed or at least cushioned, in Venezuela privatization has not only been preached until the beginning of 1999 but it has also been partially achieved through *Apertura Petrolera* (Oil Opening).

Another trick was to egg us on to believe that the solution

lay in increasing the volume of production, even though the price was $8 per barrel, 5 cents for each liter (less than bottled water), a price that hardly covers the costs of extraction. Pressures to increase production were so intense that they continue even today, when we see important representatives of our local academe propose a weird thesis, according to which if Venezuela produces 3 million barrels of oil per day and sells it at $30 a barrel, we will find ourselves in the immoral grip of living on rents whereas, if, on the contrary, we produce 7 million barrels a day and sell it for just $7 a barrel, it would reflect an immense and praiseworthy productive effort.

Finally, with respect to OPEC, we can only say it has just saved itself from extinction—for the time being.

With this on record, who can doubt that, in fact, I have produced enough material to inspire a thriller script? If anyone out of curiosity wants to know what the imaginary Kohlenweiss fifth pillar was in the hope that (as my daughters say) recounting a nightmare makes sure it will never happen, I confess that recently I have been waking up each morning bathed in nervous sweat, fresh from the nightmare that the EU has plotted to plant an environmental extremist in the White House.

From *El Universal*, Caracas, August 2000. Translated by *V-Headline News*.

### The search for transparency in an oil-consuming world

Sir, There has been a lot of talk lately about a curse that, through corruption and other distortions, is stopping oil-rich countries from turning income into development. The Extractive Industries Transparency Initiative, championed by the United Kingdom and endorsed by the World Bank, has been named an exorcist and is starting the rites by applying a much-welcomed transparency to projects such as the Chad-Cameroon pipeline.

In the name of that same transparency, let us also remember that for every $1 received by any oil-producing country (which forever sacrifices a nonrenewable asset), the public treasury of many oil-consuming countries receives, net, at least $4 and is therefore a likely victim of the same curse, albeit stricken by different symptoms. For instance, in many oil-consuming developed countries, the curse has now created such an addiction to petrol taxes that their whole fiscal structures would be completely unsustainable without them.

Transparency would also, perhaps, not be a bad rite to use to exorcise this tax man's curse, since most of the gasoline consumers in these countries are not remotely aware of the real extent of the taxes and much less of how the proceeds are used.

For instance, having been told that these taxes were environmental, they would be surprised to learn that probably less than 0.5 per cent of the 100,000 million dollars collected yearly in Europe, just in taxes on lead-free gasoline, goes to the environment; and, worse, that much of it goes in subsidies to the even less environmentally friendly coal.

Also, today, as the possibilities of satisfying the world's demands for energy seem quite uncertain and the world becomes more aware that the ultimate cost of cutting, or not cutting, the trees of the Amazon will be paid by all, whether they like it or not, it is clear that the world needs to become much more penny-wise when developing alternative energies; and we all know that the best and only companion of the penny-wisest is transparency.

So, after the pipelines, when do we start with the Exchequer's bag?

*Financial Times*, Letters, December 24, 2004

### We need the world price of gasoline (petrol)

When discussing how to protect the environment, we frequently hear about the importance of having the prices set by free and liquid markets. In this respect, I would like to point out that one of the most relevant markets from an environmental perspective, the gasoline (petrol) markets are not allowed to function at all.

Currently we can see prices ranging from less that twenty United States cents per gallon in oil-producing countries such as Venezuela, to US $ 2.40 in the United States, to over 7.00 US$ in all of Europe. These enormous differences in the price of petrol, at the vital point where the market should be expressing its final verdict, have almost nothing to do with real economic factors, such as transport costs, but are solely a consequence of manmade artificialities such as subsidies and taxes. This introduces serious distortions that make it so much harder to find solutions to our growing energy-environment problems.

With this in mind, I wonder whether we should not start looking for a real-world price of gasoline, at the pump. To do so is no easy task, as it obviously requires the world to agree on a common petrol-consumption tax. Nonetheless, if we were successful, the rewards could be immense as this could open the door to the possibility of using some of these revenues for many global urgent distributive and environmental needs. Let us never forget that the only way of avoiding becoming a one-country world is to behave quite frequently as a one-country planet.

## Sovereignty

Recently, at a conference on environmental protection in Russia, scientists from the University of Uppsala (Sweden) declared that there are not enough remaining reserves of hydrocarbons to cause the environmental damage that some scientists predict. They maintain that world gas and oil reserves will begin their downward curve as early as 2015, long before 2050, the conventionally estimated date. I suppose that declarations of this kind must have come as a shock to the great number of environmentalists present there.

Neither, I imagine, was this thesis well received by those who rally around Sheik Yamani, relying on the false analogy that the Stone Age ended with plenty of stones still around, and offer us their services to free us of oil as quickly as possible and get rid of it at any price before the Oil Age ends. Talk about a career change, Sheik Yamani used to be Saudi Arabia's oil minister and the de facto spokesman for OPEC during the late 1970's and early 1980's.

Still on the subject of oil, we learn that the government of Chad has announced that a London-based trusteeship has received an initial deposit of six million dollars corresponding to the net value of the first sale of oil from the Doba fields, followed by the long trip to Kibliz terminal, via a 1,070 km pipeline through Cameroon.

Ten percent of the deposited funds are to be set aside for a Future Generations Fund; and the remaining 90% are to be shared with 5% for regional development in Doba; 80% for education, health and social services programs, rural development, infrastructure projects and water management, and 15% to state coffers. All withdrawals must be authorized by a commission made up of representatives of civil society, parliament, the Supreme Court and the government of Chad. The account will be audited annually, and the results will be published regularly. It is estimated that over 25 years, two billion dollars will pass through this account.

Friends, Venezuela has already received vastly more oil income than Chad will ever receive, and to no avail. Given what the Uppsala scientists tell us and with even greater income in mind, don't you think the time has come for us to consider schemes like Chad's?

Some will undoubtedly argue that this would affect our National Sovereignty. Nonsense! The only sovereignty affected would be that of our politicians. And isn't that precisely what we all want most? In our own sovereign way!

*El Universal*, Caracas, December 2003

P.S. A sovereign country is not a country that is able to do as it pleases but a country that is willing to take on full responsibilities for its own actions in an interrelated world.

## The Oil Referendum

WOULD YOU BE IN AGREEMENT if the Bolivarian Republic of Venezuela were to sign an oil contract with the United States of America (U.S.A.) under the following conditions?

The U.S.A. and Venezuela agree that starting today and for the next 50 years, the U.S.A. would buy and Venezuela would sell three million barrels of oil per day with Venezuelan characteristics. The Reference Price (RP) would be US $25 per barrel, indexed to the U.S.A. inflation rate, plus or minus an adjustment equivalent to 50% of the difference between the RP and the spot-market price.

As a consideration, Venezuela would also keep an additional 2 million barrels per day at the preferential availability of the U.S.A., which could be bought by the U.S.A. at spot-market prices, provided there were an emergency that made those prices exceed the RP by at least 100%.

In order to guarantee to the U.S.A. that Venezuela would always be in a position to meet its supply obligations, Venezuela would agree that it would not, under any circumstances, contract a new public debt, so as to make sure that the oil revenues to be received over the next 50 years would not be given as guarantees for new fresh loans today, and thereby risk wiping away the value of those reserves in a mere 50 days.

In order to ensure the enthusiastic applause of environmentalists, Venezuela would earmark 3% of oil revenues to planting trees in our country, trees which would capture carbon from oil emissions.

In order to ensure that the Venezuelan citizenry would get its fair share of the revenues (and vote "YES"), 30% of Venezuela's gross oil revenues would be directly distributed in equal amounts to each Venezuelan. That distribution could be made in cash or in vouchers for health and education services.

If the "YES" vote were to win the hypothetical referendum described above, Venezuela would have macroeconomic stability, enabling it to formulate a true development plan, and the U.S.A. would have a larger, more secure supply of energy.

But so long as the natural market for our oil, the United States of America, remains incapable of gauging its interests beyond the current quarter, and doesn't care if oil falls to 7 dollars a barrel, and prefers to create costly strategic reserves by burying crude oil or exploiting environmentally delicate areas, then any Venezuelan president trying to defend his or her country and keep the price of oil somewhere above the miserable marginal cost of extraction has no alternative but to strengthen OPEC and seek alternatives elsewhere, if for no other reason than to incite jealousy.

To the best of my understanding, this is what geopolitics is all about; and that's why it might not be such a bad idea for the United States to study realpolitik—especially when, as happened forty years ago on a Caribbean island, they flunked that subject royally.

Published in *El Universal*, Caracas, June 7, 2001

The above is what I wrote in 2001, but no one in the U.S.A. picked up on the idea or proposed anything similar. That is why today, when oil is up around 60 dollars, I don't care a lot about some of the crybabies.

### Why do they point their finger only at us?

Why are oil-producing countries receiving so much hell for keeping their production of a valuable nonrenewable resource down while the critics of OPEC find no fault at all with the lack of investment in oil refineries? It is a shortage of new refineries and a failure to update existing ones that have created so many bottlenecks. They, in turn, have had a considerable impact upon the final availability and price of gasoline at the pump.

### About accountability in energy planning

I just can't believe that professional organizations—such

as the International Energy Agency, and even the WBG for that matter—were unable to warn the world about the ever narrowing gap between the demand for and the supply of oil. Much more so, they should have been able to warn us about the shortages in refining capacity. Equally, I find it unbelievable to observe how no one really kept track on the building up of demand for natural gas, resulting from so many pursuing the same "clean" though in reality not so clean generation of electricity. Why were they not able to warn how this could affect the price of gas?

This year, for instance, many consumers in the United States are going to pay much higher prices for their electricity bill. That means that we, the rest of the world, besides paying our own higher electricity bills, will of course also pay one way or another for the higher United States dollar inflation. I doubt that the poor planners who got us into this mess are going to pay for their faults, by getting fired, as they should. As I see it, as long as there is more risk for planners in being politically incorrect than just factually incorrect, it will be very difficult to find our way out of this energy labyrinth which we're facing.

Another problem that is hindering the correct design of our energy strategies is that most of our energy sources are really competing against one another, and so the professionals tend to identify themselves with just one energy source. "I'm an oil man," "I'm a natural gas man," "I'm a solar man," and so on. We need to be able to look in a more neutral way at all of our energy options.

# Trade, agriculture, services, and growth

### On the road to Cancun...with new proposals

Venezuela has clearly fulfilled its share of opening up its markets, as testified by all the abandoned industrial zones, today cemeteries where its hopes for industrial development and a professional, diversified middle class have been left to rest in peace.

For this sacrifice, Venezuela was to receive some compensation. That is why together with other developing countries, it must be eagerly waiting for the meetings in Cancun to start, in order to ask developed countries to make good on their promises, especially in the agricultural sector. Its feelings, like those of anyone feeling cheated, should be those of a contained rage, but—Why should Venezuela believe it will be better off just because the European farmer and the Floridian orange grower also get entrapped, lose their jobs, and have to feed the cancer-like growth of the cities? I myself, as a Venezuelan, certainly do not think so.

On the contrary, we probably will be much better off if we learn from those farmers how to defend our own interests, how to avoid being cheated by false promises, and finally how to keep alive and vibrant a totally unproductive economic activity, based solely on its social importance, as the Japanese rice farmers get their subsidies. In this respect, I refuse to believe that our future depends on turning their green fields into parking lots—in a suicidal vendetta.

I therefore propose that we should go to Cancun equipped with a set of new proposals designed to conquer the agricultural impasse, and with a greater potential of job creation than that implied in a simple zero-sum game.

So, friends, let us offer the developed countries to liberate them from their impossible agricultural commitments—which, in theory at least, should be causing them some bad conscience—in exchange for the following:

1) A commitment to have 50 percent of all the caring services for their elderly provided directly in and by the developing countries, and

2) A tenfold increase in the opportunities for developing countries to exploit the only clearly identified economic activity at their disposal, namely that of sending their workers to developed countries in exchange for Diaspora remittances. Of course, just as most capital flows in the other direction are treated now, these salaries should be tax-exempt.

Yet there are some excesses in agricultural protections that should anyhow be revised.

For instance, the use in the United States of specific duties (cents per pound) for orange concentrates should be eliminated, as this leads it to import only the best and, consequently, forces the rest of the world to compete for leftovers, in a sort of quality dumping.

Also, the so European tradition of paying US$2.50 per day in cow subsidies, with funds obtained by charging US$1 in taxes per liter of gasoline is just a little bit too much.

From *El Universal*, Caracas, February 2003

\*\*\*

My editor Jim: "Quality dumping" is not very clear" I: "Price dumping takes place when products are exported at lower prices than what they sell for in their own land, and so, when you export products the quality of which is lower than what your home market demands, we could say we are in the presence of quality dumping. For instance, exporting chicken wings from a country where its own consumers demand only chicken breasts.

\*\*\*

### Place us next to something profitable…

I recently visited a country here in the Americas where I flew over a valley that appeared very fertile—a vast, thick green carpet beautifully woven by plantations of African palm trees. I was enthusiastic, thinking that at last I had discovered development in action—that is, until I landed.

The contrast between the wonderful view from above and the misery below screamed out that the African palm, far from being a motor of development, could be the mother of all poverty traps. By contrast, take, for example, a coffee bean. It may be worth very little in the field, but at least it lets us dream of the chance of capturing a bit more of the value suggested by the fact that some people pay four dollars or more for a cup of it at Starbucks. But in the case of the African palm, no dreams seem possible. Just for a starter, its saturated fats are considered undesirable.

In this sense, the difficult cultivation of the African palm would seem to be doomed to mark the borderline of lowest overall marginal cost, that is, where the least is paid to farmers for their labor. Palm farming now has such a small margin of profit that it does not even cover the costs of registering a union, and so, Mr. Planner, just in case, don't place us next to the palms, please place us next to something profitable.

When analyzing agricultural margins of profit, we must not forget that in most cases in which farmers' margins allow them to maintain a decent standard of living, this is due to some kind of subsidy, protection, or market interference. So, of course, if we're offered the chance to grow African palms in France, we might just consider it.

It is one thing to be a marginal agricultural producer and it is another very different thing to be an agricultural margin capturer. In a supermarket in the United States I came across 11 kinds of eggs, ranging in price from 95 cents a dozen for caged, industrial production to $3.99 a dozen for eggs certified as coming from organically-fed free-range hens.

For countries whose hopes focus on Cancun and on agricultural opening, I hope that the above leads them to stop, think, and realize that opening in itself does not work miracles if farmers do not also receive other kinds of aid, such as those offered in many developed countries.

Friends, as I have said many times before, if we let globalization simply pursue the lowest marginal cost of labor, then Great Bad Deflation will inevitably come.

From *El Universal*, Caracas, July 2003

### Time to cover up?

Because of its oil, Venezuela has foreign income that in normal times would keep the value of its currency relatively high, making it difficult to compete abroad and generate domestic employment. From this limited perspective, Venezuela selfishly has little to gain from more open trade.

However, we cannot consider Venezuela in isolation, but rather in its global context: only by broadly opening up trade can the necessary economic growth be generated to avoid the collective suicide that would eventually occur if common solutions are not found for poverty and inequality. The world is increasingly interrelated. Evidence of this, for example, is how the world would be affected if its green lung, the Amazon, were to disappear one day simply because settlers there chopped down the wood they need to cook and stave off starvation. From this kind of global perspective, Venezuela, for equally selfish reasons, does indeed have much to gain from freer trade. And so?

Given the above, it is clear that the dilemma as to whether or not Venezuela ought to open its markets comes down essentially to a question of the right opportunity to do so.

Venezuela and a few other countries, deferring to world interests perhaps too soon, stripped off their protective clothing. With the failure of the recent World Trade Organization meeting in Cancun and the minimal advances made in opening trade (and labor) markets, they must now be realizing that far from having made a common cause of group nudity, they are now the only ones left stark naked. And so? Is it time to cover up?

It is hard to decide whether we are saints or sinners. In the same way that for some it is spiritually comforting to cast off all material possessions, for others it is not. What is certain is that if we decide to carry on in this nudist colony, we should at least expel the Peeping Toms.

It may very well be the very World Trade Organization process that makes freer trade unviable, because when everything is more a product of negotiations than of truly convinced beneficiaries, the results will reflect only the powers and the doubts of the negotiators. In such circumstances, the only alternative may be to set up a real colony for trade nudism, where only those willing to go a *Full Monty* would be welcome. If not...Let's cover up! Quick! I'm dying of embarrassment!

From *El Universal*, Caracas, October 2003

### An encore on nudism and WTO negotiations

The worst part of free-trade agreements might be the negotiation of free-trade agreements. I am not at all recommending nudist camps—after all I am the father of three girls—but, if you really have to speak out in their favor, you do so in the understanding that all those who are present in the camp find nudity perfectly normal. But what if those who were to approve entrance to the nudist camp derived *special* enjoyment from playing strip-poker? That would certainly go against the spirit of it all. In this same vein, I believe that many of the negotiators of trade agreements do not themselves believe in free trade but are taking a perverse satisfaction from the negotiating process. I refer especially to those from the developed world who are especially good at poker and have much more clothes on to start out with. The spirit of free trade does not stand a chance against these saboteurs.

### Hosting the spirit of free trade

A couple of months ago, Mr. Andres Oppenheimer wrote that Miami should host the Permanent Secretariat of the Free Trade Agreement of the Americas (FTAA) and as arguments he presented a list of available infrastructure—as if free trade was to be the result of the availability of infrastructure and not of the spirit for Free Trade.

In that respect it would be useful to remind Mr. Oppenheimer that it was Florida that not long ago prohibited the use of the Venezuelan heavy oil "Orimulsion" for environmental reasons, while permitting the use of their local clean coal. Likewise, it is in Florida where the present governor recently promised its orange growers to maintain the specific duties that at times provide them with an impressive 80% protective barrier.

*\*\**

Jim, my Editor's Q: "What is your "80%"? Eighty percent of what? Floridians, who in places can literally pluck fresh oranges off the trees, wouldn't want to buy imported, necessarily less fresh, oranges and orange juice even if foreign oranges had no import duties. It would be like Venezuelans importing oil."

My A: "Jim, it is what the duty paid by solid pound of orange concentrate represents as a percentage of its value. Without those duties Florida would not be able to compete with imports, and most of Florida's orange groves would be malls or extensions to Disney's parks. Your comment illustrates well the fact that in the same way Europeans citizens are basically unaware of how amazingly high the taxes applied to gasoline are; you in the United States are also in great ignorance about how high protection some groups have been able to negotiate."

\*\*\*

Clearly, the host of FTAA should be in a place that really and truly believes in the principles of Free Trade. According to this criterion, in the Americas, Chile should most certainly be the favored place, but, unfortunately, the geography is against them. I have heard that Venezuela is lending its support to Trinidad and Tobago, which sounds quite reasonable, but, nonetheless, I wonder why our beautiful Island of Margarita (Venezuela) has been left out.

Clearly, too, our Island of the Pearls—where the pearls were freely extracted and traded away unto extinction of the oysters, and where also we have enjoyed a very long and honorable tradition of smuggling that with time turned into a duty-free zone—can provide plentiful evidence that it definitely possesses the spirit of free trade.

\*\*\*

Jim, my Editor: "Of course, Latin margarita means "pearl," and was borrowed from the Greek (s)margarites, in turn borrowed from some Eastern language such as Sanskrit or Persian. It is related to the name of Saint Smaragdus. But will your readers know this?" I: "I didn't. Are you putting me on? (Of course he's not)

\*\*\*

To top it off, the Island of Margarita is also part of a country that is so in the forefront of opening up its borders that, according to some, it is even outsourcing its military command to Havana, Cuba. I am absolutely certain that the

United States of America is still far away from using Bangalore for that function.

## Time to scratch each other's backs

Do you remember the 'no-driving day' in Venezuela? Somebody's brilliant idea to ease congestion! Depending on your license plate number, there was one day a week when you couldn't drive your car. Even if the idea had worked, I still would never have liked it because, as traffic kept growing, logic would lead us towards a blind alley as—inevitably—the next step would be two no-driving days, then three, all the way up to seven, when everything comes to a complete standstill. It's rather like applauding the fact that a patient's breathing problems have ceased—because the patient died.

There's a hint of all coming to a standstill in the theory about how globalization will optimize the world economy, by ensuring that merchandise will always be produced at the lowest marginal cost. What good does it do us to have products where the cost of the labor component gets smaller by the minute, if workers can't buy the very products they produce? (Jim, my editor: "That's why Henry Ford shocked his fellow businessmen by paying his workers the unheard of high wage of five dollars a day—so they could afford to buy his cars." I: "Congratulation Jim. I see you got through Economics 1.") What could be waiting for us at the end of that tunnel is a world of desperate wage earners, willing to work for pennies, who might never be able to afford even a reasonable part of the fruit of their efforts. Doesn't it seem as if we're getting nowhere?

This wouldn't be as much of a problem if there were more jobs than workers, but unfortunately, that isn't the case. Just ask the millions of professionals competing for jobs as taxi drivers in the world's capital cities! Not even the United States has managed to escape unharmed from the pangs of globalization. In fact, over the past few months, for the first time, we have seen economic growth in the United States coupled with an increase in unemployment. As it turns out, over the past three years, the United States has "exported" 2.5 million jobs to low-wage countries like China.

I don't have a solution. How can we increase profits, create jobs, increase wages, put an end to poverty, and make everybody happy? Nonetheless, sometimes I've toyed with the idea of a macro global fiscal reform aimed at creating jobs. The principle behind it would be that whoever requires the most services ends up creating the most jobs, and so should end up paying the least taxes. Under such a system, you'd pay double sales taxes on a frozen pizza you eat at home; standard sales tax on a pizza you order over the phone for home delivery, while a pizza eaten at a restaurant wouldn't just be tax free; it would automatically be credited on your income-tax return.

Friends, let's give one another jobs, scratching each other's backs—paying each other good salaries of course.

From *El Universal*, Caracas, August, 2003

### Of Mangos and Bananas

For several reasons, the debate about the global economy has recently reminded me of fruit. The wise Henri Pitier wrote his *Manual about Common Plants in Venezuela* in 1926. In it he wrote the following about the mango:

> It is harvested in abundance, and there are many who, during the season in which they are ripe, dedicate all of their time to the search for this fruit which for some time then becomes their only source of nourishment, very often to the detriment of their health. One can vacillate, then, on deciding whether the introduction of this tree [from Asia] has been a blessing or a curse. The writer of these words is inclined to believe the latter since the mango leads to idleness, to the invasion of another's property and to vagrancy; additionally, no matter how good

or healthy it may be, when ingested in moderation, it sometimes provokes digestive disorders and is far from being wholesome food. It alters, then, both morality as well as public health.

This interesting quotation shows us that, in addition to oil, the mango should be classified high on the list of culprits that have been the cause of our poor economic development. Most assuredly, in addition to the mango and oil, we must also add to this list the sun, the beaches and all those variables that undoubtedly make it easier to survive an economic recession in a tropical Caracas than in a wintry Moscow.

Since it seems evident that the simplicity of living in the tropics leads to laziness while the hardship of winter promotes the discipline and work ethics that have ultimately inspired today's global economic development, it behooves us to view global warming with renewed preoccupation and from a totally new angle.

I belong to a group that is identified in Venezuela as Contemporary Adults (sounds better than middle-aged). This implies being up-to-date with current issues such as the environment. I have, with certain frequency made own individual observations about the evolution of global warming. Every Carnival weekend, for example, I stroll out to the beach in Margarita, the tropical Venezuelan island in the Caribbean Sea, in my most casual, monarchic pace, and with all seriousness and responsibility, take note of the width of the shore from the water line to the roadway. Even when I had terrible difficulty in finding a spot in which to anchor my garishly multicolored beach umbrella, I never really worried about it. I simply attributed this difficulty to the increased popularity of the island and not to an invasion by the oceans.

Today, however, I harbor serious doubts as to the validity of my method of measurement. Wherever I look I find evidence of the advanced state of warming in the world.

How else, other than by assuming a certain displacement toward the north of the geographical boundary of the *Banana Republics*, can we explain the opposite positions sustained by superpowers like Europe and the United States on the issue of bananas, as if they were some modern versions of Lilliput and Blefuscu. (The current enormous fiscal and commercial deficits of the North might also lend further credibility to the thesis of the displacement of the parallel of the Banana Republics.)

How else, other that by assuming the creation of climatic conditions conducive to the cultivation of mangos, can we understand why Japan has not been able to combat idleness and stimulate the reactivation of its economy? We have all read that Japan has reduced interest rates to an annual rate of one per one thousand. Can you imagine how impressed a botanist like Henri Pitier would be upon observing this unique specimen of a mango?

From *The Daily Journal*, Caracas, March 1999

### Local strawberries in season

Although I appreciate being able to eat *strawberries-in-winter* I still miss those very special strawberries that you could only get only once a year, early summer, in strawberry season. As an economist I would have to say they had that very special taste of scarcity—and scarcity allowed them to provide their growers a quite decent return. Their disappearance happened when such strawberries were forced to compete, marginal cost against marginal cost, with other brutally efficient quasi-strawberries that could be transported overnight, into your local supermarkets, at anytime and in any quantities.

As the world allowed those coming from anywhere at anytime to count as the same as your neighbor's at-their-right-time strawberries, we—if I may mix a metaphor—mixed apples with pears, created confusion, and destroyed important economic value. This mess in the strawberry patches of the world can still be corrected though. Currently as a result of World Trade Organization's negotiations only champagne from Champagne can be called champagne and the rest has to be labeled as produced by the Méthode Champenoise. If we were to broaden these criteria there is nothing that stops us from marketing any local-strawberries-in-season as strawberries, while requiring all others to label themselves as close-to-being-strawberries berries—and this way all strawberries would survive.

It is quite clear from the awakening of protectionism that something dramatic has to be done, and perhaps a much clearer market segmentation could be the key to keep borders from closing up, and having to wave good-bye to all those ersatz strawberries that even while never the same as their summer cousins, are still quite nice to have in winter. But if the worst happens, let's find some consolation in the fact that strawberries-in-winter could turn out to be a new and profitable smuggling alternative for some of the uglier cartels, while being much less harmful to us all.

# About remittances and immigration

### The nature of remittances

Mr. Chairman, I see references over and over again to the remittances of foreign workers in developed countries back to their not-so-developed homelands and so I feel once again compelled to remind my colleagues about the true nature of these flows. The remittances come from very private earnings.

Picture yourself working in a foreign country for less than minimum wages, alone, perhaps sleeping in lousy quarters, not understanding all that they say to you, and still you take a substantial part of your earnings and send them home. That's what these remittances are all about. They are quite close to being like sacred religious donations.

Please do not confuse these flows with other financial flows. Do not even think of taxing them or assisting third parties to lay their hands on them. Be extremely careful. Do I exaggerate? I hope so but I have already read in World Bank publications about the securitizing these flows! Come on!

### Remittance fees: The tip of the tip of the tip of the iceberg

There has been an incredible fixation by many institutions with the fees charged by the banks for the service of making the remittances. Yes, of course it is good that these fees become more competitive but it is almost laughable to think about all the resources used up in analyzing this very minor issue in an immigrant's reality. Just the money spent on communicating by telephone with home or buying yourself over the border surpasses by far the sum of all the fees paid to the banks. Stop talking about the fees, and help the immigrants make more money with which they would happily pay even higher fees to the banks, if asked. Boy. Talk about shortsightedness!

\*\*\*

Jim, my editor: "Recently a Canadian client sent me a $175 Canadian check. I was shocked that my nice bank charged me $17.50 to convert Canadian money to United States money. I don't want the client to have to pay some huge fee in Canada in order to send me money either. What is the best way for him to send me money in the future? Thanks!"

I: "Jim, as you see, it is not only immigrants who are affected, and also the $17.50 is before you know what exchange rate they used! That's why some of Europe adopted the euro. But, I will not try to convince Canadians about anything similar, as two of my daughters study in Montreal, and so I have to be careful with the consequences of what I say. Do you want me to take up this issue on behalf of the citizens in developed countries with The World Bank?

\*\*\*

### The knowledge Bank and immigration

I have luckily been able to assist some seminars organized by the Bank on the issue of immigration of labor, or Mode Four as it is known in World Trade Organization language. That said, I am still surprised at how little the World Bank gets involved in this area, especially as it should have a very important advocacy role to play. I hope the Bank soon starts accumulating some knowledge about what works and what does not work in temporary immigration programs. I have long been advocating that we could develop programs where, for instance, an immigrant had to deposit a percentage of his earnings in a special savings account to be disbursed to him upon his return to home—instead of continuing to criminalize it for the sole benefit of the professional criminal smuggler who will charge the poor immigrant thousands of dollars to get him over the border.

## What GDP?

The GDP (Gross Domestic Product) for 2003 of El Salvador is calculated by the World Bank to have been 14.9 billion dollars. Now, if you consider only the highly probable estimate that their one million emigrants working abroad manage to earn only five hundred dollars each per month, then this figure totals 6 billion per year, and we could ask ourselves whether this should not appear accounted for...somewhere.

When we consider that about 40% of the workforce of Central America really works abroad, are then their GDP or even their current GNP (Gross National Product) figures really relevant? Is it enough just to include the remittances? What would happen if one of the countries would start to regard the nationals working abroad as part of their own economic reality? Would they then give them more classes in English?

Given the ever-increasing importance of cross-border work and cross-border services in general it is surprising to see that emigration/immigration and remittances are not even mentioned among those 204 Development Topics previously listed in the introduction.

By the way, note when resettlement is mentioned in that list, it refers only to the involuntary resettlements of tens or perhaps a few hundreds resulting from projects where the WBG is involved, and not to those millions who are being forced to resettle by the facts of life.

World Bank Group does definitively not go around naked and it surely wears a lot of fancy accessories that are bound to razzle-dazzle you, but, with so little reference to immigration and remittances, at least to me it does not seem quite fully dressed.

## Family Remittances

In recent publications of the World Bank and other multilateral organizations, there has been emphasis on the significance of family remittances for many developing countries, such as El Salvador, where these remittances reached $1,900 million dollars in 2001. This phenomenon has many bankers scrambled, trying to find out ways to attract part of the financial gains that such an influx represents, ranging from transfer services to the issuance of bonds backed by the projections of future remittances.

Likewise, they are studying the impact on a poor country when hundreds of thousands of its workers could be sent to developed countries on a temporary visa, where they could have access to greater remunerations which could even have a greater economic potential than the long-promised agricultural openness and liberalization.

After allowing their markets to be captured by external suppliers, after allowing free flow of resources, after forcing themselves to respect foreign income sources, such as intellectual property rights and patents, and finally, after many of its educated professionals have been captured by better economic gains somewhere else, poor countries, it would seem, have all the reasons to request greater access to global markets for their unskilled workforce.

Nevertheless, during our technical discussions, we should not forget the human aspect of migration, with the enormous incurred sacrifices and the generosity with which immigrants share their income with family members who were left behind. It has been more than 150 years since big groups of Europeans had to emigrate due to famine in their countries, among other reasons. They left their homes knowing that they would not see their parents, siblings, and everything they had known and cherished in their life. Even though today's emigrants have in general greater possibilities of returning to their home countries, their vicissitudes are not necessarily negligible, since they are frequently victims of rejection and marginalization.

In this sense, all that is left to do is to stand in awe while observing the significant amount of transfers that Salvadorian emigrants, among many others, send to their homes nowadays. These are only one example of family values, traditions, and solidarity that our countries still possess. They might be poor in monetary terms, but thank God these countries are rich in human, family values.

From *El Universal*, Caracas, August 2003

### Some notes on the securitization of remittances

Some financiers have come up with the idea of using the future growing flows of cash from workers remittances to create values that could be used as collateral to loans made to those foreign banks that are specializing in processing these transfers. Since these collateral accounts are located in the financial centers, the loans so backed carry a lower interest as they manage to avoid some of the country-risk margins.

There is nothing illegal with this securitization as clearly the transferring bank is in no obligation to deliver exactly the same physical funds received; in fact, he will normally be delivering local currency to the beneficiary. Also the bank is never released from its obligation to transfer the worker's money to the family back home and all the bank's general funds, including those received from the loans, should back up its commitment.

Nonetheless perhaps we should ask ourselves whether the fiduciary duty of the transfer agent is being fulfilled when this securitization occurs, especially since the foreign worker trying to send money home is in blissful ignorance of the arrangements.

Also when you walk into a bank and order a transfer of money to someone, you presume that the bank will execute the transfer as expeditiously as possible, and never would you imagine that it could be delayed by having to go through a collateral account or, God forbid, that the final beneficiary never receives your funds, because the collateral was seized and sold to satisfy the claims on the local bank.

Any problem that would occur with a securitized remittance, besides dramatically increasing the cost of that particular transfer, could lead to a worldwide scramble back to more "trustworthy" informal channels...and we do not need that.

Also, if one of these collaterals was executed, in what jurisdiction should a foreign worker and his beneficiary complain...are they also released from country risk?

### Credit rating agencies and the securitization of remittances

It is to be expected that when the country or the bank through which the remittances are sent enters into problems, these will stop. Emigrants are far from stupid. As we also know that the collaterals built around these remittances cover basically only the current service of the loan, a minor part, some doubts remain as to why then the ratings by the credit-rating agencies improve so much. Are we not here facing exactly the type of systemic risk that I frequently observe could be present by using few opinions of credit-risk agencies as proxies for the real market?

The first time I heard about the securitization of remittances I thought "How creative, I have heard about securitizing accounts receivable but this is the first time I see it done with accounts payable".

### Keeping them stupid?

Based on the argument that workers do not have as much information and do not react as fast in a crisis, we can frequently hear the opinion that the securitization of worker remittances is better and more stable than that of general company remittances. This might very well be true for the time being, but it sure feels sad to get involved in programs that are based on keeping the workers in the dark.

### Formalizing remittances

Development institutions are working hard toward making more and more of the remittances from foreign workers in the advanced countries to their relatives back home go through formal bank channels, and that is well. Nonetheless in doing so there are some things to be avoided.

First, do not deride in the process the informal remittance channels. It would do good always to remember that, in time of crisis, they are normally the only ones functioning.

Also never confuse formal with official. Remember that the remitter should receive the same guarantees of privacy from the banks that he believes he gets from informal agents.

Finally seeing that the World Bank Group could get involved in some projects to securitize projects funded by such remittances, let me remind you all that the first peso an old Mexican does not receive from his son because it got withheld in a securitized collateral of a defaulting bank—whether fact or rumor—is going to make all run back to the shelter of informality. Be very careful with those projects.

### Safeguarding resources

The reverse flows of the remittances to their homelands from immigrant workers are the capital flights that so frequently occur in many developing countries. I wish to make the following observations about some perhaps conveniently ignored aspects of these flows:

First, before condemning capital flight as something bad per se, which is what we normally do, we would do well to remember that in many cases the flight is indeed a "flight to safety". In this case, "safeguarding capital" should be lauded instead, since with it, I hope, the citizens of a country might be saving resources for a more propitious development moment. The implication of this possibility would then be that, for some countries and at some times, the acceleration of remittances might not be beneficial at all. In fact, it might indeed be better to delay them instead. This is something development entities like the WBG need to consider very carefully when looking for ways to channel remittances because the last thing they can afford to do is to waste scarce resources by eagerly pushing them into a dangerous money pit.

The second fact, also basically ignored, is that quite frequently the capital flight is a direct result of local capital being crowded out by foreign lenders willing to lend to the governments at lower rates than what the local markets deem prudent. If locals, with their local know-how, feel that their government should only be able to borrow resources at, for instance, 7%, then what on earth are foreign investors doing lending at 6% just because some credit-rating agencies so validate?

Closely related to the above question we also hear often about the need to develop deep long-term domestic financial markets, into which governments can dip for their borrowing needs. This is of course a very good development goal, but, unfortunately, to do so does frequently require offering, at least initially, much higher rates than those required for foreign borrowings. I cannot help but get the feeling that, in the back of the head of the market-developers, there is always the underlying assumption that inflation or devaluation will take care of those high rates, and so in real terms they will in fact be lower than foreign rates. This type of approach, almost based on bunching up against the local investors, is something that I found quite odious and that quite frequently forces me to defend capital flights as good per se. I understand and applaud the concept that the WBG and similar entities should work hand in hand with the governments of the developing countries, but this should never go as far as to cooperate against or behind the back of the citizens or the private sector of that country.

\*\*\*

In August 2004, I spent my two weeks of the board's summer adjournment putting together the following piece for a contest arranged by *The Economist* on the issue of immigration. I very much liked all the other five pieces that won, but that does not stop me from being proud about my effort.

### Scaling up imagination about immigration

A short while ago, A. T. Kearney/Foreign Policy published their *Globalization Index* (Foreign Policy, March/April 2004), which assigns points to countries by measuring the number of Internet users, hosts, and secure servers—without even considering the contents transmitted online or through other media. In July of 2004, one of the many lists of favorite Web hits ranked Paris Hilton as No. 1, Howard Stern as No. 50,, and in between—besides the Bible, diets, marihuana, and beheadings in Iraq—nothing that could be even remotely related to any type of useful learning.

Who is more global, a family in a rich country with 10 televisions for 10 local sitcoms or a family in a poor country with only one TV on which they watch foreign programming? Who is more global, a family from a rich country that visits Paris or a family from a poor country with loved ones working abroad on whose remittances they depend for survival? Clearly, the index developers need to go back to the drawing board.

Just like the *cause celébre* blamed in the 9/11 report for the failure to prevent those horrendous events, the current debate on immigration suffers clearly also from *failure of imagination*.

Already there are developing countries where up to 40 percent of the work force has migrated to work in developed countries instead of staying to become a burden on society. Through their remittances, emigrants now constitute the main source of their homelands' foreign-currency earnings. Against this backdrop, it is amazing to hear relatively little discussion about how to exploit these opportunities further—"scale them up," as they say—especially when compared to the immense attention given to marginal issues such as the transfer cost of remittances…or the very negative spin given to the debate with the argument of "brain drain."

There are also developed countries that for many reasons—demographics just one of them—have gotten themselves into fiscally unsustainable welfare systems. The question politicians should be asking constituents is whether they wish to have foreigners assist in the upkeep of their systems or whether they prefer to fade away in splendid isolation. If in favor of getting help, they might as well start early, and so that their future nurses will at least understand them…when they need to go.

From the perspective of the donor country—in this case, the country supplying the workforce—a brain drain should not pose any problems, unless it were to be accompanied by a heart drain. That could cut the ties with home and stop the remittances as well.

From the perspective of the recipient country, immigration should help citizens raise their quality of living to a standard fitting their level of income. A rich country where people with high incomes can afford to pay four dollars for a latte but cannot afford to pay someone to help them with the housekeeping has not begun to optimize its economy yet.

Donor countries should also consider how to prepare their workers before their landing, teaching them foreign languages and providing them with an understanding about how the work they are supposed to do is normally done. This will help ensure that they get off to a flying start and will be saved from some of the hardships of life in a new land. Of course, this will also accelerate and increase their remittances.

Recipient countries should be contemplating how to maximize the economic return of an imported workforce by ensuring that it really complements its own workforce or, when it doesn't, that it at least generates important fiscal savings that allow some benefits to trickle down to everyone.

Both types of countries should be thinking urgently about how to get the programs going. In this respect, one must remember that just as it is extremely difficult to guarantee the behavior of any individual it is fairly easy to establish some measurable parameters for an entire group. This, by the way, is exactly how the insurance industry works.

I do not intend to preempt the imagination of willing and inspired immigration-program designers but, for them to have a real chance of success, no stones should be left unturned.

The complete identification and real-time knowledge of the whereabouts of all immigrants in a formal program is something that could be discussed, no matter how much some libertarians scream. If a future English king can accept having a tracking device implanted for safety reasons, why should an immigrant object to it, if that is what his host requires to give him a chance? I am sure most immigrants would consider this somewhat exaggerated concern about their persona blissful when compared to how they frequently are ignored by their own countrymen.

If the program is temporary, perhaps it would gain a lot by forcing workers to deposit a percentage of their earnings in a savings account that will be released only if they comply with the program and return when time is up. Insurance companies will be able to provide any individual worker with protection against losing his savings, if destiny decrees that he (or she) fall in love, for instance, and never return.

Both donor and recipient countries should also have the direct costs of the programs reimbursed, but this should not be hard to achieve. Just consider the savings an immigrant will realize by going legal. The financial consequences for donor countries of educating its people and then losing them in the brain drain could also be taken care of, for example, by ensuring that education programs are duly repaid by the immigrants, with their new formal employer withholding part of their salaries for this purpose.

Program designers should consider how to maximize their economic efficiency. Although nurses might be what a recipient country needs, it should not allow these slots to be filled up by doctors, as currently happens when Filipino doctors find it easier to get into the United States as nurses.

The programs need to be credible, and both donor and recipient countries should make compliance with the agreed rules an absolute must. Clearly, an immigrant who misbehaves should be named and shamed and made aware that he is hijacking the opportunity of one of his countrymen.

The days when a Swedish mother[3] felt that watching her son board a schooner to America was like burying him alive, are—thank God—gone forever. Nevertheless, many current illegal immigrants do not dare go home, as they cannot afford the risk, cost, or logistics of another illegal entry. They are living in a de facto prison. The programs, although welcoming video conferencing and *Messenger* technology, need to stimulate frequent home visits, in order to keep the hearts warm.

The world should also not ignore the tremendous capacity building which immigrants can bring to their own homeland—for instance, by the way they direct remittances or by the way they convey to their countrymen some know-how about current best practices for good governance.

Traditional economic analysis about how to produce something for which a market needs exist starts by looking for the best mix of labor and capital. Aligned with such thinking, the world wisely decided that it would benefit from free trade and proceeded to open up markets and mobilize capital resources on the belief that the whole world is our playing field. Unfortunately the payoff, although great for some big winners, has not been distributed equitably—perhaps exactly because the world has not investigated new means to mobilize labor.

One does not have to be an economist to perceive the economic growth potential of massive legal temporary immigration plans. Travel, language laboratories, employment agencies, restaurants (where the wealthy could find more time to dine, thanks to their new housemaid) and, of course, all those remittances that—one should never forget—are immediately recycled into the world's economy.

Investment in globally mobile brainpower and skills is a good option for many developing countries—especially when compared to the alternative of having everyone competing against one another in the rat race of agriculture and manufacturing. To make the most out of their investment, donor countries need to consider demands, as it is clear that a certified bilingual nurse stands a much better chance of repaying her education costs than all those economists and engineers you find driving taxis in New York.

It is not only the developing countries that are affected by a kind of negativism in relation to outgoing labor mobility, as a five-minute search on the Web would confirm. Just the title of one Canadian article—"Are we losing our minds?"[4]—seemed to say more about the state of mind of the debaters than of the pros and cons of the issue itself.

Many are confused about the consequences of receiving a massive number of guest workers, and they clearly need to be better informed. Even such a highly reputed academician as Samuel Huntington (Foreign Policy, March/April 2004) gets all tangled up when on the one hand he worries about the sheer volume of Latin American immigration, but on the other begs immigrants to learn to dream in English—something that could classify only as an incurable heart drain. He forgets that if he really does not want them in *his* land, then they better keep on dreaming in Spanish and keep alive their hopes of going back home.

Unions might also be a bit confused. Unions played a vital and historic role in developing, while defending the weak, many essential safeguards that guarantee basic justice in our modern societies. But after a certain wealth plateau was reached, dynamic modern societies outgrew them, and some may have ended up doing more harm than good. Early retirement must be hard on many unions, but if I were in charge, I would see immigrants as my new market and jump at the opportunity to get back into the game.

The global implications of a shrinking world on all its common goods is changing political realities, as for example when the sovereign rights to clean air are proved incompatible with the sovereign rights of airspace. In the same vein, it might not be long before we hear from immigrants, with their power to vote with their feet and with their remittances, the cry of IMMIGRANTS OF THE WHOLE WORLD—UNITE!

*Maria Full of Grace*, a film about drug trafficking, illustrates how horrors surge when the supply is not allowed to satisfy demand legally. The same movie has a scene in which Carla, one immigrant woman, describes her feelings when she collected her first salary in the United States and ran to the bank to wire most of it to her family at home: *Her heart felt too large for her body*. We should remember these feelings when discussing remittances in order to remember their true nature. Remittances are not just cold financial cash flows to be taken for granted and securitized; they are human offerings of deep significance, for giver and receiver both. As such, they deserve a lot of respect.

Shall we keep the barriers to migration entrance impossibly high? Well, if you want to look at it from a Darwinian angle, you might make a case for allowing only the fittest and strongest to pass, like salmons going upstream. Nonetheless, the realization that the primary driver of emigration is despair—which might not be the best basis for moving the world forward—would indicate that reasonable, accessible, and equitable temporary immigration programs might be the best long-term alternative. Also we should not ignore the possibility that those who stay behind might turn out to be the truly strong, being able to make it anywhere.

Growing worries about the lack of employment opportunities are just the tip of the iceberg. To paraphrase the Bible, if "give jobs unto others and jobs will be given unto thee" is true, then the world must change its glass-is-half-empty perspective on immigration, unleash its imagination, and launch massive "Brain-Circulation-With-Hearts-Firmly-Kept-At-Home" temporary immigration programs.

### The Skin of the United States

The immigration procedures of a country should be like a good skin, providing barriers against dangerous elements but at the same time sufficiently porous to breathe and benefit from nutrient opportunities. As it also is one of the display windows unto the world, it should perhaps also try to look beautiful.

Attending a recent seminar in New York arranged by The Center for Migration Studies, at the Fordham University School of Law, I found that most of the participants believed that the current conditions of this country's skin were not that good, if not plain awful. Good-intentioned treatments, nips-and-tucks, such like a Premium Processing Service that allows anyone who pays a thousand dollars to jump the line, will not produce good and sustainable results as they seem almost to reward inefficiency. This program in particular is also an embarrassing blemish for a land that preaches equal opportunities.

It would be almost impossible to resolve the weaknesses of

the current system by just tweaking it, and there is no reason for even trying this route when a true state-of-the-art system could offer so many benefits for the United States and the world. For instance, as we know that information that cannot be obtained in very few hours will most probably never be obtained at all, the current efforts to reduce procedure times from six months to one month must have very little to do with an as-good-as-it-can-get modern system.

There is a lot of nervous sensitivity with respect to immigration in the United States, perhaps even to the extent of preferring a system so closed that the American citizens themselves would be precluded from being able to leave the Unites States. Recently even a program on a global TV news channel has been calling for some close-the-doors-and-build-walls solutions.

As a temporary visitor to this country I know it behooves all of us from the rest of the world to understand that the more United States citizens feel comfortable in their own skin, the more they would be confident enough to open up and mingle with us.

### A de-facto USA enlargement

When we read that in the greater Washington metropolitan area alone, there already are 550.000 persons who come from El Salvador, there can be no doubt whatsoever that the Central American countries are already a de-facto part of an extended USA Commonwealth. Put another way, the USA—surreptitiously perhaps—has gone through its own European-style enlargement. This demographic fact shows that the current debate in the USA on immigration reform could benefit by being split into two parts: immigration reform as such; and a debate about some laws and regulations affecting cohabitation in a commonwealth. Doing so would allow urgent reforms to proceed more constructively and keep the debates from being taken hostage by extreme proposals like building new Maginot Lines or Berlin Walls.

Not long ago, some enemies of the recently negotiated CAFTA agreement started spreading rumors that, through it, the United States had accepted conditions that in effect bypassed current immigration laws. This is not true, far from it. However, perhaps the CAFTA negotiations were indeed the perfect opportunity to start open and transparent discussions about what I call the de-facto enlargement of the USA. As it is, trying to look for solutions to some huge but still quite particular problems through a general immigration law is really picking the wrong instrument of change.

By the way, if I were a truly desperate builder of a wall to surround the United States, looking at the map, I would perhaps have to settle with some water barriers such as the Bering Strait and the Panama Canal.

# About cross-border services and emigration

**The prisoners, the old, and the sick**

We read that in the United States there are approximately 2.2 million people devoted to capturing and keeping behind bars two million prisoners. Imagine what capturing even 1% of that market (22,000 prison inmates) would mean to any small developing country.

The elder-care industries are another buoyant market in increasing demand in developed countries, as young people are becoming proportionally fewer than the old. This is also the case of the extended-care industry, where continuous medical advances seem to generate almost infinite demand.

It is therefore strange that developing countries give so little attention to these services when negotiating their trade agreements, considering their currently competitive wages. On the contrary, these same countries are forced to open up their own service sector for banks, insurance companies, auditing agencies, and so on.

Consider, for example, the potential economic impact on a poor country of a school that annually graduate several thousand excellent bilingual nurses to work around the world or in their own country: this could surpass the benefits that a trade treaty would provide to the agricultural and manufacturing industries combined. What's more, the nurses would likely be able to pay off their student loans more easily than economists like me.

\*\*\*

At this point, Jim, my editor, raises all type of numerous obstacles that he urges me to consider before my readers do. I: "Dear Jim, the *Washington Post* recently reported about an open-heart surgery that was budgeted at an unaffordable 200,000 dollars in the United States, but then finally carried out, successfully, in India, by doctors educated in the United States, for only 10,000 dollars, an airplane ticket, and a little side trip to the Taj Mahal included. The tide of globalization is unstoppable, unless you prefer your open-heart patient to stay home and die. As Jim also mentioned the hurdles of language, I also found it timely to remind him of the call centers in Bangalore where all those modern switchboard ladies that answer your information needs on the phone day by day are speaking better and not at all phony English. I have also read somewhere something to the effect that lately, the true defenders of true British English, are all from India.

\*\*\*

Also, given the tensions caused by millions of people looking to emigrate any way they can to the labor markets of developed countries in order to send remittances back to their families, it is surprising not to hear that the best way to prevent illegal immigration (which is often destined one way or another to caring for prisoners, the sick, or the old) would be to send this very clientele to developing countries where they could be cared for.

A real opening up of services would give poor countries access to sources of sustainable economic growth, while at the same time relieving the financial pressures on developed countries of attending to prisoners, the old, and the sick—pressures that threaten the fiscal sustainability of their own welfare economies.

Are these new ideas? Not at all! Henri Charriere (nicknamed "Papillon") was sent to French Guiana as a prisoner, and Australia was founded by exported convicts. There are already European governments that one way or another pay for their old people to stay in places like the Canary Islands [Jim, my editor: "The name refers to dogs, Latin canis, not to canary birds." I: "I guess this is the price I have to pay for choosing an editor with linguistic interests...I can live with it!"], and history is full of examples of people who had to go to other places because of diseases like tuberculosis or leprosy.

From *El Universal*, Caracas, February 2004

### A wide spectrum of services for the elderly

Talking about services to the elderly and seeing that "the higher you aim, the higher your arrow will fly," I need to make some brief comments about the two ends of that rainbow of possibilities that I have seen over the last couple of years.

On the one hand we have the very high-end market, illustrated in my mind most vividly by a Classic Residence by Hyatt that happens to be very close to where I currently live in Bethesda. To me it is virtually a luxurious cruise ship docked in the port of choice. Though I do not know her personally, from what I have seen, I get the feeling that the company's founder current chairman, Penny Pritzker, must be a true visionary.

On the other side of the spectrum, the services to the truly poor, there is Albeiro Vargas, a young Colombian. As an eleven-year-old boy he was portrayed in a French television program, together with his group of young friends in a barrio of Bucaramanga, taking care of many abandoned old people. When my eldest daughter and I watched that program, and saw Albeiro bathing an old poor lady with so much love and respect, we were humbled into a silence of deep admiration and of shame for our own shortfalls. To us, Albeiro deserves a Nobel Prize.

And, of course, in between Classic Residences and Albeiro lies a world of different needs and opportunities that all represent an enormous economic growth potential for developed and developing countries alike—if done right, of course.

Some are already catching up on this reality, and LaSalle College in Montreal is already offering a "Managing Private Senior-Citizens Homes" specialization. Right on the dot! And, I recently heard about a Chinese company looking in the Washington area to contract for further education of Chinese nurses. Why? It wanted to have them certified and then have them go back to China to serve the many foreigners moving to that country. Can anyone doubt that the world is really moving!

### The ethics of solving the shortage of caretakers

An older population, many of whom will experience longer periods of chronic illness and dependency before dying will require a growing number of caretakers. If there are enough caretakers, the issue will be to find the resources to compensate them. However, if there are not enough trained caretakers, no financial resources would suffice, and you have to find practical solutions.

The practical solutions available for solving the shortage of caretakers in developed countries are the following four:

1. Increase their productivity, but unless you wish to run the risk of being dehumanized on a Charlie Chaplin Modern Times assembly line cared for by robots...there might be a limit to how much this can help.
2. Move the careneeders to another place (if there are caretakers available anywhere else), and this you should do as early as possible if at an older age you do not appreciate finding yourself in strange surroundings as much as you did when younger.

3. Import caretakers, and this you should do as early as possible if when older you do not appreciate finding yourself in the company of strangers as much as you did when younger.
4. Give incentives for having more children and grandchildren—which is not such a crazy idea when you start considering how much society is, one way or another, currently rewarding people for not having children. (Talk about externalities!)

The Presidents Council of Bioethics www.bioethics.gov (USA) published in September 2005 its report titled *Taking Care*. It makes all types of thoughtful recommendations about the issue of *Ethical Caregiving in Our Aging Society*. As much I appreciate its effort, I do not think that the report spells out sufficiently the need for much more forceful and immediate work on achieving practical solutions. If those solutions are not found, the frontiers of what is currently considered ethical caretaking will just have to move to take up for the slack. No matter how horrendous it sounds, euthanasia and other flexibilities needed to bridge intergenerational conflicts might then turn out to be thought of as the only ethical solutions to the problems. In this respect, the most clear and real unethical behavior today is that of not anticipating and providing timely solutions.

### Are we truly a World Bank?

Dear Colleagues

Recently I attended a seminar in Berlin on the financing of houses in poor and middle-income countries. Most of the seminar came down to a very interesting duel between the extreme rationality of the Danish Mortgage System (with its almost magically low 0.5% margin of intermediation) and the very gung-ho attractiveness of the cooperative type Bausparkasse system of Germany.

Close to the end I, daringly, made the following comment:

"The final purpose for building a house for a poor person is not to have him starve now under a roof. So, before we build, we need to be certain that there is a reason for him to live there, since otherwise, with the house, we might just be shackling him down to misery.

In this respect and in relation to your interesting mortgage systems, I would like to know whether a Danish or a German citizen could finance through his own financial system the purchase of a second home for vacation or retirement, for instance in Central America. If your answer is yes, then we might be able to sell you some houses and not only find thereby the reason to build for our citizens, but also generate the sources of income they need to pay for it.

Many of the immigrants in your countries frequently want to buy a house back in their own homeland, which is great. This, unfortunately, puts a lot of pressure on the very scarce financing resources available in these poor countries from which they emigrated. If they could access your credit markets for this purpose, this should bring benefits for everyone. I know it's not easy but, tell me, what do you need? Expropriation-risk insurance, for instance…We could get you that!

As you can suspect, my intervention did not produce any immediate response, but I believe that at least I got some interested head-scratching going.

\*\*\*

Jim, my editor: "Suppose a crooked Mexican gets a mortgage from a German bank to buy land and build a house in Mexico. He takes the money, buys the land, builds the house, and sends the bank a letter saying he's not paying them a cent, and what can they do about it? Would the Mexican government have the sheriff evict the guy who cheated the German bank on his mortgage?"

I: "Jim, if there are thousands of Mexicans whose chances of buying their houses depend on how this Mexican services his loan with the Germans, you will see them all putting some pressure on fellow Mexicans and their own government to behave better."

\*\*\*

Back in Washington, I found a brochure from our Bank Fund Staff Federal Credit Union titled "DREAMING of a second home for vacation or retirement?" Great! However, further down we can read, in bold italics, *"anywhere in the U.S."* Well, colleagues, shame on us! Are we not just being a very a local World Bank?

Per

### Get moving!

Dear Colleagues,

While getting closer to the Central American economies, I realized that the recently signed free-trade agreement with the United States of America, CAFTA, did not carry sufficient punch to deliver the much expected economic growth, if it was to focus primarily on agriculture and manufacture.

But, by 2030 there will be around 80 million citizens in the United States of America and Canada who are over 65 years of age and also, by 2005, the United States government has predicted a shortage of 250.000 nurses. If Central America could somehow be made to provide healthcare and housing to only 1% of these elderly citizens as well as supply 100.000 bilingual certified nurses, to work either abroad or in their own country, then we could perhaps bring real prosperity to this poor subcontinent. Besides, would this not be the most constructive way to release the ever growing tensions around many immigration issues?

In discussing the issue with authorities and representatives of the private sector in the region, I sensed that there is a growing realization that their growth opportunities lie in finding ways to develop the Service Sector intelligently. Some of their initial thinking has revolved around the following aspects:

- The Third & Fourth Age Service Markets are in for tremendous growth, because of baby-boom demographics and increased length of life. As the fiscal systems of most developed countries will evidently not be able to deliver on all the social promises made and expected without generating new cost efficiencies, this situation creates many interesting opportunities to offer many new service products of the highest standards. Doing so would require from the host governments to take concerted and supportive actions on many fronts, such as, for example, guaranteeing the adequacy of visa procedures and tax exemptions.
- International credits for retirement homes. Clearly the financial markets of most developing countries are not deep enough to service any important demands of financing. Unfortunately the banking regulations coming out of Basel make it extremely onerous for banks in developed countries to finance foreign homes. Some discussions with international agencies have been initiated in order to design those instruments needed to overcome these obstacles, for instance, the issuance of some guarantees against political risk, such as expropriations.
- Bilingual Licensed Nurses. If their education programs focused more directly on professions like that of the nurse who can speak a foreign language and who is sufficiently qualified to be licensed in a developed country, this would clearly support the quality of the services offered.

Friends, when do we get moving?

Per

# Intermission...Out of the box tourism

### Lessons from Florence
Dear Franco and Biaggio (my two Italian colleagues), I went to Florence—and I got inspired.
### THE CONTEST!
My apologies to the Florentines, but their beautiful city is like the Magic Kingdom of the Renaissance. The inexhaustible flow of tourists, hotels, prices, and lines for attractions, fast or slow meals, and souvenirs, all makes one question, between Medici and Disney, just who copied the model of whom. In my opinion, not only are the gelatos of Florence richer, but also, with the possible exception of Goofy, Michelangelo's David and the frescos of Fra Angélico are far superior to Mickey, Pluto, and the rest.

What an inheritance the Medicis left to their city! The Florentine economy will always be easy to manage, since the only thing that their Paperon de Paperoni (Scrooge McDuck) has to do is fix admissions prices. The one little cloud on the horizon could be the quantity of English, Venezuelan, German, and other immigrants who try to take advantage of the infrastructure. What would Machiavelli have thought about entering the European Union?

We know that despite all its possibilities, Venezuela, in a local saying, still has not managed to connect the foot to the ball when it comes to developing its tourism industry. This will never be resolved by naming ministers who spend their time conducting publicity campaigns, or visiting Orlando and Florence. We are not proposing that other Medicis substitute for those who govern us—we can discuss this on another day. But in the meantime, we could emulate the experts.

In Florence 500 years ago, the contest system was used to assure that the best artistic proposals were utilized to adorn the city. So let's organize a grand contest.

It will be a grand contest to choose a grand team and a grand plan for the strategic development and management of the tourism sector for the next 30 years, with an estimate of costs and results.

A qualified panel of judges should choose the best three proposals, and the proposals should be publicly debated on television. The losers will receive an important prize, and the winners will be commissioned to execute their proposal during thirty years, with a significant fixed, indexed and guaranteed annual budget.

Since televised public contests enjoy high ratings, this contest could also be a way to build pontes novos, new bridges, in our divided society.

The Santa María del Fiore Cathedral took more than 100 years to construct, and for a long time everyone thought its dome would be impossible to build. And so, friends, let's not lose the hope of finding a local genius like Brunelleschi for our Helicoide (a local 45-year-old monstrous white elephant).

From *El Universal*, Caracas, April 10, 2003

### A niche in crookedness?

(A letter not published by *Financial Times*)

Sir, in your series about reforming Europe you refer to

Pisa's medieval tower as a "spectacular example of a grand architectural project gone awry: beautiful, still in existence, but wrong nonetheless," and you got it all wrong. It is just because the tower is leaning that it has turned into one of the most outstanding commercial successes. What would a straight tower have meant to Pisa?

I wish to make this point since when trying to pursue an "antidote to decline" in today's difficult environment, trying to straighten out Italy in too many aspects might actually break it. There might very well be interesting little niches in crookedness to pursue, and, besides, without some of it, the world would be an unbearably boring place.

But, if I am really coming out with my out-of-the-box thinking, then why should I withhold the following quite daring piece I wrote on a plane during an ED trip after having being challenged to it by a colleague who is a true Robert Louis Stevenson fanatic. (In the end the article might have been too much even for the Rolling Stone magazine)

### Dead and Useful

A friend, upon hearing that I was going to Samoa, reminded me that I could not miss the opportunity of visiting Robert Louis Stevenson's grave. "Of course I won't," I said, but it got me thinking.

Would my friend have suggested seeing RLS' grave, were he buried in London? Of course not! The fact that he is buried on an island without an excessive abundance of so-called big tourist sights presents a win-win situation in terms of development strategies. For instance, if Mick and Keith, on account of their Voodoo LP, were to be buried in Haiti, they still might provide a much-needed and useful boost to the island.

But that's not all. We all know that "location, location, location" is the mantra for any real-estate affair, and this burial site alternative has the potential to create its own location value, since many Mick and Keith fans could find merit in having their own graves located next to them. As most of the gravesites for these graveyards could be negotiated on a pre-burial basis, and as the state of the clientele permits overcrowding the venues with little added risk, the business opportunities are immense. This goes not only for the initial ticket offering (nothing to do with offerings) but also for the secondary market where scalpers (nothing to do with scalping) should be able to enjoy a strong and renewable support level, provided mainly by visiting family members.

The constraints are few, and the potential huge. You need not locate Mick and Keith in the same spot—you could rotate them from graveyard to graveyard, giving a fresh meaning to a Farewell Tour. Flexibility in product design could also allow marketing the graveyard as timeshare units, providing the possibility for an exchange of a week or two, perhaps even with Eleanor Rigby's Resort-yard.

But, of course, it's not only about rock and roll. Just think of all the very powerful and attractive burial arrangements you could achieve by mixing yesterday's and tomorrow's lovers, friends, or foes. Personally I find the foe niche especially interesting, since it would give a much more profound and proactive significance to the whole concept of a peaceful rest.

P.S. I finally went to visit RLS' grave in Samoa and although I never made it up to the mountaintop, I must confess that it was much more than a grave. His former residence houses a splendid museum where, guided by a classy and knowledgeable local girl, we were shown interesting glimpses of the five final years of this famous Scottish author. I submit that this little detail does not invalidate the general dead-and-useful proposal.

And don't believe my out-of-box tourism started within the WBG box. Here are a couple of oldies, almost a floodgate, almost a hobby.

### Adventure tourism

Nag, nag, nag about not being able to develop our tourism as we should...but perhaps there's still hope. On this marvelous island, where the ingenuity and genes of its native and assimilated population are put to work full-time to confront all adversities with spunk and élan, new promotional strategies for increasing tourism are being designed.

As a sales tax was recently introduced in this previously unspoiled paradise, the merchants, instead of despairing, have instead taken it as an opportunity to offer all those tourists, who are so burdened with taxes in their homelands, the possibility of participating in the exhilarating experience of evading taxes. Just a variant of adventure tourism! To that effect some Tax-Evasion-Certificates are currently being designed, and there is great optimism that these will be able to compete successfully with any of the dried and lacquered fish sold in other souvenir shops around the Caribbean. The local authorities, not wanting to be left behind, are also studying the possibility of raffling one citation by their taxmen among every five thousand tourists. Clearly it should be the highlight of a trip for a Hans from Hamburg to be able to frame and hang a citation in his living room from which he escaped by taking the plane one hour before he was to appear in tax court. It sure must beat a couple of hours of those boring videos that friends abhor.

The same goes for corruption and, just to prove they have nothing against videos per-se, a local production company is setting up arrangements so that tourists can fall into the local nets of the slightly overweight transit police who have bugged everyone on the island for generations, and thereafter work themselves out of the mess, on camera. Clearly a video of one bribing the authorities must beat any African antelope head on the walls, no matter how wide its horns.

From *The Daily Journal*, Caracas, May 14 1999

## Vanity tourism

I received an e-mail saying: "Take this one! Attached is one article published by ABCNews.com which states that without a doubt, Venezuelans are by a long shot the vainest people in the world." The index reveals that 65% of Venezuelan women and 47% of Venezuelan men say that they "think about what they look like all the time." In Germany, for contrast, virtually no one confesses to this habit.

From the tone of the e-mail, I suppose that the sender considered the high ranking achieved by Venezuela in this index as being unfavorable, and I also suppose that he would like me to share some degree of guilt. Well, I DON'T! Intuitively, I am pleased to be part of a country in which my compatriots are worried about their appearance instead of rubbing shoulders with those ranked among those who "never think about how they look." The fact that our society holds dear to the heart a feeling of vanity over and above levels in other countries certainly differentiates us from the rest and perhaps we should analyze this fact within the context of comparative advantages.

The dedication of persons like Osmel Sousa to the Miss Venezuela beauty contest has elevated our country to the apex of world perception of the beauty of Venezuelan women. By using the word "perception," I do not intend to question the objective beauty of our women (God forbid, I have four of them at home!). I wish to make a point of the importance of the general perception per se. This, by the way, renders even the less pretty Venezuelans beautiful.

Any country culturally geared toward taking care of physical appearance for centuries, that has managed to develop methods and formulas that have been time-tested and proven to the world by live TV transmissions of Miss World, Miss Universe, and similar mega events, has in its hands a tool to attract tourism that other countries would give one arm and half the other to have.

And so I promptly pushed the "reply" icon on my computer and sent off the following message:

"Thanks for having sent me the Vanity Index. I think there must be certain mistakes in the Index since I believe that the figures for Venezuela are too low. In Venezuela, I would say that 100% of the population worries about how they look."

"While we talk about appearances, you should see the results we have achieved with a treatment supervised by the stylist school of Caracas which includes massages in the turbulent waters of the Caroní river and scrubbing with powerful and mystic Orinoco algae, while listening to the sensual rhythm of the beating of the herons' wings and drinking a skin reconstituent malt-based beverage.

And all this under the indiscrete tropical moon, for only US $1,680 per day!

Extracted from *"Vanity and the nation's economy"* published in *The Daily Journal*, Caracas, October 1999

## Guaranteed boring

In a world with so much entertainment available anytime and anywhere there might be a niche for a tourism that guarantees a boring experience. "Get a good reference point. After a week with us, we guarantee you'll enjoy much more the rest of your travels and even perhaps the rest of your life."

# On our own governance

### A real choir of voices
Dear Colleagues,

Experience is said to be something you can gain only when things don't go as you've planned. In the same vein, what is the purpose of an Executive Director if he is just going to sit around and agree? Friends, as we recently spoke again about the importance of voices let us remember that 100 voices saying the same message might sound nice but still be only a Gregorian chant, while a harmonious choir requires many different voices (and now also some noises).

Per

### Voices, Board Effectiveness, and 60 Years
Dear Colleagues,

The World Bank is soon to be sixty years old, and I think that it is a tribute to the foresight of its founders and the capacity of its managers to know that if it did not exist, we would have to create it in order to do very much of the same things which it currently does, in very much the same way, and with very much the same people.

That said, it is clear that with time the Bank must naturally have lost some of its original vigor and that most definitely the circumstances, challenges, and resources are not the same as those present sixty years ago. So, if we were to recreate this multilateral development effort today, a "new" World Bank, it might turn out to be a somewhat different organization from ours.

I mention this as lately, for instance in the discussions of *voices*, it is clear that having to look through a glass colored by the Bank's day-to-day realities (and all the special interests that have evolved with time, whether internal or external) makes it very difficult for management and ourselves to visualize what changes are required.

In this respect I would suggest that, as a Board, we could benefit immensely from an in-depth and outside view as to how the World Bank should have been organized, had it been born today. The nonbinding conclusion of such a study that could be provided for instance by a diversified work group of creative, wise, and credible personalities, could most probably provide us with a better vision of what we all should strive to achieve. It is only by painting the green valley you want to reach that you can muster the sufficient will to get there.

Is there any support out there to make the study I propose a part of the roadmap of voices and the so many other issues we are grappling with? Perhaps a 60 Years Development Committee?

Per

### WB-IMF Collaboration on Public Expenditure issues

Collaboration between the Bank and the Fund is great, but its final worth should not be measured in terms of how it assists expedience and effective management between the Bank and the Fund but rather in terms of what that collaboration really means in strengthening the voice and the participation of developing countries. A country's voice is always strengthened by learning to manage the differences of opinions in a debate, not by having these differences disappear through a prediscussion between the other debaters. Collaboration should never be allowed to silence the fundamental differences between the Bank and the Fund. Collaboration should, on the contrary, make those differences stand out very clearly. And we must learn to live with them.

### The Normal Distribution Function is missing
Dear Colleagues,

The 14th of October we discussed the 2003 Annual Report on Operations Evaluation, and I must admit that I felt a bit unsatisfied with the debate because, when it ended, I left without a real feeling of what was working well in the Bank and what was not. It was only later that I suddenly realized what was missing from the report, so although perhaps a little late, let me share this worry with you.

The standard feature of any evaluation and monitoring system we know of, is the use of some sort of distribution function, be it the normal bell-shaped curve or any other type. It somehow indicates the extremes; for instance, the worst 5% of the organization's performance and the best 5%.

Any board, if it wants to be effective, cannot spend a lot of its time in the grayish middle area of the function, but has to concentrate its attention on the extremes of the curve, weeding out poor performance and learning from bad experiences, so as to avoid being dragged down into mediocrity, while guaranteeing the promotion of the best and learning from its successes, so as to advance the organization's goals

Only hours away from completing my first year at the Board, I cannot honestly tell you, with any degree of certainty, about what is working and what is not, and this is quite frustrating. I know I share this sense of frustration with most of you and perhaps the root of our problem lies in the fact that these distribution curves are totally absent in the evaluations brought forward for the Board to consider. If so, it behooves us to make certain they are adequately introduced.

In general terms, I have felt a generalized difficulty of the Bank to manage criticism, as just the utterance of minor questioning, or even withholding praise, makes one sometimes feel somewhat of a traitor to that esprit de corps that is expected to prevail. We have also reached a point where it is even hard to congratulate one another on extraordinarily good performance as the value of praise has been diluted by its ridiculously excessive use.

All this is wrong and clearly to the detriment of the efficiency of our development work that so many poor depend upon. On a daily basis, the needy people of our constituencies are harshly evaluated by life in very cruel terms, so we might as well ask ourselves whether we should not be a little stricter in our assessments, living up to the accountability we so much preach to others.

I wonder: does anyone join me in challenging our evaluation and monitoring systems to come up with a list of the 4 worst and the 5 best activities? of the WB? What if our own Board effectiveness is among the worst?

Per

## Board Effectiveness and the ticking clock

Dear Colleagues,

One year gone and less than one to go, so excuse me if I am getting a little anxious and want to share with you some concerns related to Board Effectiveness in a slightly more formal way than through our many brief corridor meetings. I know many of you share them.

First, the truth is that our Board is simply not functioning the way it should and that it really comes down to us to improve it since, unfortunately, in this matter we cannot instruct management to do it for us.

What is wrong? Well, in very few words, that we are drowned in too many written and spoken words about too many topics so that our power, as a body, is completely diluted to such an extent that we could easily qualify as the most expensive rubberstamp in mankind's history. Think about the following facts:

Our yearly workload consists of about 850 formal Board documents, 3,700 other documents like project assessments, besides technical meetings, informal meetings, bilateral meetings, contact with our capitals, seminars, retreats, executive travel, spring and fall meetings, 11-hour communiqué-drafting sessions, plus, of course, hopefully, some life.

Being 24 EDs, means that very rarely a sufficient number of us are simultaneously focused on the same issue and, if it were to happen, like boats passing in the ocean as they say, chances are that there would always be a need for additional documentation that, presented in some future fall or spring, would at least mean having the issue to be revisited and analyzed by different EDs altogether.

Yes, we have our 24 Alternates, "with full power to act for him when he is not present," plus the valuable additional resources of about 80 Senior Advisors and Advisors that could act as temporary Alternates, "in the event that both an ED and his Alternate ED are unable to be available." Unfortunately, sometimes this could make for some additional dilution by splitting us up even more.

Many of us do receive good support from our capitals and so we might reasonably be fulfilling our role as a communication channel between our constituencies and the Bank. Nonetheless, when it gets down to that very personal fiduciary responsibility to "exercise individual judgment in the interest of the Bank and its members, as a whole," it is clear that we are lacking, in too many ways. My reading of the Articles of Agreement makes it clear that someone counted on our own consciences, as individuals, in order to find some reasonable cohesiveness in this world full of uncertainties and contradictions, and this could perhaps require us to be somewhat more than management—not less.

The Bank is in itself a very peculiar organization and truly difficult to assess. That, together with the extreme sensitivity the Bank shows against any type of criticism, which stops the development of reports which would show clearly what does really work and what really does not work, clearly makes it currently impossible for us to prioritize in any sensible way our workload.

I know that when anyone starts hinting at these problems, the wet blanket of the dangers of micromanagement by the Board are quickly thrown over the discussions but, my friends, in this case what I really am referring to is the problem of the Board's having a sub-micro influence on macro issues.

In the end, it really doesn't matter if you are a Pavarotti, if you have to sing in Madison Square Garden during a Knicks' match or in the deserts of Arizona, because in both these cases you will not be heard anyhow. In this respect, our Board's acoustics are currently so bad that I have to repeat what I've frequently said in our discussions on the issue of voice for the developing countries, namely that, in reality, no one has a voice.

Where do we go from here? I do not know, but it really behooves us all to find out. This is not a matter for the management of the World Bank since they are not doing anything else than what normal management normally does, which is to maximize their own control of the organization by minimizing the Board's interference.

Nonetheless, there are some ideas that could provide the basis for some discussions among us. For instance, there is always the possibility of splitting up more of our workload into more committees. Although they should have their own powers of approval, these powers should be subject to our possible objection. This would still mean that the Board does not relinquish its final say in any matter. This way we could perhaps create four committees with responsibility over geographical areas and so at least have more of a chance that, when we convene to discuss a matter, enough of us will have really read and analyzed that particular case in depth.

We know that the CODE, the Committee on Development Effectiveness, is reputed to be the most important committee of the Board, although that might just be false since CODE probably is just as weak as the rest of us and could in fact have the lowest functional-strength/importance-of-issue ratio. Nonetheless, many of the current issues of CODE are exactly those extremely important issues that should always be discussed at Board level, and so we might therefore be delegating in CODE some nondelegable issues, while retaining at the Board the workload of some less important tasks.

Another thing we should do, as I indicated before, is to be more straightforward in demanding from management evaluation reports that clearly identify what is working and what is not. Management should be able to come up with this overview, and, if not, we need to worry even more.

In conclusion, we all know that the needs of our world are almost unlimited, and I am certain that we never discuss something that does not have its very clear and urgent merits but, nevertheless, as every single effective hour of our Board discussions ends up costing us around 80,000 US dollars, we absolutely have to find better ways of prioritizing our time if we are to have a chance to fulfill our mandate as EDs.

I am aware that COGAM (the Committee on Governance and Executive Directors' Administrative Matters) is planning to take up the issue of Board Effectiveness very soon and I know that it shares many of the concerns. I am certain this step will be a good opportunity to take this issue forward.

Meanwhile, and knowing that so many of you share these concerns, excuse me for reminding us all that our clocks are ticking.

Per

### WBG's fight against corruption

Dear Colleagues,

I sincerely believe that the World Bank Group could lose

its entire capital, and could still count on the full support of its shareholders, as long as they believed that this was just the financial consequence of a bona fide development action. But I also think that the Bank could lose all support, if its willingness to fight corruption is put in doubt.

I have seen some very important advances but I also believe that the Bank still has some way to go before it can fully live up, in actions and in spirit, to its commitment of being a prime force in the battle against eternal corruption. The fight against corruption really boils down to the continuous setting of good examples, and therefore there could never be a real fight against it if you are unwilling to communicate very openly with the world about your struggle.

I have repeatedly noted concerns that publicity related to fraud and corruption in any Bank project could make it appear that the Bank has acted negligently in its supervision and thus impeded the good work of many; and, on the other hand, that disclosing more detailed information could provide a basis for litigation or other challenges. And this, in turn, might be indicative that a somewhat nonproactive state of mind still exists in some quarters of the Bank. Of course disclosing corruption always presents risks but those risks clearly belong to the "getting up from bed" risks, and, as such, are totally negligible when compared to the "staying in bed" risks.

The Bank, in order to have the moral strength to fight the corruption externally, needs to demonstrate that it is doing its best at home. As no one could expect the Bank, where thousands of individuals move billions in resources, to be immune to human shortcomings, fighting corruption can only mean being very forthcoming on the issue.

In the same vein, as corruption has many tentacles and is certainly not limited to individual wrong-doings, the Bank could perhaps be well-served by appointing an Ombudsman for Corporate Behavior to ascertain whether there is a logical and moral relation between its almost sacred mission of fighting poverty and the way it goes around the planet earth doing it.

Per

## The Annual Meetings Development Committee Communiqué

I must confess that I do not really understand how it gets produced. We sort of start out by pitching out a lot of issues to ourselves and then we go over to the other side and bat the balls back for about eleven continuous hours just so that we can later have a chance of fielding them again in our Board meetings six months later. It is hard to tell whether we are in a virtuous or a vicious circle or, if at the end of the day when we get some issues out of the loop, it is because we have adequately exhausted these issues or because they have just exhausted us.

Nonetheless in this unpleasantly volatile world we might find comfort in the thought that our communiqués provide an inspiring source of stability—as they always read the same.

Any readers who do not understand what I am talking about should not worry. The preparation of communiqués is like one of those strange initiation rites impossible to describe to anyone not part of them...and to most who are part of it.

## Hurrah for the Queen

Dear Friends,

Facing, involuntarily, the need for a career move in the month of November (as I suppose many of you also are), you might understand why I found it interesting to find in The Economist, the announcement by the Buckingham Palace requesting an Assistant Private Secretary to H. M. the Queen. Colleagues, don't fret, I did not send my C.V. to recruitment@royal.gsx.gov.uk, not because it was not tempting, but because I believe that, although I could perhaps help to offer a global perspective on many issues, the Queen might really be looking for someone with more local know-how (cricket) than what I (baseball) could provide. By the way, for those who believe they might indeed qualify, go to www.royal.gov.uk.

That said, I do think Buckingham's announcement is in itself noteworthy as it evidences that, even in the Monarchy, good governance issues are deemed so important, as to require the inclusion of a notice that "The Royal Household is committed to equality of opportunity."

But, my friends, in terms of transparency and equal opportunity in hiring, how really does the IMF currently stand up in its search for a Managing Director, when compared to the British Monarchy? Even though being a born republican (in its original meaning), I cannot refrain from a Hip Hip, Hurrah! For the Queen!

Per

### Diversity

Dear Mr. Bourguignon:

I wish to extend to you my most sincere congratulations for your appointment as World Bank Chief Economist and I am certain we will all benefit immensely from your presence among us.

Though I feel that we need always to have one foot firmly placed on each of our development pillars, I very much welcome your "plan to focus more on the second goal, that is, social inclusion," as inclusion is exactly why I want to make the following comment.

When the search for a new Chief Economist for the World Bank was announced we were told that although it was obviously quite a delicate task, it should not take too long, as the search had to be carried out within "quite a small and exclusive community of development economists."

As I am certain you realize, that characterization illustrates in itself one of the many daunting challenges we face in the WBG. I beg you, in parallel to your many other responsibilities, to dedicate some time to the challenge of developing that small-and-exclusive-community, so that perhaps in a couple of generations, the Bank could choose one of your successors from a larger and more diversified group—even though that would mean a somewhat more extended search. Again, very much welcome, do count on our support and I wish you a very heartfelt good luck.

Yours sincerely,
Per Kurowski
Just one of 24

### About the board and the staff

Not long ago in a personnel committee I was reminded (I am not sure why) of the saying about why grandfathers and grandchildren get along so well: they have a common enemy!

But then again I must confess that I have been through some experiences that point to the existence of a big divide, Mr. Chairman. On some occasions when I have been speaking with staff members who were unaware that I belonged to the board, when they found out, some of them have actually panicked, trembled—and that to me is not a very healthy relation. What does the staff think of us? I know that I think very highly of them, generally, and I know I treat them all with respect but...do we all? Or is somebody setting us up?

And while we are on the subject, when are we going to end the tradition of praising one another so much that we dilute the traditional meaning of praise? Colleagues, do you have some special words or a code that you use when praise is really for real? Can you share it with me?

I must be a total stranger to this community because there is no way on earth I can come to understand why all the quite reasonable discourses I keep hearing about development and helping people out always need to be praised as courageous or fearless. They probably know something I don't. I'd better watch out.

### A very local World Bank or…the not in my backyard syndrome

Just weeks after I had arrived and perhaps because I had already been screened for the Personnel Committee, I got called to an emergency meeting.

The problem on hand was that there had been many complaints and difficulties with the handling of the G5 visa program, through which World Bank staff could bring with them to the United States domestic help from their homelands. Apparently different religions, customs, and what have you, plus some bending of the rules on how to pay for domestic service, and perhaps even some tax evasion, had given the human-resource department so many headaches that a proposal to give up the G5 program altogether had been formulated.

My opinion was, and so I told them in very clear terms, that if we as The World Bank were not prepared to face fully up to the many difficulties that come with globalization, then how on earth were we going to ask others do so? The World Bank needed urgently to abandon this not-in-my-backyard attitude and look at the G5 program as a learning opportunity, instead of comfortably hiding our head in the sand.

# Budgets & Costs

**On the urgency and the inertia of our business**
Dear Friends and Colleagues,
Board effectiveness

If we, the Board, work on our own effectiveness (the numerator) without making sure that all our improvements are not diluted by the ever-increasing complexity of the Bank (the denominator), we will be doomed to eternal ineffectiveness. The Bank claims that the world gives broad support to its current agenda, but perhaps it is just that the world finds the agenda so broad that it makes possible for everyone to find something to support, without anyone having to support the Bank fully. Management might have some inkling about what could be satisfactory and what not, but that is not enough. We urgently have to know what is really good for development, to focus and concentrate on it and scale it up, and to know what is really bad, to expel it before it rots the rest.

### Budgeting the World Bank's Strategic Framework.

I am sorry if I feel a bit confused but having to go so fast from strategy into budgeting makes this all seem to me a bit like a budget-driven strategy. Should we not instead be looking for a strategy-driven budget?

### We need to reach out…further than the NGOs

On this side, all the world's daunting needs and, on that side, all the immense resources needed. Is it not the Bank's primary role to act as an effective matchmaker? I am sure that there must be a way for the Bank to sell a Home-Globe Security Program and, if it is credible, I am sure that the world, in its own interest, will provide the funds. In Jim Wolfensohn we have one of the foremost salesmen of the world, and in the Bank I am certain we have many of the best products produced by the very best people, and yet, somehow, we just cannot seem to get the packaging and the promotional material right.

### Are we not a development holding?

Yes, we should care about IBRD, IFC and MIGA individually, but as Executive Directors our principal role should be to look at the accumulated results of our development portfolio. I am not sure I have yet seen the aggregate figures anywhere. Much less have I seen us act as active portfolio managers.

### Medium Term Strategy and Finance Plan

Dear colleagues,

In light of the immense needs, the Plan gives the impression that we are not going anywhere. Looking at the 9-year horizon provided, we see a projection that we will reach 141 billion United States dollars in loans for Fiscal Year 2013, which means a net growth of about 3 billion US dollars a year. Friends, what on earth does this have to do with the estimated development needs, which range between 50 billion to 175 billion US dollars a year? For those poor countries that are fully dependant on aid, anything will be well-received, of course, but to think that with this we are making a real dent in reducing poverty is laughable. It is never enough to be moving forward in the right direction, if your target keeps moving faster and faster away from you.

Before energy and water scarcity and environmental damages really set in, the world has a very small window of opportunity for peaceful global solutions, and the Bank was founded as part of a system to provide them, although it might have forgotten this central core of its heritage by being busy providing for its own institutional life. The way I read the budget, it almost seems to allocate the scarce resources to the various working units of the World Bank on a per employee basis (internal equity?) instead of on the basis of performance indicators and real deliverance of countries from poverty.

When the windows finally close for peaceful solutions, it will be too late for the World Bank, and it might even be too late for the Red Cross. Are we doing enough? If the known big oil tanker can't turn fast enough, should we keep steady course turning full speed ahead towards further mediocrity, or is it not better to split up into smaller and more maneuverable boats? Boats where Boards can be effective, where results might stimulate real scaling up, and where the smaller units together stand a chance of doing a much better job than a big single Bank?

Dear colleagues, we need to find urgent ways to break up our own inertia. One alternative might be turning our "Knowledge Bank" into a holding and monitoring bank of development banks which in their turn will be the real competitors for resources based on the performance and lending portfolios of their development operations.

Meanwhile, in the budgeting process, I would like to listen to at least one single VP unit openly arguing, with management and the Board, why it believes it can use resources better than others.

Per

## Unbudgeted costs

Dear friends,

Last Tuesday, we approved an investment in a pipeline in country X, as indeed we should since the project, although risky, seems to offer the chance for some positive developmental impact in a region with so many needs and, frankly, no one really came up with a truly convincing argument against it.

Nonetheless, buried within the project, there was an element that I believe should perhaps have caught more of our attention. I am referring to the additional costs that the IFC will be incurring in the long-term as a result of the project.

In answer to one of my questions during an informal meeting, the IFC has said:

"It is envisaged that during an actual monitoring visit, IFC and EBRD will invite national and international NGOs/civil society, as well as other parties mentioned above, to a meeting to be held in the region to comment upon and discuss the project implementation. This will of course entail additional staff and other transactions costs, which will have to be budgeted (MSF: US$300,000 + substantial travel costs and about 30 IFC staff-weeks for preparation)."

If substantial travel costs are 50,000 US dollars and a (low) per week cost of the IFC staff is 5,000 US dollars, are we then perhaps talking about 500,000 additional US dollars, per year from now on?

We need to be careful with the long-term budgetary implications of our decisions and therefore, as a minimum, when we approve any project where IBRD, IFC, or MIGA are undertaking future commitments that may call for new, not-budgeted costs, we need for these potential costs to be made explicit in the project proposal. Of course the costs could always be recoverable, for instance by larger IFC margins but if that is what is intended, then we should be informed of it beforehand, not after the fact.

Although somewhat irrelevant to the specific issue at hand, I still dare to comment that 500,000 US dollars invested in Education for All, perhaps instructing about the environment, might be a more productive use of scarce resources than a monitoring gathering with NGOs, on the site of already irreversibly laid down pipes, more like sightseeing, most especially when this may be better monitored through alternative and more creative means.

Or is all this just a price tag needed to keep some particular NGO happy and in consensus with the Bank? Is it then in effect a kind of bribe?

Per

## Budget tools

Dear Friends,

At the end of an informal meeting on Budget and Strategy you implored for a more concrete expression of what we, as a Board, really wanted and needed in relation to the budget process. Well, this is what I would love to have.

With our very serious time constraints, to be able to participate in any constructive discussion on the budgetary implications of the Bank's strategy, it would be very useful to receive from management the following two lists:

Management's choice of the five (5) least developmentally productive uses of funds currently approved within the budget, the ones that foreseeable could be eliminated, and,

Management's choice of the five most developmentally productive uses of resources currently not approved within the budget, the ones that foreseeable could be implemented.

With this information, I would then be able to:

Have an opinion on whether the budget should be reduced, which would be the case if I do not agree with the current uses but remain unconvinced by any of the new proposals;

Have an opinion on whether the budget should be reshuffled replacing some of the current approved uses by some of the new proposals instead, or;

Have an opinion on whether the budget should be increased, as well as getting the arguments I need to join management wholeheartedly in requesting or finding the necessary resources.

Of course, as we know the immensity of the needs of the world, there could always be a presumption that all requests for funds are valid. Unfortunately, exactly because these resources will always be scarce, it is important for us on the Board to feel that we are at least truly participating, in a concrete way, in the setting of the priorities of the Bank or, as a bare minimum, in understanding how management does it.

Per,

## The remuneration of our President

Q. Why should our President have a lower salary than his IMF counterpart?

A. Well, you know we are a Development Bank, while they are...well, who knows? It's hard to tell about an institution such as IMF that has its own logo on its own golf balls.

Q. Why should our President have a higher salary than his IMF counterpart?

A. Given the much wider range of issues that he has to handle and that he also has to promote the development agenda continuously by traveling all over the world, on job description alone he clearly deserves it. Moreover, if you top it off by considering how well he has performed, and that the Bank does not have its own golf balls, the question might be somewhat rhetorical.

Q. Would an average of the salary paid to the managers of the 10 most important multinational organizations be a good reference to establish his salary?

A. It does not sound bad, but perhaps put some 20% on top of that average and let the IMF be part of the reference group.

Q. Would a multiple over and above the Managing Director's average, or a multiple over and above what is paid to the Executive Directors work?

A. That sounds good, as that way you will achieve good internal salary consistency.

Q. Would parity with IMF be good?

A. To pursue parity with someone who does not really want to have parity with you does not sound reasonable, although it squares with Groucho's remark about not wanting to be in a club that would accept him as a member. No, the IMF should not be our Piper from Hamelin and besides, in confidence among us, who dares to pair up with an IFI that has its own golf balls? How on earth would our Financial Sector hedge the risk of their going really bananas with their salaries?

Q. Would you adjust our President's salary now?

A. The way I read it, I feel that our guy has every rightful reason to believe that essential parity should be maintained, and so we need to increase his salary immediately. That said, I also agree we need to review the whole system. Now, whatever we do, let us do it fast, since discussing a forty-thousand-dollar adjustment at a going cost of about eighty thousand dollars per board hour seems to carry a big reputation risk of its own.

[Here again I leave a comment from my too clever editor. "For a while, my college hired a retired admiral who had been in charge of the Navy's multibillion-dollar budget. He said that they had agreed that any item under a million dollars would be approved without discussion, because they couldn't afford to waste time on something that was less than one-thousandth of one billion dollars. He added that it was a relief to be back to the real world, where even half a million dollars was real money worth real discussion." In fact, I was thinking more in line with Parkinson's Law.]

Q. Did not the IMF create this current incident?
A. Yep! Let's bill them for the 40,000 US dollars!

## About our central travel agency

Dear Colleagues,

The WB staff travels a lot and naturally organizing those travels is a very important part of the functioning of the organization. Although I never really understood how and why, we were informed that all of our first-class or business-class flying basically cost us the same as tourist (it has to be a volume discount as we surely fly a lot). On long flights, with my back, I sure appreciate business. Nonetheless the truth is that flying with class to fight poverty must unavoidably create some dissonance with donors—but I guess that's life. Perhaps it could help if all short flights, less than three hours, were in tourist and at least in my office I have made it a rule. But this is not really my travel-related issue.

No, what I find quite unacceptable is that the Bank had awarded to one single and central travel agency basically all its travel business, locking itself up with specially favored airlines. Therefore when I, for example, need to travel to countries in Central America, it is much too difficult for me to include among my options those local airlines that if they charged me less, I would have loved to use. I guess if any of our borrowing countries would set up a similar procurement system that so much favors so few, all hell would break loose. Honestly, the WB might in fact currently have the best system but, if it really wants to live as it preaches, as it should, it needs to change it.

Per

P.S. Let me add that another reason why the WBG could need a central travel office is actually not the traveling itself but all the work needed to fill out so many visa applications. Nonetheless this is perhaps not enough justification to stop us from freely using the market and the Web to obtain the best fares—as all human beings currently do.

# Reshuffling our development portfolio

**Let us scale up the IFC**

Dear Colleagues,

Do Ministers, the representatives of the WBG shareholders, agree that the World Bank should make a capital contribution of five billion dollars to the IFC, our private-sector lending institution, fully paid in cash? That is a question I believe we should raise in the next meeting of the Development Committee.

Why? Even though we regularly speak about the role of the Private Sector, the outstanding credits of the World Bank to governments are currently ten times those of IFC credits to the private sector.

The Bank has entered into a somewhat stagnant mode from which it will not be able to pull itself out, until it is better able to focus its activities. With so many things going on, it is very hard to see where capital and budgets should be allocated to get the best results, and there should be no better stimulant for getting the house in order than to see important capital resources diverted to a sister institution.

Currently the World Bank has, according to its own finance

department, an unused borrowing capacity of over 40 billion dollars at rates lower than Libor rates (Libor being the rate the best banks pay for deposits in US dollars, in London), and that only seems to be growing, and so to dedicate a small fraction of it for an increase of IFC's equity does not seem at all incompatible with our constant declarations about the importance of the private sector.

\*\*\*

My Editor's Q: Do you mean that the World Bank has to pay interest? I thought that much of the money it lends comes from outright grants from donor countries. I thought much comes from successful countries repaying earlier loans. Surely the World Bank has good credit. If the World Bank were in a financial pinch, wouldn't the United States government lend it billions interest-free?

My answer: Jim, the world has put about 12,000 million dollars into the bank, plus the promise of an additional 178,000 million—if needed. In addition the WB (1994 figures) has been able to accumulate 24,000 million dollars in profits over the sixty years of its existence. On the basis of these resources the WB borrows around 110,000 million dollars from the market and lends about 110,000 million to the developing countries, keeping its own 36,000 million dollars in income-generating reserves. If the World Bank gets in a financial pinch it is not that the United States and the rest of the world would assist it with interest-free loans; it is that they would have to cough up an important part of the 178,000 million in subscribed, but not paid for, equity. Of course, a normal bank would have to pay in the capital before authorities were to treat it as capital, but this is no normal bank, as you should have gathered by now. The IFC, on the other hand, has a fully paid equity of about 2,360 million dollars plus retained profits of another 5,420 million. They also borrow in the markets, but in their case they do not have a huge reserve of unpaid subscribed capital as the World

Bank does, which is also one of the reasons I am proposing to put some substantial new equity, in the form of cash, into the IFC.

\*\*\*

The IFC might not feel that it really needs capital at this stage, because it is doing fine and is not thinking about really expanding. In this respect, a substantial capital injection, thereby clearly signaling the wish of its shareholders, would perhaps force a quite naturally somewhat comfortable and thereby somewhat reluctant IFC to come up with a substantial growth strategy.

The IFC would perhaps reply that it does not need more capital in order to sustain growth, given its strong balance sheet. This might be true, but the fact is that its loan and equity investments of 10,279 million dollars are primarily financed with their own equity resources, 7,780 million dollars. In fact, were the IFC to adopt IFRS (International Finance Reporting Standards) and adjust its probably excessive loss reserves, its equity would be even higher and their ratio of loans and investment to equity would almost reach 1 to 1.

Since almost all of the IFC's current borrowings go to maintain the financial "hoopla" (liquidity) that makes up more than 50% of its balance sheet, and the loans and investments are financed almost completely with their equity, then, whether we like it or not, there might be no other way to accelerate the IFC's credit growth substantially than through a substantial capital injection.

"If it ain't broke don't fix it." That might very well be so, but the fact is that IFC's mission is to take risks in order to assist the private sector in generating sustainable economic growth in the world, and not just to avoid risks in order to guarantee the sustainability of some initial capital contribution and some private development jobs.

"If it ain't broke don't fix it" is clearly irrelevant in IFC's case since, as we look to its general performance, it is not that they are broke; just the opposite, it is that they are doing too well for them not to be forced to expand.

There have been some calls for flat budgets and, in the IFC's case, this policy would quite obviously produce something much worse than suboptimal results. As for those colleagues who in any circumstances are hooked on a flat-budget concept, let me remind them that this goal could be obtained equally by letting some entities grow strongly, compensated by the slower growth of others. This is the way equity and budget resources are, and should be, allocated in the real world, year after year, and so perhaps we should think about adopting some external best practice. If for instance, the World Bank were formed by five regional subsidiaries, perhaps the pressure for results, to validate the fight for resources, would provide us with a very stimulating competitive environment.

Friends, when I see the challenges of the PPPs, (Private Public Partnerships) the MDGs, the immense market and needs of sub-sovereign lending, all the regional initiatives just waiting for support, and all the South-South investment and private-sector business waiting for help and guidance, and I place all these needs in the perspective of IFC's results, my conclusion is that we are obliged to provide IFC with much more long-term development resources. Would our ministers agree?

Real fresh capital increases take ages to negotiate, a check from the World Bank to the IFC could be negotiated in months—hopefully even before our ED group leaves.

While management has the task of budgeting for the best use of resources allocated to each entity, the Board has the responsibility for channeling the resources to the most productive entities. Actively shifting resources from low-productivity entities into higher ones is an absolute requirement to achieve productivity increases, and we may have been doing this insufficiently.

Per

### An encore on the BIG capital increase for IFC

"But really, if IFC is not in need of capital to grow at this moment, why should we increase its capital? Is it not enough just to ask IFC to grow more and take more risks?"

Yes, you could go that very timid route if you wish, but what I am proposing is to give IFC a completely revised new mandate for growth, and there's no better way to do that than putting the big money on the table, up front. "But what if IFC does not want that capital increase and refuses to accept it?"

Then perhaps that would be all for the better, since we could create an IFC II with access to all the know-how of IFC I, and then have them compete!

The immense needs, the ample resources, the more-than-reasonable results seen in IFC, our endlessly repeated talk about the role of the private sector—they are all out there, and so, why don't we put our money where our mouth is? Might it be because we also are comfortable with the current level of efforts? If so, shame on us!

### The Multilateral Investment Guarantee Agency—MIGA

And we really did not hit it off...many were the reasons, and at one moment I even told my colleagues that if we were the shareholders of a private MIGA, we would have long ago asked for the keys—to close its doors. Let me try to explain my reasons for such misgivings.

MIGA's purpose is to provide various political-risk insurance so that investors will be willing to invest in developing countries where they, or the markets, perceive that the risks of misdoings, such as illegal expropriations, are too high. This mission sounds all very well and has in fact been partially carried out by all those official export agencies through which governments of developed countries have tried to assist their exporters in selling their goods to difficult markets.

But and this is just the first big but, the developing countries that are being guaranteed through MIGA are themselves shareholders of MIGA, and so this leads to some very strange and incestuous relations that are hard or impossible to administrate. Think of it as a grandchild selling insurance against the risk that any of his grandfather's misdoings might cause. If the grandchild tells the world his grandfather is OK, which he should, then no one will buy the insurance at the rate he is quoting; but, it would not be right either to tell the world that his grandfather is not that OK, just to sell the insurance at the right price. The perversity of having to signal to the market low risks but not too low rates, without any reference price available, represents for MIGA, in my opinion an unsolvable conflict of interest.

My second but takes off from where the previous one ended. Because the grandchild, having two grandfathers, can also not be seen as telling the world that one of them is worse than the other, in terms of the political mischief he could do, this now leads to the need for absolute confidentiality about the pricing. Now, you tell me, applying the most generous version of Murphy's Law, where will an organization end up if the price of the products it is selling must be kept confidential, even to their Directors.

Once, when I wanted to understand a specific MIGA request better, I was forced to sign all types of confidentiality agreements, but even then, just being able to analyze one case at a time, without being able to place it in any perspective by comparing it to the other cases, it turned out to be a quite useless exercise. By the way, I was told that I was only the second ED of MIGA who had ever looked at the specifics of case. In fact, because of the confidentiality issue, the EDs never approve any operation of MIGA and they have to settle for a "we concur," a sort of blind man's consent. As confidentiality goes squarely against the transparency which the WBG so much preaches, I guess that this is also an unsolvable conflict.

My third but has to do with whom MIGA can provide

with insurance. Although the finance that is provided with a guarantee against political risks by the export agencies must be related to goods and services provided from the agencies' own country, the buyers can be anyone. MIGA though can only offer its political-risk insurance to foreign investors, thereby giving them an additional competitive advantage in relation to the local investors, as clearly the insurance provides access to cheaper financing. It is clear that differences in relative competitiveness will always exist but perhaps it should not be for the WBG to stoke that fire. At least in theory this but could be solved by amending the statutes of incorporation: if the Bank preaches globalization then it should treat all investors as equals.

My fourth but is a minor but, but still a relevant one. In order perhaps to calm any of the previous doubts, MIGA always makes a big splash about guaranteeing that its guarantees promote development and growth. That might very well happen, but there is no way MIGA can guarantee it. The premiums charged by MIGA does simply not allow for any major analytical effort, and in reality it is the client who in his application form describes his development impact, and the government, of the county being guaranteed against political misbehavior, that attests that this is so. As I do not know of any comparable export-credit agencies that would be required or have the resources to do the assessments of development impact, profitability or environmental effects before extending its coverage, there is perhaps nothing to do about this, except saving the costs of the charade.

So should there be a future for MIGA? I am not really sure, but as it sometimes harder to kill these organizations than create new ones, perhaps MIGA could start to look into alternative specializations such as sub-sovereign financing or international mortgage finance.

Finally I should make clear that my concerns about MIGA as an institution should not be construed as a criticism of those working there, as I much commiserate with any management expected to carry out such a crazy and confusing mandate.

# On some varied homespun issues

**The Poverty Reduction Strategy**
Many commendable results have indeed been achieved through the implementation of the participatory PRS. That said, we would like to reiterate some of warnings that need to be repeated over and over again.

Order of factors

In multiplication, it is said that the order of the factors will not alter the results, but this might not be applicable to a PRS. Frequently it is said that *the PRS initiative has led many low-income countries to focus more squarely on poverty reduction to achieve development* while, in fact the truth is that low-income countries might better formulate their development strategies so as to achieve sustainable poverty reduction. One might say that the previous distinction is pure semantics but starting with poverty reduction could signify a trap, as it creates the illusion of the possibilities and sustainability of instant gratification instead of the long-term sacrifices that true development always requires.

Participatory process

In order for the whole PRS initiatives to contribute

to long-term development, it is of utmost importance to ascertain that participation and consultation channels are laid out over sustainable paths that include the traditional representatives—like parliaments, private-sector associations, unions, and others—and does not just provide access to temporary participatory tourism, no matter how good its intentions are, or, much worse, whether they constitute a Trojan Horse for hidden agenda.

There is much more to it

We must bear in mind that the concepts of participation and ownership do extend much further than the PRS process, and one should be aware of the temptation of using them as an OK-now-we-have-complied excuse. In this respect, we believe that the PRS would benefit by including direct references to issues that are closely related, such as the use of country systems. A PRS that does not evolve almost instantaneously into a sustained effort to develop country-owned systems, and use them, is a contradiction in terms.

### There should be life beyond 2015

Yes I agree that the Millennium Development Goals, or the MDG as they are known by those petit committees that specialize in development, are undoubtedly useful to focus and to call to arms all those willing to fight for a better future. Nonetheless I have currently the uneasy feeling that the year 2015, more than the general timeline it should represent, is turning more into a finishing line, after which all the runners might lie down to catch their breath. Colleagues, when I look around the table I imagine that most of us will have grandchildren come January 2016, and so we should think of life after 2015.

### There should be new life beyond HIPC

The High Indebted Poor Countries (HIPC) is an initiative that aims to wipe out significant amounts of debt that I assume seemed anyhow almost impossible to collect. Nothing wrong with that, although sometimes I wonder whether there is enough effort to ascertain that history will not repeat itself. The write-offs are declared final only when the countries have complied with some established goals, but as this sometimes seems to take forever in some countries, the initiative seems to have a life of its own. The end, what is quite poetically known as the Sunset Clause, gets postponed and postponed, making it very hard for the cowboy to fade away and the movie to end.

Dear colleagues, this initiative and the many others that in similar fashion manage to display such a joie de vivre need to be disposed of with firmness, so that the sun can rise on new and improved initiatives.

**We need to make more transparent our harmonization.**

Some of my colleagues have expressed concerns that the paper leaves open the possibility that the World Bank Group and the International Monetary Fund may express divergent views in their assessments. But to me it would be very disappointing if diversity of opinions is not brought to the forefront of the debate, truly transparently. We and the International Monetary Fund have different development agenda, and sometimes and somehow they could be in conflict. Nothings wrong with that! What we cannot do is to sweep our differences under the rug in the name of some wrongly understood harmonization. What we need to do is to learn to take more of the full debates to the different capitals instead of the prefabricated and well-packaged consensus.

We might also otherwise instead of the Good Cop—Bad Cop strategy end up with just a totally Blah Cop.

**Transparently Understandable Debt Management**

Dear friends and colleagues,

In an annex of a recent Country Assistance Strategy (CAS) for a developing country that we discussed, after thoroughly reviewing the serious problems related to that country's

public-debt management, the following suggestions were indicated:
1. The (debt management) strategy should include the systematic use of active debt-management operations (exchanges, swaps, buybacks, and so forth).
2. The Ministry of Finance should...define mechanisms and procedures for
3. preserving the confidentiality of information and operations of the Debt Office; and establish a code of conduct to guide the behavior of the Debt Office staff, consultants, and all other entities or persons rendering services to the Debt Office.
4. ...or (b) creating a separate institute under the Ministry of Finance...there will likely be more salary and structure flexibility that will help increase the capacity of the Debt Office.

Frankly speaking, these suggestions make me shiver, most especially in view of the recent experiences in nontransparent financial engineering around the world.

As I see it, all of the above recommendations, if implemented, could only lead to diminish even more the ordinary citizen's comprehension of his country's financial affairs. Even educated professionals will find it harder and definitively more time-consuming to evaluate whether their financial authorities are doing a good job or not. All this will, of course, work against the much predicated "transparency" and will also imply the strengthening of special-interest groups with privileged access to facts and truths.

I believe that it is more productive for the good governance of these countries, if the Bank, instead, were to promote a road to simplification. For instance, by limiting the public debt to only four issues that cover the short, long, local, and foreign currency matrix, this would not only help to make the true financial cost of the debt much more transparent, but perhaps also reduce its servicing cost by deepening their respective markets, which means having more investors trading in the same security, competing, instead of offering a myriad of investments to the same number of investors.

By the way, one single long-term bond, if adequately designed, does not mean less access to varied term markets, as the private sector (through stripping and other tools) could easily perform that function much better than the public sector.

I think we can all understand how difficult it may be for staff—who normally guarantee their own professional advancement through deepening and sophisticating their own respective know-how—to advance agenda where "small is beautiful," "lean is mean," or "perfection is the enemy of success." In this respect, it might rightfully behoove the Board to find means to impose some wisdom upon the Knowledge Bank, no matter how immodest it sounds.

I believe that the potential benefits for many developing countries of a "Debt simplification" are immense and that the Bank can and should act as a promoter of it. If, with the Bank's technical assistance, countries could be able to convert their actual skewed short-term maturity schedules into long-term, while simultaneously committing themselves to limit their overall debt level to absolutely obvious manageable levels, just think of the effect this would have on credit ratings and interest costs, and how much resources could thereby be released to foster growth or so much needed social spending.

As I am not certain about what actions an individual director can take without breaking the protocol, I would very much appreciate your comments and assistance in advancing this little quest of keeping dangerous and unnecessary financial engineering out of the public

Per

## The Financial Sector Assessment Handbook—a postscript

In September 2005, the World Bank and The International Monetary Fund published the Financial Sector Assessment

Handbook and as I read it, it is a perfect example of what I mean by excessive harmonization, so I need to make a special comment here.

You might have already read extensively in the chapter "BASEL—Regulating for what?" about my strong belief that the world is giving too much emphasis to how to avoid crises potentially occurring in the financial sector, as opposed to how that sector is performing its role intermediating credits, generating growth, and distributing opportunities for access to capital. Yes, bank crises are setbacks, but, if in their wake they leave continuous step-by-step advances in development, we might still prefer that to a financial sector that receives a perfect bill of health but does little for the rest of the economy. In fact, such avoidance of a crisis is most probably just a temporary mirage. Developing is balancing various risks, not looking to eliminate one.

Well, in this handbook, which is more than 450 pages long, only a very few pages, perhaps fewer than ten, salute the flag of assessing and helping the banks perform their true function in development, the WB's basic agenda. Instead, most of this handbook centers on how to supervise banks and minimize the risk of bank failures, the IMF's basic agenda. Chapter Four contains most of the little there is about development, and "4.6.4 Development Obstacles Imposed by Unwarranted Prudential Regulation," gives us sixteen complete lines about how entry or start-up regulation and uneven supervisory practices can hamper competitiveness and create "undue reliance on tools that are likely to disadvantage small new firms (such as excessive mandatory collateralization requirements for bank loans)." If I have ever seen what amounts to mere flag-waving, this is it, but, on the other hand, I must admit that these flag-wavers are at least quite transparent. Under the interesting subtitle "The Demand-Side Reviews and the Effect of Finance on the Real Sector," we can read, "development assessments are interested in the users and the extent to which the financial services they receive (including from abroad) are adequate to their needs. Development assessments must express a general view on this issue, though in many countries, especially low-income countries, *detailed quantification may be beyond the scope of the assessment.* Friends, I rest my case. It is quite obvious that on this vital issue, WB has been harmoniously silenced.

Pssst...just between us, I feel that what's valid for us is equally valid for the IMF. The Fund could also benefit from the clarity of not having to harmonize with someone who has other institutional objectives.

### Too sophisticated

We were discussing (sort of—most frequently it seemed that some others were doing our discussing for us) whether to continue to use something called Rolling Reinstatable Guarantees that under some circumstances could help developing countries benefit by being able to issue less expensive debt. The Bank by issuing any guarantee is taking on a risk and when it so does it should expect results. In this particular case it did not seem that the markets valued sufficiently the Bank's involvement and so there seemed to be no reason to keep alive this RRG program.

That said, more than the specifics of the RRG program what really interested me was that the markets had not really understood what we were offering, and this should be of importance when considering ways of how to develop the financial markets. Sometimes, by overfinessing, we might end up confusing, them...and us. Perhaps developing countries instead of looking at thousands of proposals put forward by ever so creative investment bankers, need to restrict themselves to the issuance of very few debt instruments. Only by doing so will they ever have a chance of developing deep secondary markets. Only by doing so will their citizens, and government, ever understand what is going on.

Yes, the markets did not value adequately our RRG.

However, on our side it is not enough to leave it like that and withdraw the instrument, with our institutional ego somewhat hurt. No, the Knowledge Bank needs to understand why the markets did not value it correctly. In economics class we learn that sometimes something can be a great product but still not sell, just because the vendor does not believe enough in his own products. Of course, we Executive Directors are way past our courses in introductory economics, but maybe this is an old lesson we need to study anew.

### About the addiction of guarantees to municipalities

It is really good to see that IFC by providing partial guarantees to bond issues is getting involved in providing assistance to the financing of municipal projects, most especially since in this case it seems to be for a very good project and for a strong municipality. Municipal finance is a very important area but always remember that it is vital that our guarantees are used to hook the market on good projects and good municipalities and at any cost avoiding that the markets get hooked on us.

### About risks and the opportunities

I truly believe that the World Bank Group's Financial Complex is staffed by very qualified professionals.

That said it is precisely because they could become too good for our own good, falling into the very human traps of complacency and excess of confidence, that I frequently made some comments, if only to pinch.

Phrases such as "absolute risk-free arbitrage income opportunities" should be banned in our Knowledge Bank. From what I have read and seen, I believe there is a clear possibility that much of the world's financial markets are currently being dangerously overstretched through an exaggerated reliance on intrinsically weak financial models that are based on very short series of statistical evidence and very doubtful volatility assumptions. Just as an example, let us not forget how all our risk-assessment models had to be "recalibrated" just to take into account Argentina.

If the Financial Complex identifies an arbitrage opportunity where it feels reasonably confident that it can close out positions in a brief period and register a profit, so be it, but, if it starts building up quasi arbitrage positions, that have to be carried in our books for a longer time, then we might be incurring some important opportunity costs.

For example, when we refer to the value of "borrowing flexibility" but discuss it primarily in terms of the need to borrow while the conditions are good and the markets are not closed, we might blind ourselves to the possibility that we could perhaps obtain even better conditions tomorrow. Even our finance department points to this possibility when it reminds us that they were able to "record sub-Libor rates during the Asia Crisis as a consequence of the flight to safe haven."

We all share the concern of the recent lower lending activity by the Bank but, in fact, this could also allow us to assist more forcefully in urgencies. Of course we are not and we should never be a lender of last resort. Nonetheless, I believe we could gain some wisdom by reflecting on what we could have done now, had we not participated in the buildup of the debt of Argentina, while their markets were open, perhaps too open. Today 10 billion US$, in long-term loans from the World Bank, could have helped achieve a more satisfactory restructuring of their current debt, against which the only conditionality that I would have suggested is for Argentina not to incur any more public foreign debt, allowing instead the private sector to breathe.

In good times, the differences in basis points of the funding costs between the World Bank and Argentina might have been 100, while in bad times they might easily have reached 2,000. You tell me…when is the right moment for the World Bank to help out?

## Financial Outlook and Risks

We wish to free ourselves from certain financial risks and therefore we tend to like to borrow and lend our funds on a floating-rate basis. But do we really think about our clients, our shareholders, many of the developing countries? Are they not increasing somewhat their risks by using floating rates? Somehow it all reminds me of my days in the leasing industry about thirty years ago. One day I proudly sold a substantial lease contract to a state-owned oil company, based on the tax savings it would accrue, only later to reflect on the fact that all those savings were to be paid for by its own shareholder, the state, receiving less tax income.

We need to reflect on the fact that as a development bank we are actually here to have a different view than the market. If we just believe what the market believes, then there is no real reason for our existence. This makes it much more difficult, as it is not enough for us to take a good measurement of risks by just using standard instruments.

Oh yes we have had a period of low rates and we hear how they have had an impact upon the earnings of the Bank. Are we then supposed to ignore the fact that during this period our borrowers, the poor developing countries, many of our shareholders, have also had to pay low interest on their debt? Are we to hope for high rates as this could be a reflection of high economic growth? No, definitely it is not easy to be a development bank.

# Some political incorrect Private-Sector Issues

**Is the private sector the same private sector everywhere?**
Dear Colleagues,
The recent evaluation of the four IFC-supported Small and Medium Enterprise (SME) facilities provided us with a good opportunity to think about the private sector in the world and about its particularities and complexities. This is something we clearly need to take into account if we want to draw the lessons from these evaluation exercises that could contribute to the success of future WBG operations.

The report seems to indicate quite meager results of the program, attributed primarily to a weak strategic focus. As the SMEs are very important in our overall strategy to foster economic growth, this should require us to sound the alarm.

Nonetheless, as the report also states that "The facilities have helped many SMEs boost their sales, profits, and employment," it is also important to remember that we should never welcome an approach with a strong strategic focus, if it does not provide results in terms of sales, profit, and employment.

Now what I really wanted to say about this report is how

it completely ignores the possibility that the private sector would differ country by country and, therefore, the responses to programs might turn out to be different.

In his book *The Future of Ideas* (New York: Random House, 2001) Lawrence Lessig reminds us that "a time is marked not so much by ideas that are argued about as by ideas that are taken for granted" and, I ask, might we not be taking for granted that, given an "appropriate investment climate," all the private sectors everywhere will respond with equally enthusiastic and good initiatives?

We are continuously mentioning governance issues and even developing performance ratings by which we look to evaluate the governments of different countries. But, when have we differentiated—much less ranked—different private sectors? Is it not time to think about it? For instance, the private sector of an oil-rich country could be quite different from the private sector in a country that is poor in natural resources. Consequently, in some places, those who might need or benefit the most from a capacity-building initiative that goes beyond education might be precisely the private sector.

Reading through The Private Sector Development Strategy for WBG of April 2002, I find only a one-sided causality analysis one that is based on the assumption that if the government does something (or at least does not interfere) then, automatically, it is presumed that the private sector unleashes all its potential. In that document, there is not a single reference to the possibility that, although all men are created equal, perhaps the societal aspects of the private sector in various different countries and regions might nonetheless be dramatically different. Do we dare to ask these questions?

Among the aspects related to an individual private sector that could benefit from a further analysis are the following:

Work ethics, corporate responsibility, attitudes towards tax payments, attitudes towards workers and relationships with unions, effectiveness of business associations, entrepreneurship, investment attitudes and risk tolerance, and differences between the local and foreign investors.

For Bank business, operations and evaluations in general, we as a development group always take into account local knowledge and the local particularities that shape governments and civil society in different countries for our operations to be successful and have a developmental impact. When operating with the private sector in 70+ countries, we need to do that as well with this sector, so that the lessons we learn from the evaluation exercises contribute to the cumulative knowledge of the Bank and the success of its operations.

Per

**Private vs. local investors**

Whether there are some differences between foreign and local investors that the Knowledge Bank should be aware of, while helping countries develop, is most probably a very sensitive issue.

Just like the saying that goes "Of course all men are created equal, but some are more equal than others" (Dear editor Jim, as I am much better off avoiding any reference to animals when talking about foreign and local investors I'll just skip on your suggestion on making a reference to George Orwells' *"Animal Farm"*, especially its reference to pigs as the privileged animals.) I cannot see why we should not be able to acknowledge and discuss differences between local and foreign investors. I know that this is a very sensitive area and frankly I never found time to write anything about it during my two years. Nonetheless as I now and then conversed with some of my colleagues about it, I guess I should put some of my observations forward.

Let us paint a mental picture of a big company with a sizable debt in a country where devaluation rumors abound. In that case I submit to you that if the owner of the company was a foreigner he would look to saddle the company with as much debt as possible, local or foreign, and try to get out his own capital investments as fast as possible, weakening, of course, the company in the process. If, on the contrary, the owner were a local citizen, he would do his utmost to come up with local finance to pay off as much foreign-denominated debt as possible. Is this true? I do not know it for sure…but why have I seen this over and over again, and what does it imply for a developing country?

Let us now take the case of that sort of easy and quite profitable business that in small local markets could tend to develop into a quasi-monopoly—like a brewery. My impression is that if the owners are local they would tend to reinvest much more of the easy earnings in their own country than if the owners are foreign and all surpluses have to be sent to a central treasury. Is this true? I do not know it for sure…but why have I seen this over and over again, and what does it imply for a developing country?

But then again, in some circumstances, I have also seen the local investors escaping the country much faster than foreigners…but perhaps then also doing the right thing!

By the way, when I say foreigners I do not mean foreign citizens who are residents in the country; they are sometimes the most resilient nationals of them all; no, I mean all those foreigners who are really foreign everywhere, except perhaps in business-class lounge at some airports.

## Some thoughts about financial good governance
### Big Responsibilities

Sir, The Big Four accounting firms became that big by marketing the value of their size, and now they want to have their cake and eat it too, claiming that they should be sheltered from ruinous lawsuits. If accountability is to mean anything in accounting, we cannot afford to turn the whole concept of professional responsibility into a risk model of affordability.

Individual professionals and small firms lay their names completely on the line, day after day. If the Big Four cannot

handle it, they better let go. Perhaps then we might all be better off, as at least the risk for systemic risks will be smaller.
*Financial Times*, Letters, May 29, 2004

## On global accountancy

I have seen how the Bank has had difficulties explaining that the current accountancy rules do not really reflect the Bank's business. If this is the World Bank, can you imagine the difficulties of others? Can we afford the very relaxed and leisured way in which all the private and official accountancy boards are trying to come to grips with their Tower of Babel babbling? Should not the World Bank play a more active role in these global issues? At least so as to try to hold the accountancies rule-developers more accountable?

## What is lacking in the Sarbanes-Oxley Act.

Requiring all senior management and board members of companies to disclose publicly what they understand and what they do not understand of the business they are in charge of would do wonders for corporate governance, especially when we start hearing so many cries of "I did not know". For instance, when using sophisticated financial instruments such as derivatives, we could suddenly realize that no one upstairs has a clue of what they, the experts downstairs, are up to, and this could be a quite instructive for the market and the credit-rating agencies when they assess the risks of a corporation.

By having clues I do of course not refer to any specific know-how needed to take apart and put back a carburetor, as very few would be able to do that, and in fact I am not even sure carburetors any longer exist. No, what I refer to is whether they to have a good working knowledge of some basics, like how a car drives, how it brakes, how much gasoline it consumes, and what to do if a tire explodes or an airbag suddenly inflates.

To oblige recognition and acceptance of where the buck really stops both in theory and practice and before mishaps occur could also be useful for shedding light on some systemic risks that, like lava in a volcano, might be building up dangerous pressures underneath the world of finance. It could also provide immediate relief to all those executives living out there, burdened with the constant stress of having to feign that they are in the know.

### Too well tuned?

Martial arts legend Bruce Lee, whom many people regarded as immortal, died at the age of only 32 of a cerebral edema, or brain swelling, after taking some sort of aspirin. I have not the faintest idea whether that pill actually had anything to do with his death but I have frequently used (or misused) this sad death as an example of how an organism could be in such a highly tuned and perfect condition that it could not resist a small external shock. And I used this metaphor to explain why companies nowadays, pressured by the stock market's expectations for the next quarterly results; the latest theories in corporate finance as to how squeeze out the last drop in results; and, perhaps, even some bit of creative accounting, might be so well-tuned (no little reserve fat left) that they would not be able to withstand any minor recession. (Whenever I expose this theory, I can see in my wife's eyes that she believes this is just my preparing an excuse for my growing—ok, grown—midline.)

### Alternative Millennium Development Goals

How I would like to see a group of leading hands-on entrepreneurs from the private sector develop what they believe should be the Millennium Development Goals, and compare their ideas with what we currently have. We might be up for some surprises!

# Communications

### Communications in a polarized world
(A speech at the World Bank Communication Forum)
Dear Friends,

I am just a hobbyist communicator, not nearly as accomplished as Jim Wolfensohn...or Jimmy as someone referred to him today. Therefore I feel more honored about this chance to speak to communication experts than Jimmy needs to be when he plays with fellow virtuoso musicians in Carnegie Hall. As an Executive Director, I should not be seen being any less intimate with the President of the World Bank.

What I then would want to use this precious one-lunch-speech-chance-only for, is to talk about a world where opinions seem to become every day more polarized, which is an issue that has worried me a lot lately, coming as I do, from a very polarized country that is a living proof of the dangers of it.

To illustrate the problem and since we will soon host an event in Shanghai, the leitmotif of which is *learning from cases*, let me use as an example my very own amateurish case.

Every week, (while an Executive Director every two

weeks), I sit down to craft out an article to publish in a major Venezuelan newspaper.

Believing myself to be a sensible man, prone to reasonable attitudes (though some might say that's just trying to make up for other types of behaviors), I usually find myself on most issues in an in-between position, where I can identify a lot of pros and a lot of cons.

The true challenge for any writer, who is not into darkness, is to transmit the message in the clearest possible way. In this respect, I like to think of myself as a conservative jumper from a diving board who prefers executing the easy-graded jumps well, rather than going for the spectacular triple in-and-outs, where you could indeed score higher, but you could also completely lose your reader trying.

Therefore, after duly taking inventory of all the pros and cons, carefully turning them around and finding suitable allegories and metaphors and similes that illustrate the topic at hand, I finally come up with what I normally believe is quite an excellent script. Cautioned by experience, I then take the script to my editors. If it is in English, to the closest available qualified colleague and, if in Spanish, then even much closer, to my wife Mercedes.

These critical editors, who probably assess my script in somewhat more realistic terms than my self-assessment, at the best murmuring a "so-and-so," then usually proceed to split up my 5-line sentences into five 1-line sentences, to be shuffled around. Their professionalism is evident since they always seem to come up with a product that means exactly what I intended to say. I never understand how they can take it to pieces and still manage to put it back together again.

I then send the embryo away and sit down and wait until early Thursday morning, I can see the newborn on the newspaper's Web line.

Let me now describe how my readers, through their e-mails, react to my babies.

They mostly start with a direct Per Kurowski, as many

believe that "Per" is my title and not my name and just as many think that Kurowski is not my name but my alias. In life, I am frequently greeted with an "Oh! Per Kurowski, I didn't think you existed."

\*\*\*

Jim, my Editor interrupts again: "Tell me, since you and your daughters were born in Venezuela, does that make "Kurowski" a Hispanic surname? If you should have a grandson born in the United States, would his name "Kurowski" be a Hispanic surname, a Polish surname, a hybrid surname? This could be a very practical question, since there are scholarships for some persons with Hispanic surnames." Me: "Dear Jim, as I have an accent in all three languages I speak, I guess Kurowski is a just another globalized surname." "Three? Spanish, Swedish, English? Not Polish?"

I: "Yes, Jim, even though I very proudly carry a Polish passport in addition to my Venezuelan passport, I do not speak Polish. I just suppose that makes me perhaps even more globalized. You know, it's all a gender issue—it's not called your mother-tongue for nothing. When my father met my mother, they spoke German with each other until she said "Tillräckligt!" And so thereafter my father duly spoke in perfect Swedish with us."

\*\*\*

(And back to my speech again)

Their responses classify then in the following three significantly different categories:
- "I hate your yellow...despicable...how could you.... Have you no shame?"
- "I hate your blue...despicable...how could you.... Have you no shame?"
- "Oh, thank you for explaining it so well and in such clear terms!"

Although I obviously prefer the amicable intentions of the

third group, and they do help support my ego, I am still never sure whether their praise of my explanatory power is because they managed to see the green I wanted to show them, or just because they saw an even brighter yellow or blue.

And this is the big polarization that is blocking communications and creating worldwide divides.

In 1872, the British Parliament decreed Speaker's Corner in Hyde Park of London as a place reserved for free expression, and initially it attracted all those extremists who, although qualifying as nuts, still had the right to vent their opinions. Lately, we have all witnessed how the original Speaker's Corner speakers moved into Speaker's Studios and now radicalism, anarchy, or fundamentalism is voiced on prime-time television. All of us others, modest low-key analyzers or rational in-betweens, have to settle gratefully for slots in after-midnight cable television, dubiously sponsored by the most traditional professional services. As rationality could soon be viewed as symptomatic of a modern nut, we might all have to line up at Speaker's Corner.

As you understand, this polarization poses many challenges.

How on earth, in an ever more colorblind world, can we be sure the reader knows what color we talk about?

How on earth do we know that we have communicated, when clearly rating is not all nor should be an end it itself and, on the contrary, sometimes a big rating just guarantees a bigger confusion, as when everyone finds it easy to read in his preferred color.

How on earth do you communicate, when the receiver is no longer decoding the message into its yellow or blue components, but only receiving the whole message, as is, through his one and only yellow or blue pipeline? There are times I actually suspect we are going through a genetic mutation, in response to modern information overload.

And friends, this is not a problem just in communications, as color blindness can hit us anytime, anyway, and anywhere.

For instance, in the World Bank, most of those who currently speak about Public-Private Partnerships do so only because they feel they have found a more politically correct way of defending a 100% private or a 100% public alternative and not because they would truly believe in PPPs, or even understand what they are.

As you can understand, this raises all types of serious issues, especially for a World Bank that wants and needs to communicate so much Knowledge with Yellows and Blues but that—for it to become the development Wisdom the world so urgently needs—must all be mixed into various degrees of Green.

So, what do we do? You tell me. You are the experts! Anyhow, armed with the blissful ignorance of an amateur, let me daringly point out some directions.

We can perhaps keep it a very simple green so that there is no way it could take a blue or a yellow meaning, though running the risk of watering down the message so much, that it is just ignored.

Or—we can complicate it so much that the receiver is blocked from any channeling of the message, as he cannot even start to understand it. Though this does not at all sound very promising, it might in fact be the route some researchers in the World Bank are exploring. Just last week, I read a document that was very cleverly obscured in academic jargon, mentioning "modeling this in a tractable way using autoregressive conditional heteroskedasticity" and including so many footnotes that a comparable reference to healthful food would most certainly have included a note: "(Mother. 1958. Published on the magnet memo board on the Fridge)

Or—keep the colors so pure that a blue channel would choke on a yellow message and vice versa. This could be a stupendous idea, but only if we were looking to be ordained as High Priests of the Purist Blue or the Purist Yellow Churches.

Or—do we need really to diversify and open two or three

Web sites? One for each color extreme and one for the mix, and how do we hyperlink them?

Or—should we use ex-ante censorship, like some radio and TV channels, where you are only allowed to call in your opinions on line yellow or line blue, to help the producer avoid mixing colors? By the way, this new era of media apartheid seems already to produce its counterrevolutionaries as we can already hear an insurgent movement of color cheaters, the blues on line yellow and the yellows on line blue.

Or—set up ex-post filters with questionnaires that the receiver is obliged to answer before being allowed to leave?

Now, as long as I have you all sitting there, let me also dare some recommendations that could generally help the World Bank in reaching out to a world that does not seem to hear even our loudest fire alarms.

First, I dislike the concept of "The Knowledge Bank," as it sounds too much like arrogant yellowist or blueist to me, and I would much rather prefer a more humble "The Search for Solutions and Answers Bank" or, even better, "The Learning Bank": knowledge comes from learning, and the Bank—although having acquired a significant stock of cumulative knowledge over sixty years of operations—has still a lot to learn from its clients. Such an approach would stand a better chance to transform its knowledge pool into wisdom, which, at the end of the day, is what the developing and the developed world really needs.

Second, we need to start talking more with the world instead of with one another, hoping the world listens in. I myself would prohibit the use of all acronyms. I am certain that Mary Poppins would never have been able to communicate as effectively had she used an SCE instead of supercalifragilisticexpialidocious, much less Shakespeare had he used a TBONTB instead of a To Be Or Not To Be. Today, I tell you after having asked around, the sad fact is that our lead product, the MDGs, has very low name recognition among the NONNGOs, the normal citizens, and this does not bode well for our future. Do we need a flashy MDG logo?

Third, whatever we do, let us not badmouth the NGOs, since they might very well be, at least for the time being, the only wall that echoes our voice and so, without them, we could find ourselves with virtually no voice at all.

Fourth, we all might benefit from better focusing. Doing and communicating about so many things, ninety and then some thematic themes, might signify, or at least leave the impression, that we are not doing anything at all—which might also be true. For instance, the way the Board is drowned in tons of communications, might be exactly the reason why, frankly, it is currently quite nullified.

Fifth, I believe that it would not hurt if we also lighten up our ways of verbal expression. It has lately become an unbearable fashion to speak in a grave voice, in a tone of solemnity, and with an accent that could come only from using the same tutor as Robert Williams used for the role of Ms. Doubtfire.

Finally, as for myself, as a true green, a radical of the middle, an extremist of the center, with perhaps poor ratings and condemned for ever to Hyde Park Corner, I will go on, doing just the best I can, searching to communicate with simple natural and organic ingredients, while following Dori's safeguards of...just keep swimming...just keep swimming.

Thank you and, now I am ready for your answers.

NO ANSWERS...just questions, some on the issue of voice.

Q. What do you think about more voice for the developing countries?

A1. Before we worry about our voices in the Bank we should perhaps worry about the voice of the Bank. The sad fact is that were it not for a couple of NGOs, the whole world might be unaware of our existence. Hey! They even ignored our 60th Birthday. We were not able to rouse up even 60 protesters. Is that not a sign of irrelevance?

A2. I could have a big voice and still not be heard at a Knick final at Madison Square Garden, or out in the desert of Tucson. I could have a small voice, and still be heard a lot, if the acoustics are right and so, let us work on the acoustics. At this moment, with about a thousand formal board documents that come our way each year, plus about four thousand other projects, plus about a hundred seminars and brown-bag lunches, plus having to call home now and again, in fact no one at the Board has a voice…and so in the famous words of Alfred E. Neuman: "What, Me Worry?

## Some other global communication issues

### A comment about Web pages

When I have tried to print some of the bank Web pages they sometimes did not fit. Please remember that most of the citizens in our constituencies do not usually have laser color printers, and much less can afford color inks, and so, before you put out material on the Web, check the printing result on a simple black-and-white daisy-wheel printer on an A4 page, and not in the European larger-page format.

### A comment about the translations of documents made by the bank

Before spending money on translating any World Bank document we should carefully identify the target and how the translation should reach him. If it will not be read anyhow, by anybody, at any time, why spend money on it?

### Videoconferencing—their choreography

Most of the videoconferences that I have attended seemed artificial and arranged only in order to display the availability of modern technical gadgetry—forcing poor blokes to utter platitudes at unearthly hours because of differences in time zones to an audience that in their turn are forced to assume bad postures to get a glimpse at the screen. And of course they must utter platitudes back, or they will be suspected of sleeping discreetly in their seats. Only once did I attend a videoconference when it all really came together, and one of the tricks, I believe, was that the person on the video screen appeared in natural size between the other persons on the podium and therefore blended in very well. It was great! I even remember telling some of the people there that we need to learn a lot more about the choreography of videoconferencing. I made a mental note to tell my daughters about it since it would be a great profession.

### WB Coffee Shops

Instead of running our own World Bank public-information centers why do we not franchise them as WB coffee shops to people willing to serve regular real organic coffee from Honduras (not that oxymoron of organic decaf) and to arrange small conferences on development issues? That way we could be much more effective spreading the word around the world—not having to rely so much on our President's hectic travels.

### On putting things into perspective

Here we are presented with a document that in relation to one absolutely miserably poor country with a per capita income of 100 dollars a year tells us "in order to reach other MDG targets...XXX needs to accelerate its policy efforts aimed at gender parity, health outcome and environmental sustainability." That might all be true in theory but unfortunately in a country with an income of 100 dollars a year, the priority for most of the people is just survival until tomorrow, and not an MDG for 2015. We need to phrase things better.

### What do our figures mean?

We need to measure, and without measuring there would be no accountability; there is little indeed as it is. Nonetheless, when we read, in some documents, statements like that without NAFTA, Mexico's per capita income of $5,920 would have been 4—5 percent lower ($5,620), do we know what this really means?...if anything?

### When wishing no voice

Representing a varied constituency and expected to speak out for all, I find that the *sound of silence* turns out to be the most appropriate language for me and most other Executive Directors in some delicate issues. There are occasions, such as the war in Iraq, when even outspoken persons like me prefer not having a voice. That said, as an Executive Director of a development institution, I supported multilateralism and expressed confidence in how the management was handling the issues. I admit I did it through some statements that would have made Cantinflas proud, something that only my fellow Latin Americans could understand. (Jim, my Editor: Who? I: A genius Mexican actor who reached sublimity with his marvelous discourses that said nothing. His own voice is very much missed in today's world.)

### Red and blue, or, red or blue?—a postscript

On the radio, C-Span recounted details about "Intelligent design," which according to its defenders is a valid scientific alternative to the evolution theories of Darwin. I could not resist postscripting the following to my American friends.

Unity is a very precious thing for a country (I should know as a Venezuelan), and there are some issues better left alone. This is clearly one. Pitting "intelligent design" against "evolution theories" can never lead to anything good, and you surely must all be aware that you will never ever reach something close to a mutually satisfactory conclusion.

As a Christian, I know we are challenged by a lot of apparent contradictions in our faith but, as a Christian, I also believe that we are supposed to find ways to make peace with those demons of contradiction, so as not to let the devil triumph.

Friends, how can I put this warning any clearer to you? Well, if we were still in the "good old days" of the Cold War, I could have advanced the thesis that the very bad Communists had seeded this destructive and divisive debate in the heart of your heartland.

That said, I cannot refrain from mentioning that, if you absolutely have to, I would prefer the term "Divine Design," since "Intelligent Design" sounds to me like opening the door to an equally unnecessary debate about more mundane issues such as quality controls.

I switched channels and I heard Faith Hill singing "Is everything A-OK in the good old USA?"

# Some admittedly lite pieces

---

### The World Bank Special
Dear Colleagues,

On the corner of K Street and 18th, one bloc away from the World Bank, they are today serving a World Bank special, made up of chicken breast, onion, green peppers, bacon, and Brie cheese. Not bad, but some questions beg for answers.

Are they really authorized to use the term "The World Bank" in their marketing? Do we not have the copyright of our own trademark? Can we not strike a deal with them, or any other users that could help us to scale up? Do we all concur in the recipe? Could there be reputation risks if the food is not liked?

You know have I often have expressed amazement at France's marketing capabilities, as when our many diverse multiethnic coffees all get reduced to being just French Roast. Well, now they've done it again. Not only have they been able to place their Brie cheese on The World Bank Special, but they also got it all placed on "a whole French wheat roll" Chapeau to them!

Per

## Thou shall not PowerPoint

- Dear Colleagues,
- When we were small, our fathers taught us never to FingerPoint anyone, and today we also need to teach kids not to PowerPoint one another.
- Yes, I have seen some splendid use of PowerPoint presentations, but, in general terms, the world is not a better place for it.
- PowerPoint has empowered so many people with so little to say with a deep belief that the world is waiting for them to predicate, for hours.
- PowerPoint is little by little replacing all decent readable issue papers with thick bundles of copies of PowerPoint sheets, each one containing less than 15 words, in beautifully irrelevant colors, except when replaced by thin bundles containing miniature unreadable copies of aforementioned sheets.
- PowerPoint is forcing the world to structure its whole thinking process in terms of bulletpoints.
- NO, thou shall not PowerPoint me and I promise not to PowerPoint you…too much.
- Happy Holidays
- Per
- December, 2003

## Deep pondering on labels

### Warnings

The label of a pure chocolate bar containing no peanuts or almonds nevertheless informs its allergy-prone consumers that the product was "manufactured on the same equipment that processes peanuts/almonds." I had no idea that chocolate consumers could be that sensitive or that manufacturers could be so adverse to the risk of being sued.

On the other hand, after having watched 18 hours on DVD with no commercial interruptions of a highly addictive

TV series that without the slightest of warnings broke away from the time-honored American tradition of happy endings, my wife, my daughters, and I felt like suing the producer for having wasted our time, aggravated by an emotional letdown. And therefore to label or not to label seems to be a very pertinent question for our times.

For instance, when appointing individuals to some very sensitive government positions of authority there is a special need for a warning along the lines of "this idea was generated by the same mind or mindset that came up with such-and-such an idea." Taking such an approach seems to be an ideal function of the confirmation hearings of Congress. It is ironic though that in this case it is exactly when they are ordered to follow their respective labels, Republican or Democrat, that we then need a label stating "Warning, following the labels precisely might also be dangerous."

### Guaranteed—100% Artificial

Many years ago, on a Caribbean island, on a bottle which contained a greenish liquid of very dubious quality, I read "Guaranteed 100% Artificial." I thought this slogan that so shamelessly capitalized on what was obviously negative by turning it into something positive was a real marketing masterpiece. That was before I started to analyze similar examples provided by our politicians. Since then it is but an example.

### Remove all packaging and labels!

I just purchased a porcelain enameled casserole dish to use in the oven, and read on the label that before using it I should remove all packaging and labels. I understand the vendor's concern with lawsuits from suing-for-a-buck entrepreneurs, but should they in that case not also worry about someone suing them for disrespectfully considering a consumer stupid, ex-ante, or for whatever this stupid consumer might cook, which, presumably, could be much more dangerous and addictive than some old burned labels? (A frozen pizza I just bought had a label instructing that it should be cooked heated before eating!)

## Pure water

On the flight I was handed a small picnic-like bag which contained the modern substitute for the traditional on-board meal. I suppose this is aimed at cost reduction. The bag included a bottle of pure, natural water and a "globalized" menu made up of a Manhattan deli-sandwich, Dijon mustard, and Tortilla Chips.

The water is contained in a clear plastic bottle, good and very expensive, retail. Its label told me that the water originated, and is bottled, in France, vintage 2005, and can be consumed safely until July 27, year 2007. (What should one do in August of year 2007?) It also included a bar code, which evidently makes logistics easier, considering the fact that the water must be transported long distances from its source to the ultimate consumer.

On the backside of the bottle, another label gave me valuable information as to its "Nutritional Content" broken down into units per serving, which in this case was conveniently the same as the content of the bottle, that is, 11 fl. oz or 330 ml. The information was as follows: Calories = 0; Total Fat Content = 0 g. = 0% of the Daily Value (DV); Sodium = 0 mgs. = 0%; Carbohydrates = 0 g. = 0% of the Daily Value (DV); and Proteins = 0 g. = 0% of the Daily Value (DV). All was, as one should expect, from the ingredient "water," although, curiously, no info at all was provided in respect to its purity.

While I drank the water, I asked myself, why do they cut back on flight attendants in order to give you this expensive water? Why do people scream bloody murder when nonrenewable gasoline hits two dollars a gallon and then willingly pay up to eighteen dollars a gallon for pure water without even being thirsty? I guess that's life!

## Warning against warnings

We all know of the crying-wolf-too-often risks, but I also just heard an amazing new twist on it on C-Span. In a hearing about the frauds committed against elderly people, Denise Park from the National Institute of Aging, after explaining that the elderly were more prone to give credibility to anything sounding familiar than young people, told about an experiment that showed that the likelihood of a statement being considered true after having been declared false three times was, for older people, larger than for a statement that had been declared false only once. To me, the implication of this thesis—closely related in its significance to Goebbels' odious theories—is that we need also to include in our warning labels something to the effect that "this warning should not be read too often, especially by those over fifty."

## Fair prices!

And while waiting in the line I see a "Fair Trade Certified" coffee that on its label promises that its purchase will improve the lives of coffee farmers by insuring they receive a guaranteed "fair price for their harvest". I could not resist such an enticement and I bought a cup of it. It was great, and like any truly good coffee it made my mind wander. What does a fair price mean? That the coffee grower can afford to send his kids to school, afford good decent healthcare, and buy a car? Or that his kids will not go to bed starving. I hope he gets at least the last. Or does fair in this context mean that he is getting prices that are fairly similar to those quoted for coffee on the commodities exchanges without risking being taken to the cleaners by some savvy distributors? Who knows? I finish up my coffee with a lingering suspicion that perhaps a fair price might still not be enough. Would it not be better to certify "unfair prices" or, in perhaps more marketing digestible terms "fair price plus 100%"? Whatever, at the end of the day, if I were a farmer, I know that I would much rather get European farm prices than fair prices.

## To write or not to write...by hand

My father always thought good handwriting to be one of the foremost proofs of a good education and he was most certainly right, in his own time and way. Unfortunately, nowadays, you do not have that many opportunities to show off your good education by handwriting. Every year that goes by, the less I write and the more cramps I get in my arm when I try. As an economist, concerned about input/output productivity, I have to question whether there still is a valid reason for including learning to write by hand in the general school curricula. Just think of the number of hours you put into that effort and then calculate the estimated number of letters you are expected to handwrite in the future where even your signature is perhaps about to be supplanted by a scanned image of your right eye pupil.

"Dear God, another economist gone mad believing life is just about efficiency!" I can hear the purist cry out. No, friends, I am among the first to acknowledge a real human need for inefficiencies but perhaps even from this perspective, we should be able to find more enjoyable and useful inefficiencies than writing—and also with much less potential for creating conflicts with our perfectionist fathers.

Many write-defenders will put forward the argument that it promotes coordination of mind and muscle. However, if this were the whole purpose of the exercise and if we look at what seems to be future needs for coordination, derived from the many hours children invest playing handheld games, then I would argue that what we have to do away with is single-hand writing. Forget about right handed or left handed, let Darwin work, and have children learn to write with both their hands.

"But writing helps you to understand the language!" Nonsense! That you do by reading, listening, speaking, and nowadays by typing. If you really must cling to writing because of contractual clauses carefully crafted by your writing teachers association, then, at a minimum, you should convince them to use those sessions to teach writing in Chinese.

Want your children truly to stand out and be able to master future technologies with the same flair as Cirque du Soleil acrobats? Let them then practice to write with both hands in Chinese and Arabic, simultaneously, while humming Bob Dylan's "The Times They Are A-Changin'." That should do it!

But my purpose is not to eliminate writing as an art form but to recapture it as a true art form. You know how much I worry about how the world seems incapable of creating new good-paying jobs. Well, limiting the teaching of writing now allows us to visualize in a couple of years the resurrection of the profession of writing clerks. May I offer you my services then?

What on earth has this to do with the World Bank? If you can't figure it out, you should not be in the business of development!

A quite interesting spin on this same issue is made by Willam Easterly in his book *The Elusive Quest for Growth*, since when he argues that "the productivity gains of the computer are slow to be realized…because there are still too many traditional people out there with ink and paper," he is actually making the point that perhaps we should prohibit handwriting as such, so that the world can move forward. [Jim, my editor: "Plato suggested—I suspect jokingly—that the invention of writing was a bad thing that ruined human powers of memory."]

In the WBG cafeteria, we read that by using its napkins made with 100%-recycled paper, the WBG Food Services was proudly saving 268 trees annually, 110,000 gallons of water, 47 cubic yards of landfill space, 65,000 Kwh of electricity, and 945 pounds of greenhouse gas emissions. As the WB Board's 100% paper-intensive proceedings alone might consume several times these "savings," not being able to write by hand could presumably also have some favorable environmental implications.

## Three bullets on punctuality
## Time and human rights

I have no intention of putting the right to punctuality in the same category as the right to education, security, health care, food, and work. However, in a country such as ours (Venezuela) where we because of sheer lack of punctuality can easily lose up to three hours per week waiting for something or another, this, over our an average active life span of 55 years, adds up to around one year. As civil-rights organizations normally go ballistic whenever anyone is arrested without justification even for a couple of hours, I wonder how they let this pass.

There can be no doubt that the majority of our countrymen do, without any remorse whatsoever, blithely ignore the existence and purpose of the clock, and so it is evident that in terms of punctuality we need a total reform of our civil society. How do we achieve this?

One alternative would be the creation of a "Punctual Venezuela," parallel to the actual one. For example, if we start to use a little symbol that could be printed on all invitations to those activities that really require punctuality at the risk of being either excluded from the event or publicly chastised, we could possibly begin to create some semblance of civility. This symbol could be a watch, but I'd rather leave that up to the specialists in advertising.

The interesting part of this alternative is that it would allow us to impose, as of today, a heavy public and social sanction for those who lack punctuality without having to request that "notorious and incurable sinners" kick the habit cold-turkey. Also, maintaining the option of a not punctual Venezuela alive would allow us to continue to humor those foreign visitors who with a tropical flare that rivals our best take every chance they get to free themselves from the yoke of punctuality.

From *The Daily Journal*, Caracas, June 11, 1999

## About parallels and meridians

We have recently witnessed public spectacles such as the fight the United States has sustained with Europe about bananas. Perhaps the effect of global warming has been much greater than we suspect as it seems to have moved the parallels normally identified with Banana Republics northward.

However the meridians might have gone haywire as well. I often take my daughters to parties that begin at midnight, which to me simply seems like a real and crude version, in cinéma vérité, of Saturday Night Fever. I cannot but suspect that their generation has simply decided to substitute the East Coast's meridian for that of the West Coast. Some of the television channels seem also to suffer from the same syndrome. Somehow, I always seem to go to bed at night watching their afternoon comics while, if I am not careful, my daughters could wake up with their XXX-rated after midnight material.

From *The Daily Journal*, Caracas, June 11, 1999

## My daughter's cult

She is rarely late but she is absolutely never ever a minute early. She follows that Just-In-Time cult that drives us inhumanely nuts.

## My wife's cult

She is never late, but she is absolutely never ever just in time. She follows that better-early-than-late cult that has made us use years of our life waiting in airport departure halls.

## My reality

Being squeezed between the just-in-time cult and the better-early-than-late cult is probably one of the reasons why I have been harassed into developing a radical middle mumbo-jumbo philosophy.

# On common goods and some global issues

Dear friends and colleagues,
I wonder whether we, as directors of the World Bank, are discussing sufficiently the difficult global issues. Here I introduce some combustible material to fire up some debate.
Per

### Towards World Laboratories

Few things inspire one to question globalization—with the heart—as the sight of a father in front of a pharmacy in a poor country, unable to buy the medicine his sick son needs because even though its direct cost is only two dollars, patents raise it to twenty. Nonetheless, we all recognize—with our heads—that without patents to guarantee laboratories a temporary monopoly with which to recover development costs, there would surely be less investment in the field of medical research. As always, the challenge for humanity is to use our heads—with a lot of heart.

When we hear the record industry defend its property rights against piracy, we sometimes feel they are trying to make us feel guilty, presenting us with the image of the poor musician unable to reap the fruits of his talent and efforts—but ignoring the fact that it is the musician who receives the smallest part of the remaining margin of 18 dollars.

As a solution to the dilemma of the price of medicine, perhaps we should begin by studying the components of the profit margin, especially taxes. It seems obvious that although the poor father may pay his share of development costs, he should not have to pay a penny in taxes to any other country, which may use them to provide free medicine to the child of a more fortunate father.

Today, when the developed world has managed to convince us of the global value of respecting patents, it may be time to investigate whether the concept of globality should not be broadened, classifying the development of most medicines as a global public asset. Consequently, in the same way that the Amazon rainforest does not charge us for purifying the world's air, no country should tax laboratories or the people working in them.

This implies placing laboratories under a kind of global jurisdiction, which could also facilitate the solution to problems such as when medicine must be sold at different prices to those who simply cannot pay more, and to guarantee research on diseases that will never be able to generate profits to pay for their development, such as certain varieties of AIDS in Africa.

From *El Universal*, Caracas, March 2003

## Daddy...the original or the copy?

I am a law-abiding citizen but that does not mean that I should never question some laws. Having grown up during an era with a lot of Japanese product copying, I must say that the way the world now looks to impose on poor developing countries the obligation of investing scarce public resources to enforce Property and Copyright Laws has always made me feel a bit uneasy. Somehow poor and developing countries are now expected to behave ex-ante the way rich and developed countries do ex-post, sometimes even better!

In an article that I published in Venezuela in October 2000, I posed the following question to my readers.

Two teenage twins, with that typical teenage eagerness of being praised shining bright in their eyes, stand in front of their father in a relative poor developing country and ask him to determine who did right, the one who purchased an original CD at 16 dollars or the one who got a pirated copy that sounded just as well for only 2 dollars. What should their father say?

Yes I know that probably the correct ethical answer could be neither. The first bought something they could not afford, and the second bought something stolen. Nonetheless, I think this clearly shows that there are a lot of unresolved conflicts because, even if they presumably could afford the original, we are not sure in our hearts that the one buying the copy did really wrong.

It is a very difficult topic, but it is my belief that the World Bank should debate in a more open way such issues, as they are part of the many difficulties of globalization, that will not go away just because we ignore them.

\*\*\*

Jim, my editor: "Is the question of copying CDs really related to globalization? Wouldn't it apply in exactly the same way if an American kid bought a copy of an American CD here in America from another American, an entirely internal transaction with nothing to do with any foreign country?"

I: "Jim, this is very much related to globalization, as intellectual-property rights are among the first issues discussed in most trade agreements."

(Back to my article again)

\*\*\*

For instance, let me illustrate the following dilemma. If the price of an original CD is 16 and a copy is sold for 2, then the nominal temptation factor is 14. But is this 14 the same everywhere? In countries with a per capita income of 28,000 this nominal temptation factor represents only a one two thousandth of one's income, but, in a country were the per capita income is 2,800 it would represent a full one two hundredth of one's yearly income, signifying a ten times larger relative sacrifice. Does this then mean we are imposing a law-enforcement obligation that might be 10 times as tough for a poor country as it is for a rich one? I am not implying any moral defense of infringing laws but, really, if Executive Directors, staff, and management of the World Bank cannot answer these questions firmly on a personal level, should they then be allowed to act with so much assuredness when preaching globally?

When you decide to respect a copyright or a patent you are in fact submitting to a monopoly right. The counterpart of that is that the monopoly rights should be reasonably exploited. What is reasonable? What the market can bear without pirating? What the market can bear with a certain percentage being illegally copied? I do not know, but seeing so little debate and research about these problems, I am not really convinced by those ascertaining full knowledge—just because "it is in the law."

### The rights of intellectual property user

Microsoft was recently declared guilty of some monopolistic misbehavior by a United States court. What would have happened if the United States, based on the fact that Microsoft is an American company, had simply ignored these problems? Would it have been up to our very humble local authorities to initiate the legal proceedings against this giant among giants? As far as the protection of intellectual property is concerned, we are still in an embryonic stage.

When I received (as did many others) a letter and brochure illustrated with a set of handcuffs, I was curtly advised that I should legalize all the software I was using before the 30th of April. Should I not do so, I would be confronting severe fines, would have my hard disk sequestered, and would be subject to up to four years in prison. I was galvanized into reflecting a bit more on this issue.

My first conclusion was that because all the legal apparatus that regulates this matter was developed in countries that represented the owners of 99.99% of intellectual property rights, countries like Venezuela that have only users and royalty payers need at least to develop their own theoretical frame of reference. The following are but some points for discussion:

It is absolutely clear that any creator, researcher, or inventor should be adequately compensated for his or her work, but in doing so we cannot ignore completely the fact that the accumulated knowledge of human civilization must also have played a role. In this respect, there is a general although not always very explicit understanding that monopoly rights obtained through the issuance of patents and similar legal means should be exploited in reasonable terms.

We can guess that when the United States authorities award Microsoft monopoly rights to a particular software they do so in the understanding that there are other parameters and competitive elements in the market that limit the capability of this company to abuse its position of advantage. But, are these control elements the same everywhere? Take for instance price setting. When Microsoft establishes prices for its software it most certainly will do so based on what it believes the United States can digest. Should instead a poor country have been Microsoft's only market, I am sure the price of its software would be much lower so as to be able to reach many more consumers.

Because of this we can at least theorize that when patent or copyright protection is transferred intact from one country to another market which is playing no relevant part in controlling how those rights are used, it could in fact produce the results of unreasonable monopolistic behavior.

What's the way out? I don't know, but we should not

ignore the issue just because it is difficult. Traditionally it was perhaps normal that poor countries sometimes copied and pirated part of what they needed in order to try to get out of their poverty. Things are different now, as poor and developing countries are expected to behave ex-ante the way rich and developed countries do ex-post.

Kurowski, are you messing with Microsoft? Absolutely not, it is a great company and all their products, that I have legally acquired, version after version, too many versions though, serve me well. What most upsets me in these matters is how we so easily agree to protect all these intellectual-property products, by definition renewable, creating Sheriffs' of Nottingham, not in Sherwood but here, compared to how little we do in order to have our nonrenewable oil treated with equal fairness. May I just recall some recent history?

Based on data taken from the "World Oil Trends 1999" published by Arthur Andersen and Cambridge Energy Research Associates in the United Kingdom, for example, taxes on gasoline which in 1985 were 85% of the pure gasoline price have now reached an absurd 456%. Evidently, these taxes have caused the increase of the price of oil-based products for the consumer. In England, the price index for these products went from 100% in 1980 to 247% in 1998. The result of this for Venezuela is clear as day. Demand for crude oil dropped and the real price index of crude oil went from being 100% in 1980 to a mere 18% in 1998. Value, as paid by consumers, going from 100 to 247 while our income went from 100 to 18. That just is not fair.

Extract from *The Daily Journal*, Caracas, May 16, 2000, my 50th birthday.

## Who can enforce it better?

If a product covered by intellectual-property rights were to be sold at a lower price in a low-income country (something which would require waiving the rules against dumping), then of course we would have the problem of these low-priced versions recycling to the rich countries. The question remains though who is better capable and has more resources to enforce the laws, the poor country's law-enforcement agency in stopping their poor citizens from trying to get access to the products at illegally low prices, or the rich country stopping the low-priced product from entering its markets. Well, it's not an easy problem...but who said that the world is a rose garden?

This reminds me of an interesting book. I read about a big international food-distribution company that in 1995 was fined 100 million dollars for having engaged in illegal price-fixing. As its illegal activity extended to the whole world, I have always wondered how much the other countries that had been victims had been able to participate in the partial indemnification that the fine represented. Nothing?

### Moisés Naím's Illicit—a postscript

We can just hope that Moisés Naím's recent book *Illicit: How Smugglers, Traffickers, and Copycats Are Hijacking the Global Economy*, Doubleday, 2005 helps to open up a long overdue debate on some very important issues related to intellectual-property rights that have been considered almost sacrosanct. For instance, when society awards intellectual-property rights and is thereby expected to invest scarce resources enforcing them, there is an implicit assumption that these rights are to be reasonably exploited. When then one of these manmade property rights is violated, as happens through the pirating of CDs, this might be the market answer to a lack of regulatory control over the monopoly. In this respect, under some circumstances, pirates and counterfeits could indeed perform a useful regulatory service to the society, as when vultures do the cleaning.

As the temptation-ratio to use a pirated good, defined as the potential savings in relation to the income per capita, is obviously larger in poor developing countries than in the rich developed countries, does this fact mean that the poor countries should have to invest relatively much more in fighting piracy?

Also, though you need an original to create a fake parasite, who is to tell us that the original is not sometimes well served by the very existence of its fakes? Might not the value and the number of buyers of truly original Louis Vuitton handbags in fact be larger because all the rest of the world has to settle for fakes? Should the pirates have a right to a fee in such a case?

Finally another related issue that needs much discussion is whether society is well served by criminalizing behaviors that are in themselves not exposed to any significant social sanction. In these Intellectual Property Right matters, some hypocrisy is truly rampant.

## Global Tax

Dear friends and colleagues,

Timidly, within brackets, and diluted by an "among others," the most recent *Development Communiqué* spells out the possibility that, in order to mobilize additional resources for aid, we should at least examine the option of a global tax. We must have touched a raw nerve somewhere, and I at least have been approached by a surprising number of persons who, moving up close, give me the what-do-you-think-of-it whisper. Colleagues, we will certainly have endless discussions about this matter in the Board, or at least our inheritors will, but, for the time being, let me share with you my not so hushed up but precocious answer.

In general terms, like any normal citizen, I hate taxes, but, in this case, that might be precisely why I find it interesting to look into a formal global tax so as to see whether in that way we could get rid of some of those informal global taxes that we are already paying or, if deferred, we will pay some fine day soon. As we live in a minuscule interrelated world, with a lot of butterfly wings flapping, no one will convince me that there aren't many problems out there that already have someone somewhere paying taxes for them, albeit not always in cash.

I come from a country where we have grown too accustomed to paying some sort of hidden taxes in many forms and ways: holes in the street gobbling up the car ties, insecurity that requires our paying private guards, a precarious health system where some even pay with their lives, poor public education whereby even if your own kids get a good private education it is worth less as they will be unable to count on the synergy of other educated citizens, and you could go on forever. On a global level, for instance in matters of the destruction of the environment, it is clear that we already are paying taxes, at an ever increasing rate.

Therefore I would analyze a new and formal global tax, not in terms of its being a new tax, but in terms of whether it is a more efficient and transparent tax to substitute for some of the current and future awful-consequence taxes. Intuitively, I would answer "yes" on both counts, and here are briefly my reasons:

In terms of effectiveness, at least it sounds quite good to be able to count on some type of centralized funds that could be allocated strictly according to global priorities instead of being captured by local interests. Just as an example, it is absolutely clear to me that, from an environmental perspective, we would be much better off allocating scarce financial resources to help Brazil cover for the fast-growing opportunity costs of not developing the Amazon, than building windmills in somebody's backyard. As you can see, this is impossible, while taxes are parochial.

In terms of transparency and coming from an oil country, what more could I say? Huge taxes are currently levied on oil in the developed world, and most of the contributors (consumers) believe that these taxes have environmental purposes that extend much beyond curtailing consumption. Well, no, the truth is that not a single net cent of each dollar goes to the environment, perhaps even less, when taking into account the economic inefficiency of investments in wind and solar energy and the environmentally negative implications of coal subsidies.

\*\*\*

Jim, my editor, goes into a fit: "You are an economist. Do you realize what Holland accomplished with wind power for centuries? Do you know what FDR's TVA is accomplishing through hydroelectric power in the United States southeast? Or what tapping volcanic power is doing for Iceland? Maybe one day nuclear fusion will provide such clean, safe, cheap, endless energy that these alternatives which I favor will become as unnecessary as coal and oil and wood, but until that happens, and in case it does not happen, wind, waterfall, tide, solar cells, and geothermal heating are wonderful improvements on gas, oil, and coal. Sure there will be initial problems. When Ford started mass-producing automobiles, there weren't many gasoline stations, and there weren't many miles of suitable roads, and there weren't many people who knew how to repair cars instead of putting horseshoes on horses, and there weren't many people who knew how to drive and could teach others, and there weren't any ways to register and regulate automobiles on the public roads. When Alexander Graham Bell invented and started selling his telephone, there were hardly any people to call, since there were so few phones in existence. Well, automobiles and phones went over despite these initial hurdles, and so would wind and solar if we worked hard at trying them, as hard as we did with cars and phones."

I: "Dear Jim, I understand you and I wish we could go that route too, but, unfortunately, the world's environment is in such a lousy shape that we cannot afford to throw away resources like that."

Back to my discussions

\*\*\*

But, as always, the devil is in the details. How on earth should an earth tax be run? I haven't gotten that far yet but, as a starter, perhaps a petit committee of experts, world leaders, and scientists (not any self-appointed eminences) could allocate the resources to development institutes, through yearly public hearings, based on proposals and performance, and could also help to fire some healthy competition and accountability into development.

And tax on what? On our airplane tickets? No, if we are going to have a chance to work things out globally, we should meet frequently, not only through videoconferences. If forced to give an off-the-cuff answer, I would mention a type of Tobin tax[5] on capital movements as a probable candidate, as that would also perhaps help us to slow financial movements down, from minutes to nanoseconds, and help the world to move out of its shortsightedness where full weight is given to the next quarter's results and nobody thinks about the next generation.

Summarizing, those opposing a global tax are blind to the fact that such costs exist anyhow. Perhaps they are living out their teenage illusions of never growing old and never needing to depend upon others.

Friends…pssst…what do you really think of a global tax?
Per

### Labor standards and Unions

Standards

While discussing core labor standards we should always remember that they mainly apply to the formal sector but it is the informal sector that is growing everywhere. What does the Knowledge Bank know about the informal sector and its informal working standards?

Unions

In general terms, jobs in the maquila industry frequently seem just like a zero-sum game in that one person gets displaced by another willing to labor for less. Nonetheless, it should not be for us to decide where the frontier of the lowest marginal labor cost should lie as we have no practical or moral ground to negate a person's right to and willingness to sacrifice himself for his family. Having said it we still believe that unions and collective bargaining play a vital role in assuring that some absolute minimum human working conditions are not transgressed. We therefore urge the Bank always outspokenly to support the rights of free bona fide unionizing.

***

Jim, my editor: Per, You must decide for what kind of readers you are writing this book. If you mean it is only for economists or only for Latinos or perhaps only for Latino economists, maquila is fine. I know that directly and immediately it is short for maquiladora, and that's American Spanish for where the miller collects his fee for grinding someone else's grain. And that in turn comes from the Spanish of Spain maquila which is the percentage of grain that is measured out for the miller to keep in return for grinding, and that it goes back to the Moorish occupation of Spain and comes from the Arabic noun makila, a measured amount, from the feminine passive participle of the Arabic verb kala, to measure, from the Semitic root kwl, kyl meaning to hold, to have a capacity, to measure. I know when Ford sends auto parts just across the border to be assembled by cheap labor in Mexico instead of paying the United States minimum wage, and then gets the parts back improved by the Mexican labor (improved in that they are now automobiles that run, not separate parts), then to make the parallel perfect the owner of the Mexican assembly plant should get the same percentage of the assembled cars that the miller used to get of the grain he ground. I suspect that the Mexican owners prefer cash to a percentage of the cars, but the analogy is fairly close. I go on at this length not only because maquila is interesting, but, more importantly for you, to suggest that you make the whole book understandable to the average ten-year-old in the United States.

I: Silent and appreciative contemplation!

# A mixed bag of stand-alone issues

## My insecurities about the social security debate

### About disseminating our knowledge

It really is not possible for the value of investment funds to grow, forever, at a higher rate than the underlying economy, unless they are just inflating it with air, or unless they are taking a chunk of the growth from someone else. Therefore when we observe how many Social Security System Reforms are based on the underlying assumption that they will be growing 5 to 7 percent, in real terms, for ever. I wonder when we are going to use our knowledge, and inform the world that this is just plain crazy.

When we speak of expected returns, let say a real 3%, this is just an average of a distribution curve where there are a lot of winners, with higher returns, and a lot of losers, taken to the cleaners. Knowing this, how come we allow the debate on Social Security reforms to use the averages? In systems where you are supposing to pay someone to manage the funds, you should expect the managers to produce different results. Yes of course the returns could be average, but for that you just buy a stock index, and pay no fees.

## A question

Are there any real differences between a pay-as-you-go, governmentally backed pension system, and a pension fund that invests completely in government paper?

## About the timing and the losers

Any individual Social Security accumulation system that has the luck to start when the markets are close to rock bottom will always perform better than those systems that start when the markets are at the top. This has been the real beginner luck of the Chilean system and future generations of Chilean accumulators might not be as happy with the results as the pioneers were.

When we now read how investment funds publicly state that they do not wish to receive more funds since they do not know where to invest them and we also observe how many private pension schemes in the United States are running for public cover, we need perhaps to ask ourselves whether the timing for those Social Security reforms that might be en route is really that good.

Those who beat the market average will always love to be on their own, and therefore the problem does always reside with the losers. The difficult question is whether in an individual security accumulation system all of the future losers have truly surrendered their expectations of receiving official assistance and, even if they have, proudly preferring to starve than to ask for help, whether the governments could really get away from their social responsibilities by answering the losers with a "Hard luck, pal, you had a private plan."

And so, at the end of the day, to me it seems that you might just be substituting a pay-as-they-fall for a mean-based pay-as-you-go system. So, when we add it all up, it all boils down to the same—except of course for the fees.

## On Social Security in Real Terms

In order for your savings and social security investments to be worth something when you need them, the real economy must be in a reasonable condition at the time of your selling your investments. When I hear the many discussions about the financial preparation needed to accommodate for the upcoming demographic changes, I find it truly amazing how little is being said about the economy in real terms.

Considering that there will be many fewer young ones to drive people around and shovel snow, much of today's beautiful real estate might drop in value when the elderly start selling their houses to live close to a metro, hospital, and more reasonable weather conditions. So, before putting the money away in a private accumulation trust I think we need to rethink the whole retirement strategy.

\*\*\*

Jim, my editor: "The Philadelphia suburbs have many Metro stations where it is safe to wait, many outstanding hospitals, and fairly good weather. Philadelphia proper has stations where it is not safe to be, hospitals overcrowded with uninsured indigent patients who are certainly not going to get the cutting-edge high-tech expensive care available in the suburbs, and somewhat worse weather (hotter in summer, less effective snow and ice removal in winter). Any sensible elder would move to the suburbs. Doing the opposite is like swimming towards a sinking ship."

I: "That's OK Jim. I did not mean that my real-terms projections are necessarily correct, but, now that I have you thinking of the future in real terms may I also suggest looking into beautiful Isla de Margarita off the coast of South America?"

Now back to my voice (and noise)

\*\*\*

Also we should never forget that historically, through all economic cycles, there is nothing so valuable in terms of personal social security as having many well-educated loving children to take care of you, and that you can't, in real terms, beat that with any social security reform.

### Two current updates on the social-security issue

Sir, Delphi's (a company that supplies General Motors) problems do indeed pose a threat to public-pension institutions, but it also evidences the structural weakness of the alternative of accumulations in private-investment accounts. The fact is that when the old retire and might need to sell their stocks, the young might not be willing to buy them.

Sir, With respect to GM's pension woes, you claim that the company recorded a return of 5 per cent in the first half of the year, putting it on track for its assumed annual return of 9% but also that if GM's pension funds produced the same poor returns as the equity and bond markets, this would of course have a dramatic negative impact. What is thereby implied makes a case for developing a formula that calculates how much arrogance it must take to promise to pay 9% on funds over a life span, and/or to beat the markets continuously.

### About the SEC, the human factor, and laughing

A couple of days ago, our SEC reported that their pension fund had also been the victim of a fraudulent stock-managing firm, and that they had lost a lot of money.

I also read recently about the Mars Climate Orbiter spaceship that, after having required an investment of 125 million dollars, had to be declared as a total loss due to a technical confusion derived from simultaneously applying metric and English measures.

If what happened to NASA or what happened to our SEC is of any mutual comfort to them, I don't care, but what I do hope is that they have learned a bit more about humility.

I bring this opinion to the table since I recently heard that our SEC was now establishing higher capital requirements for stockbroker firms, arguing that "...the weak have to merge to remain. We have to get rid of the rotten apples so that we can renew the trust in the system." As I read it, it establishes a very dangerous relationship between weak and rotten. In fact, the financially weakest stockbroker in the system could be providing the most honest services while the big ones, just because of their size, can also bring down the whole world. It has always surprised me how the financial regulatory authorities, while preaching the value of diversification, act in favor of concentration.

The SEC should not substitute the need for capital in place of the need for ethics, nor should it allow that fraudulent behavior hides amid the anonymity of huge firms. In this respect, let us not forget that the risk of social sanctions should be one of the most fundamental tools in controlling financial activities.

If there is a relation between weakness and a rotten apple, it could really be in the SEC itself, since, though they frequently complain about the lack of resources, that doesn't stop them from transmitting institutional messages about how well they are fulfilling their responsibilities. Perhaps the best thing that the SEC could do is to stop all their actions that are creating a false sense of security in the investor, acknowledging the absence of any supervisory capacity, and instead stamp each share prospectus with a big "BUYERS BEWARE."

We read an article in *Newsweek* ("Giving Big Blue a Shiner, November 1999), about the surprising 20% drop in value that IBM shares had suffered in just one day. It also states that this drop was not in any way the result of any especially surprising event. The purported lesson of the article was "To teach not to take too seriously the investigative capacity of Wall Street and to remember to laugh next time you hear that the stock-market is a rational place where the big investors know what they are doing." I would also like to suggest remembering to laugh next time a regulator presumptuously assures you he is doing his job.

Extract from *Economía Hoy*, Caracas, November 16, 1999

## Roping in the herd

We have frequently seen examples of how economies that permit total liberty for foreign investment flows, especially those that are in essence short-term investments, often must confront more difficulties than those that impose certain restrictions.

As so many things in life do, problems often have their roots in exaggeration. It is possible that on the one hand confidence and the magnitudes of the resulting flows become so great that they can actually hide problems or diminish the pressure brought to bear on local authorities to take corrective measures. On the other hand, absolute mass panic may set in, creating the medium for the type of accidents normally attributed to such a response (for example, the Mexican debacle and resulting "Tequila Effect").

Since it is very difficult in most cases to identify a special event such as war, earthquakes, or the sudden death of an important leader as the trigger for a change in sentiment, and as we supposedly live in a world of virtual and perfect information, what could be the possible origin of the overly exaggerated reactions of fund managers?

Above all, I suspect that the financial roller-coaster rides we are subjected to have their origins in the traditional search for the type of security usually found in herds. This instinct predominates in most decision making. I refer specifically to the attitude "it doesn't matter if things go well or not, as long as I'm in good company."

As an example, I can go back to the period just after Venezuela abandoned exchange stability (February 1983). I watched with surprise as the treasurers of large multinational companies blithely signed contracts that insured future exchange rates at such incredible costs that they seemed outright irrational. The premium paid easily surpassed the possible exchange losses that would be caused by reasonably predictable devaluations.

When I tried to get to the bottom of this madness (frequently assisted in my investigation by offering a shot of whisky), I invariably would receive the following explanation: "We actually have two accounting registries. In the first we register the exchange earnings or losses per se. In the second we register the cost of the insurance premiums to cover exchange risks. Our head office has become so sensitive to exchange risk that it doesn't combine both accounts to analyze the total net results. On the contrary, even if I save the company a fortune by not contracting this coverage, but incur in so much as one cent in exchange losses, I would be handed my pink slip in a flash."

What, then, does this observation aim at? Simply that even when an individual or company is perfectly amicable, capable and basically worthy of an invitation to invest in our country, if his inclination as manager of funds is to follow the herd in stampede, the nation can simply not afford to allow him and his company to enter.

In this sense, we must ask why our monetary authorities have not managed to develop a coherent set of regulations to limit the inflow of international investment when this is obviously intended to be for irrationally short periods of time, in grossly large amounts, or both, instead of wasting time and money exchanging bonds and restructuring debt that matures in 20 years.

Countries like Chile, which have earned the confidence of international markets, limit the inflow of short-term investments. This limitation has definitely not resulted in damage. On the contrary, it has helped increase the confidence of exactly those foreign investors whom the country actually wishes to attract. They are not those that come on a 30-day visa, but rather those that come to invest for the long term.

It is important to remember that when a foreign investor risks his funds in a country in the long run, installing factories, developing projects, creating employment, and in general acquiring a real presence in the country, his interest in the future of the country becomes much more sincere and similar to that of the nation's own population. Much more so than the interest of some fund manager sitting in New York or London.

When we speak of gaining the confidence of foreign investors, we must learn to discriminate among them.

Published in *Daily Journal*, Caracas, December 4, 1997

\*\*\*

Jim, my Editor: "I'll tell you my opinion about what is often behind wild fluctuations in the market. How should people invest rationally in their own best interest and that of the country and economy as a whole? They should find a few companies in different industries, buy stock in them, and hold on to them decade after decade without looking at or paying attention to the daily ups and downs in their price on the stock exchange. They should consider selling only when they have a big need, such as sending kids to college, or an uncovered health expense. The one exception would be if a company they had invested in were in the headlines for criminal activity or for mismanagement that was leading to bankruptcy. Otherwise, they should throughout a working lifetime keep investing in the handful of companies they think are solid and not selling. Over a fifty-year period of their working life, they would have made money (even if the fifty years ended in the middle of our Great Depression). The economy and the stock markets would be much more stable than they have ever been. Compare it with highway driving. If everyone tries to dart in and out, switching lanes because of a perceived slight advantage, overall traffic will slow down enormously. If everyone tries to become a day-trader, or an hour-trader, he will cause the market volatility from which he hopes to profit. This volatility will be bad for the stock market, bad for the economy, and probably bad for most day-traders sooner or later. Almost everyone would be better off buying wisely for the long term and staying with this plan. Who would lose? Obviously, stock brokers, who make a fee each time a person sells one stock and buys another. So the stockbrokers flood their investors with hot buy! dump now! and the like urgent-sounding messages occasioned by real and imagined happenings at the company (in which one owns stock) that will have negligible effect on its value twenty, thirty, forty years down the road. Why do people fall for this obvious ploy of stockbrokers to increase their income at the expense of their investors and against all common sense? Greed! The hope to make a big buck easily in a short time. These people need to be reminded of the warning about swindlers and con-artists: If it seems too good to be true, it probably is."

My comment: "Jim, I would never put this so harshly. Some sloshing back and forth of funds and the consequent volatility is good as it provides important market signals and keeps the economy on its toes. My questioning has more to do with warning about letting your huge ocean waters enter our small pools and create manmade tsunamis. As far as stockbrokers, at least when there are some human beings involved and not just huge automatic exchanges, I would say "Live and let live." Finally, on highway driving, you cannot imagine how much a little free Latin driving spirit can help to ease the car queues. I for myself always take the lane furthest to the right: since as it should be the slowest, it always ends up being the fastest."

***

### An encore on roping...strictly by invitation

It is not only because I believe that too frequently it is the absolute free inflows of funds that should be blamed for setting up economies for the future panic outflows, that I prefer placing foreign-exchange controls upon the arrival of these funds to the small developing countries. I also have a marketing reason. There are two quite distinct lines of people queuing: those running toward a fire escape and those wanting to access a very exclusive club. I sort of find the latter sending a better subliminal message.

## A paradise of customs illegalities

There is no way a country like ours (Venezuela) could manage to liberalize legal trade if it cannot simultaneous eliminate illegal trade. If we do reduce the duties, we cannot also afford to reduce artificially the values of the goods involved.

Under-invoicing (the issuance of an invoice for an amount lower than what the buyer really paid) is a problem in international trade, where the aspirations of exporters/ importers of minimizing the duties paid are in constant conflict with the interests of local producers/taxmen that these are not underpaid. For developing countries with their scarcity of resources this is a specially serious issue. Not only do they sometimes lack the resources to negotiate trade treaties as-among-equals, but also any mistake they make could later be made worse by the sheer difficulty of controlling the flow of merchandise and assessing its correct value.

How are you supposed to punish those exporters who illegally under-invoice? On this issue the only reference that we found in international agreements was in the Kyoto Convention on the Simplification and Harmonization of Customs procedures, where Annex H2, on customs offences, says "In some countries, any person who has prepared or caused to be prepared or who has procured documents which are falsified or intended to deceive the Customs authorities and are used in a foreign country is regarded as having committed a Customs offence in the country where the documents were prepared" Unfortunately, this mutual-assistance measure seems to be limited to what is "expressly provided for in certain preferential trade agreements, e.g. those concluded by the European Communities with the EFTA, ACP and

Mediterranean countries." (By the way, Venezuela does not appear among the signers of this convention, and I do not know why, since requiring the other country to be a signer of it, seems to be the first minimum step of any treaty opening up trade opportunities.)

I am no lawyer and also not an absolute expert in these matters, so there might be some procedures that I do not know of, although, in this case I doubt it. Furthermore, if they do exist, they are most probably impossible to apply. Nonetheless, in the same way that there is much international legislation in reference to money laundering, I cannot see why there should not be some legislation in relation to the facilitation of international smuggling.

For instance, although not well known, extremely flexible, and much less applied, there is a convention among the OECD countries that tries to limit competition through corruption. It establishes that the corruptor of a foreign public servant will be punished as if that corruption had occurred in his own home country...and not only in a Banana Republic. From that convention we could perhaps derive another convention destined to increase competition by fighting smuggling. This convention could perhaps include a special duty applied to all products originating in countries that are deemed to be protecting these collaborators in crime.

Extracted from an article published in *Tal Cual*, Caracas, September 18, 2002

P.S. We need to take advantage of modern technology. I am sure that in the near future we should be able to do away with the tradition of one invoice for customs and one for real, by having electronic signatures link the Bill of Lading with the one and only invoice that is valid while in customs.

P.S. Don't get me wrong. As a believer in free trade, I harbor a lot of intuitive sympathy for smuggling, but, if we are having free trade legalized, then we must act consistently and get rid of the illegalities.

P.S. I wrote the above only a month before starting as an ED at the World Bank, but, unfortunately, I never had a chance to pursue this issue.

## Human genetics made inhuman

Lately world leaders have issued statements labeling research into the human genetic blueprint as "one of the most significant scientific projects of all time." They have also suggested that "to realize the full promise of the research, raw fundamental data on the human genome including the human DNA sequence and its variations should be made freely available to scientists everywhere."

As of this moment, all I have read about the mapping of human genes has been so upsetting that it only brings to mind the title of the musical *Stop the World, I Want to Get Off*. I am very far from making my mind up about this difficult issue, but I need to share some of my initial concerns with as many people as possible.

A report cited in Reuters from the *Daily Telegraph*, London, indicates that "the government plans to allow insurance companies to use DNA testing to assess whether people are at risk of inheriting serious illness and should pay higher premiums."

I believe strongly in the importance of the market as a means for the distribution of resources in society. However, I also believe that the benefits of development should accrue to all, not leaving any behind. What we now seem to be able to accomplish with research on the human genome multiplies manifold the difficulties of harmonizing these two previously contradicting objectives.

For instance, it would be great if genetics allowed the insurance companies to decide who will pay lower premiums, that is, those with less risk of developing serious illness. However, who will be responsible for those declared genetically second-class citizens, who will be forced to pay double or triple the premium, or who will ultimately be turned down altogether?

This problem is not limited to insurance. Reuters also reported on a conference to be held in mid-April in the United Kingdom in which "Genetic testing of children and testing for physical and social characteristics, as well as medical traits, would be high on the agenda." Does this imply the possibility that even access to the university will some day be determined in part by genetic analysis?

What would parents who today limit their background search to asking their children who their friends' parents are do tomorrow? Would they be obliged to ask about their genetic charts? The potential for discrimination is great, and would only reinforce the motivations of overly twisted Darwinists.

This genetic investigation might also represent a serious commercial threat for those countries that are not participating in this area. One of the companies racing to use information from gene mapping to make profits declared that it had hooked up with a center to find genes associated with breast cancer. If the efforts of this company are successful, it will be sitting on a patentable product and would be in a position to become a monopolist in a market with very inelastic demand. Can rationality be guaranteed within the openly declared and not unreasonable intention to obtain profit from the venture?

Many countries have signed commercial agreements that obligate them to respect patents to the extent of having to collaborate with other countries and punish unlawful use of protected discoveries. In the future, advancements in genetic science may force the revision of these accords, to decide whether they are still valid or whether, on the other hand and for the good of the common citizen, they should just look the other way.

What to do? It is very hard to say. Today, and just out of practical considerations, I limit myself to suggesting that all insurance companies design a plan which obligates them to issue policies for all of those who undertake a genetic examination. This policy should cover the negative impact and consequence that could arise from anyone getting access to such information.

I know this is only a Band-Aid, but what else can I do? I am not among those that resign and lie down to cry, even though this matter actually would justify just that.

From *The Daily Journal*, Caracas, March 2000

## Justice needs to begin with just prisons

Dear Friends.

A couple of weeks ago I had the chance to participate in Madrid in a seminar about Judicial Reform in Latin America, and this made me publish the following article in my country, Venezuela. I wish to share it with you. I know the majestic emblems of power are important, but when I travel around in many countries and see all these new beautiful Supreme Court buildings mushrooming, and know about the horrendous, more horrendous, and most horrendous state of most of the prisons, I just feel that someone got it all upside down.

## McPrisons

Justice is something very difficult to understand with precision, since it is situated along a continuum that becomes finite only when it reaches Divine Justice. On the other hand, injustices are much easier to identify and, in our countries, prisons themselves represent one of the greatest injustices. In terms of the use of scarce resources, as an economist I am convinced that programs of Judicial Reforms would be better served by improving prisons than by investing in Supreme Court buildings.

I am not advocating, nor do I believe in, imported solutions. Moreover, if we were to respect individual rights defined as extravagantly as possible, for example, by guaranteeing in Venezuela access to justice similar to that which benefited O. J. Simpson a few years ago in the United States, this would, because of the cost involved, be an affront to our human rights, collectively.

Nonetheless, I believe in good examples, and I am sure that if prison franchises could be established in our countries we would all reap the benefits, as we are shamed into reforms.

When we read that one factor making it particularly difficult for Schwarzenegger, the new Governor of California, to balance his state's budget is the 28,500 dollars he has to spend each year on each of his 162,000 prisoners and that one of his options would be to use local private prison services, which would allow him to cut the cost to 17,000 dollars per prisoner per year, we see an opportunity.

If California wants to save even more, it could do so by letting our countries offer prison services for some of its prisoners. Companies could build and operate prisons and would have to apply ISO 9000-type quality certifications. This would probably generate a set of global good prison practices that would benefit everyone. Nowadays, rapid transport and facilities such as videoconferences should make such proposals much more feasible. All that's lacking is the will to carry them out.

Since some people trace the origin of the violent maras (gangs) of Central America to Los Angeles, and since crime is to some degree attributed to the violence in films, perhaps California, its Governor, and even Hollywood, all have a special motivation to welcome an initiative such as this one to help us help them.

Besides, Schwarzenegger's experience in the movies alone, which ranges from subduing criminals by force to teaching kindergarten, would seem to fit the ideal résumé for a real super prison keeper.

P.S. I just read in the press that Schwarzenegger refers to his experience in the 1990 film Kindergarten Cop as useful for handling the legislative branch in California...perhaps that too.

From El Universal, Caracas, July 15, 2004

## My Power Point for justice in prisons

- **They are sending them to another Auschwitz**

In too many countries around the world when judges

sentence people to prisons, they are in fact sentencing them to another Auschwitz in terms of the absolute disrespect those places show for the most basic human rights, and worse the judges cannot even start to claim they didn't know. When will the International Criminal Court in The Hague start to investigate these crimes against humanity?

- **To get to justice...try fighting the injustices**

Justice is something very difficult to understand with precision, since it is situated along a continuum that becomes finite only when it reaches Divine Justice. On the other hand, injustices are much easier to identify and, in our countries, prisons themselves represent one of the greatest injustices. In terms of the use of scarce resources, as an economist I am convinced that programs of Judicial Reforms would be better served by improving prisons than by investing in Supreme Court buildings.

- **We need minimum prison standards and controls**

The world needs to adhere to a minimum set of global good-prison practices and allow for ISO 9000-type quality certifications of its prisons and jails.

### Real or virtual universities?

I had the opportunity to visit the amazing campus of Monterrey Tech (I.T.E.S.M., after the initials in Spanish for the Technological Institute of Higher Studies of Monterrey) in Mexico City. It is just one of the thirty campuses that this private university, founded in 1943, operates, in which more than 100,000 persons study. Given that the ITESM, in addition to its traditional classrooms, operates one of the most important virtual universities of the world, the conflict between what is real and virtual should provide for some heated budgeting discussions.

I can imagine the discussions. On the one side, the traditionalists take their stand, the ones who advocate more and better classrooms. They must still constitute by far the larger part of the faculty. On the other side, the virtual crowd must be growing, they who most probably argue for faster and more potent servers and for more publicity to assure ITESM's place in the list of the surviving and thriving virtual universities. And, in this sense they are right, since in the coming years—or even months—it could be decided who will be the leading virtual university for decades to come.

To this date, the traditionalists would have surely based their demands on the grounds that a university with a strong physical presence is the only one capable of producing the expected results. Most of us would have had to agree with them. Nonetheless, the corridors are starting to fill with rumors that analyses of early generations of virtual students have demonstrated a surprising and very real academic superiority over traditional students. I have no real proof of this, but the rumor could end up being true, since obtaining a degree through a virtual approach must surely require some very special motivation.

What would happen if, in the not too distant future, alumni of these virtual universities were considered to be the best? To begin with, we should remember that it is the professional quality of the graduate which really matters to the labor market and not the fact that he or she enjoyed the university years. Thus, if the business sector starts demanding graduates of virtual programs, well, students might need to go the virtual route, even if it means doing it hiding in the old classrooms.

Traditional faculties need not panic. Studying the "virtual way" requires plenty of individual assistance to students by faculty members. Thus such professors will not only be necessary, but also they could even have the opportunity to teach from the beach! Considering that a certain amount of interaction among students seems important, many traditional classrooms could still be used when converted into hotel rooms to house the virtual students for weeks at a time and provide them with some real physical contact.

Published in *El Universal*, Caracas, December 2004

P. S. Three brief additional comments about virtual universities

There is an ongoing debate about the Social Responsibility of universities, and sometimes a difference is made between private and public universities. As their communities could be somewhat different, should we need to think about special Social Responsibilities for the virtual universities?

Thinking of the many emigrants, I wonder whether their homelands should not be offering them and their children and their grandchildren basic Web courses on local subjects like their own history and geography, so that they can keep in touch and perhaps have an education that is still valid at home—an education that keeps their hearts there.

From a comment that a friend made about the elderly people liking the ambiance provided by universities, and knowing about demographic pressures, we could speculate that some of those perhaps emptied classrooms and dorms could also be transformed into luxurious retirement suites. This sounds though a bit depressing since the universities should foremost be for young people and not for the just *Young At Hearts*.

## Brief thoughts on Europe

### Hang in there, Europe!

For those who believe that the world needs Europe more than ever, the latest events are very disconcerting, not so much because of the no vote itself but more so because of the ensuing reactions. What a gloom! After the incredible advancements of a Europe over the last decades it is unbelievable how this little tripping up could create so much fuss. The vote on a messy, too voluminous, uninspiring and basically unreadable document was an as-good-as-it-gets opportunity to grunt a bit about la-bureaucracy, but now they allow the same bureaucrats to deflect this perfectly valid criticism by letting them equate it with a rejection of Europe. No, Europe! Pick yourself up! Just wrestle whatever Delacroix's flags are waved from the current bearers, and keep moving on. We will be cheering.

### Where do you circle your wagons?

The European "NO" is just one of those recurring and natural cries of no that human beings scream out whenever they feel threatened by change. At this moment, through the lenses of the environmental mess-up and the technological revolutions occurring, we already know that most of the drivers point toward a one-nation world and that the question of resisting it boils down only to where do you most effectively circle your wagons: at home, in your community, in your nation, or around your Europe? The smaller the circle, the more you can keep, for a while, before totally surrendering; the larger the circle, the less you can keep, but the more you can impose on whatever is left. Europe knows it, so don't confuse a rest-stop with a halt. Anyone doubting the forces in place will do well reflecting upon the fact that even the United States with all its money, arms, Hollywood, and Coca-Cola has not been able to stand against this tide and, according to some rumblings, has already lost its own Florida to Cubans.

### And then there is the Italian lira!

Some years ago when the euro was adopted I wrote that they were burning bridges, since the agreements did not include a single word about how to manage a breakup, and I also considered somewhat unorthodox the whole European scheme of creating a monetary union before having a political union. Today after witnessing the success of the euro, even after a somewhat shaky start, we are once again rudely reminded of all these doubts when an Italian minister starts talking about reintroducing the lira. It is understandable, though, that a beleaguered Italian minister could be looking enviously at how his Argentinean descendants got away with paying only thirty cents per dollar on their foreign debt. I wonder how many new liras per old euro that would be.

## Europe, you need electrical, not financial engineers (like me)

A couple of years ago when the hundred-year-old private electric utility company that served my hometown (a South American city) was taken over by an international player, it became within a short time leveraged up to its hilt in debt, and I suspect also poison pills and golden parachutes, and I knew we were heading into the wrong direction. When I now read about all the consolidations in Europe, which can only distance consumers from their day-to-day local electrical engineers and place their needs in some distant foreign trading rooms, I feel the same, although clearly, if Europe is now an all-of-the-same Europe, I could be wrong. What I do know, though, is that all those high valuations paid by financial wizards purchasing utilities will, sooner or later, need to be repaid by all those European electricity consumers who are currently living in blissful ignorance.

## Some spins on the US economy

I am an economist. I guess that the average person would think that I spend most of my time at the World Bank Group reviewing issues related to the state of the world's economy. Not so. Early in 1999, I remember publishing an article expressing concern with the almost one-billion-dollar-a-day commercial deficit of the United States. Since the federal government was then producing a surplus, the deficit had to be blamed on the growing indebtedness of the private sector. I thought it untenable and intolerable. Some five years later, the United States public sector had joined the private going into the red and the commercial deficit doubled to two billion dollars a year. Even worse, long-term United States interests were showing no signs of heading north. I as an economist felt at a loss to understand what was going on, much less to explain it. So I sort of withdrew a bit from it. I did right! Not only had I more time for many other interesting issues but also life was made more bearable as ignoring economics helped me to ignore the contradiction of working in an organization designed to increase the flows of money toward emerging and poor countries, during times marked by the immense flows to the wealthiest economy of the world, flows that allowed it to live over its means.

I don't have a clue where all this is going to end. Currencies since 1971 no longer provide even the wishy-washy cold comfort of being backed up with some gold discipline, and so we are all down to an "In God We Trust" mode of operation. I can certainly understand why faiths of all sorts are making a comeback.

Of course as an economist, "on the other hand," I know very well what the United States can do to start correcting its imbalances. Every dollar per gallon in gasoline tax would generate more than 100 billion dollars in new fiscal income, assist in reducing the commercial deficit, and provide some relief to the environment. Currently in the United States of America they do not even talk about this alternative, probably because their political leaders, like so many others in today's world, think of leading only in terms of following opinion polls. They will, though, sooner or later. Gasoline taxes in Europe hover around five and a half dollars per gallon while in the United States they are currently only about fifty cents per gallon, so you can really say that the United States possesses a higher reserve of exploitable fiscal corrective instruments than Europe. Sometimes we need to measure the strength of a country not so much in terms of how strong it is but how strong it can be with little corrections.

But why worry so much about the United States economy? Well, coming from a developing country, I strongly believe that our best chances of doing well in today's difficult world come about when all other countries are doing well. As the United States of America is the foremost of all those other countries, we worry about it. I have never ever thought of developing in terms that require bringing someone else down, but always in terms of a win-win game, and I am not about to change now.

## A sensible country would raise tax on petrol, so what is US waiting for?

Sir, it is hard to understand the United States of America! It has a huge fiscal deficit; it has a huge current-account deficit; it is by far the world's biggest oil consumers both in absolute and in relative terms; now willing to explore for oil and gas in Alaska, it shows itself to be aware of the difficult energy outlook the world faces; it seems aware and resolute about the environmental problems (ignore the Alaska part) as it imposes other expensive environmental regulations, such as recycling—which, as no one likes to do it, requires the hiring of Salvadoreans; it speaks all over the place about having to reduce the vulnerabilities of its oil supplies.

As any other sensible country would, in similar circumstances, increase the taxes on petrol consumption and substantially help to solve all the above-mentioned problems; and as the US has always shown willingness to pull together as a nation, recently even to the extent of going to war on shaky grounds, the big question remains: why is it that the leaders of the US do not even want to talk about a substantial tax on petrol?

Published in *Financial Times*, April 2, 2005

\*\*\*

My personal editing note: Jim, you cannot imagine how much it hurts me to recommend increasing gasoline taxes in the United States after having fought for almost a decade now exactly against those taxes. I feel that I am unjustly discriminating against oil while allowing consumer countries to capture a great part of the worth of those resources that, as nonrenewable, are forever sacrificed by the oil-producing countries. Nonetheless, for many reasons the United States has to lower its exaggerate gasoline consumption, for the good of the world, and I guess that taxing it is the least harmful way to achieve it.

\*\*\*

### Is inflation really measuring inflation?

Sir, over the years, the Central Banks have grown a lot more independent, which is good, as long as it does not diminish their accountability and allow them to focus blindly on goals of their own choosing, monitor the results, and live for ever after happy in a big club of mutual admirers.

Inflation is the number one of those monsters that central bankers proudly show off as having been tamed but sometimes we must have our lingering doubts about whether it really is so. In an economy where whatever few savings we can set aside buy fewer and fewer assets like houses, it is sometimes hard to accept that there is no inflation, no matter how much central bankers tells us so.

As inflation is just the result of the formula, or the basket, or the sampling techniques that we use for measuring it and is therefore a truly incestuous economic concept, there might be very good reasons for revisiting the whole issue of what, how, and why we measure it, even if this means some new hard work load for our overburdened central bankers. With the world going through major changes, inflation, as we think we know it, might very well have degenerated into something quite different from what we initially had in mind when we first thought about how to measure it.

Meanwhile just to put some check on their egos, every time I see a central banker I urge him to take a shopping trip to the closest IKEA so as to see who really should get the credit for controlling inflation as we currently know it.

# My Venezuelan blend

Though I have most of my life been extremely and vociferously critical about how it has been and is governed, I love my beautiful homeland. Its great people both deserve much more and could give much more. It is not the intention of this book to enter into any dialogue about my country since, as most do, I prefer to wash my too dirty linen at home.

That said, and so you could just get a glimpse of my country of contradictions, let me tell you that even while social justice is preached, unfortunately more through a destructive and divisive debate than with constructive proposals, gasoline, the property of the state, is currently sold in Venezuela at about 10 United States cents a gallon. With that, around 4% of GDP is being transferred from the poorest citizens to the owners and users of cars. What about that! Is that socially sustainable development?

**A Proposal for a New Way of Congressional Elections**

Since, the expected value of a blind man throwing darts against a board on which are pasted the names of all stocks traded on Wall Street in order to pick an individual highly profitable stock is larger than the expected value of picking stocks by investing in the sage advice of an investment banker.

Since, in order to maximize the risk-minimizing benefits of diversification it is important that selection occur as randomly as possible so as to avoid systemic risks.

Since, it is to no one's benefit that members of congress, in order to be elected, should need to invest in building up relationships of dependence that later create those conflicts of interest that favor decisions that could be harmful to the national interest.

Since, a limited duration of each congressional term could stimulate the members to do the best they can during their brief tenure.

Since, it is to no one's benefit that political parties should invest so much of their scarce resources in having their members elected instead of in analyzing what they are supposed to do when elected.

Since, the Venezuelans by so ardently playing all type of lotteries have evidenced sufficiently their faith in Lady Luck as a means for personal improvement.

*The Congress hereby decrees:*

*Art. 1—Of Congress.* Congress is composed of 240 members who are elected for a six-year term. Every 5th of July (Venezuela's Day of Independence) forty (40) of its members will be retired and their substitutes elected.

*Art. 2—Of the Election of Members of Congress.* The election of the new members of Congress will be done by way of a lottery among all Venezuelans who have completed high school and who have expressed publicly their desire to participate in and to serve the nation as a Member of Congress.

*Art. 3—Of political identification.* After the elections any elected member is free to align himself or herself with any political movement.

*Art. 4—Final.* Congress will, through time, be allowed to

raise the education bar for access to the lottery but besides this limited human intervention, the system is always to assure in the random selection the good of the nation, through the innocent hand of God.

Extract from "Democracy Venezuelan Style" published in *The Daily Journal*, Caracas, December 10, 1999

### Let's all whakapohane!

I remember having read about how the Maori people of New Zealand protested when something bothered them. Their method consisted in lining up a group of Maori tribesmen, turning their backs towards the person or persons that are the target of the protest, dropping their trousers and showing them their naked backsides. This rite is named whakapohane.

Without delving further into this tradition and in spite of the fact that it seems primitive and is most certainly an ugly spectacle, I think it could be also classified as a civilized and most efficient way to protest. Civilized because it does no damage to anyone or anything (except to those people with a well-developed sense of esthetics) and efficient because it manages to consolidate into one single act and gesture all the meaning that we could possibly assign to a real social sanction.

There is no doubt that we are often frustrated at not being able to find a way to protest vehemently about the stupid, naive, and criminal behavior that negatively affects our country—and so the idea of putting together a group of citizens, family men, professionals and white-collar workers with briefcases and ties, heading out to the street to whakapohane shamelessly is appealing. Let me list some worthy causes to be whakapohaned:

The International Monetary Fund (IMF)—because of its insistence that we should give our governments even more income through taxes, even though we Venezuelans hand over to them all our oil income, and especially even though it has been demonstrated beyond any reasonable doubt that our governments are totally inept at putting it to any good use.

Those bank regulators who believe that the only mission of a bank is not to fail and who therefore continue to tighten the screws on its financial solvency without caring an iota about its real purpose.

Those national authorities who know how much damage the sloshing of short-term capital flows can cause to a small country and still don't bother to take the 48 hours required simply to copy quite functional legislation from Chile and enact it in Venezuela.

Our Venezuela's national oil company when, instead of investing scarce resources in increasing production capacity, it invests them in projects of utterly low significance such as expanding the capacity of their gasoline stations to sell snacks and in advertising so that Venezuelans buy Venezuelan oil.

All those illustrious representatives of the private sector who applauded the privatization of CANTV (telephone company) without realizing that it was all an elaborate trick perpetrated by the government to collect taxes in advance, which we now have to cover through exaggerated service charges.

All those die-hard defenders of free trade who simply do not understand that in a globalized world economy each country must, when the chips are down, still find a way to guarantee itself a minimum internal level of employment.

Finally, the entire political and economic system that is based on centralized income and decentralized apparatchiks unable to come up with some real solutions to our real problems. Members of this system who have not been able to come up with a real solution to our problems should all be given the Mother of all Whakapohanes.

We have heard that one of the people most clearly and widely questioned in our recent history is due to return to Venezuela after statutes of limitations have expired. Just imagine what a marvelous message a small delegation of our "notables" dispatched down to Maiquetía (Caracas' airport) to receive that person with a mini-whakapohane would send.

We should not discard lightly the possibility of introducing an ancestral aboriginal custom from New Zealand into the Venezuelan political scene. WHAKAPOHANERS OF THE WORLD, UNITE! The alternatives are much worse. [Jim, my editor: "To paraphrase Churchill, Better whak, whak, whak than war, war, war."]

Extract from *The Daily Journal*, Caracas, July 2, 1998

### We enjoyed

Early 1983, after Venezuela's defaulted on servicing its foreign public debt, I remember some foreign bankers visiting me. They had until quite recently been praising the country and doing their utmost to sell their unneeded credits to earn their commissions and now they were all complaining in rage. "You mismanaged, you wasted all the resources we lent you. Have you no shame?" And on and on they went. After I while, I got fed up and told them: "Sorry gentlemen. We did not mismanage or waste the resources you lent us. Let me guarantee you that we Venezuelans, we truly enjoyed them." Thereafter blissful tranquility reigned.

\*\*\*

Also coming from Venezuela I know that readers would expect me to say something at least about the very controversial Hugo Chavez and, in this respect, perhaps the best I can do is to include the following two articles.

### Hugo, the Revolution, and I

When I see our industrial cemetery where because of a stupidly negotiated trade deal and stupid foreign-exchange policies so many Venezuelan illusions lie with nothing else to show for except more unemployment, I know that Hugo and I wish for a revolution.

When I see that the United States places an effective 60% protective duty on orange-juice concentrate and allows importing only the absolute best quality, while Venezuela applies only a 20% duty, and is drowned in imports of the worst-quality leftovers, and thereby sentences our orange groves to death, I know that Hugo and I wish for a revolution.

When I see our country sign treaties on intellectual-property rights that oblige us to respect what amounts to renewable sources of income of the developed world, while we only get 25 dollars for sacrificing our nonrenewable barrel of oil, though in some places the consumer pays the equivalent of 150 dollars per barrel because of the local gasoline taxes, I know that Hugo and I wish for a revolution.

When I see the very unjust income distribution in my country, the horrendous inefficiencies of our fiscal spending, and see how the efforts to collect income taxes are abandoned for sales and other indirect taxes just because they are easier to collect, I know that Hugo and I wish for a revolution.

When with bad conscience, I reflect on how through decades we have kept silence about a lousy education system and about the obscene and violent programs through which our TV channels indoctrinate our youth, I know that Hugo and I wish for a revolution.

When I see my Venezuela submerged in anarchy without any authorities capable of or willing to control the small percentage of abusers, I know that Hugo and I wish for a revolution.

But when Hugo calls his revolution a daughter of the Chinese or the Cuban revolution, I also know quite well that Hugo and I don't speak of the same revolution.

My revolution would pursue only the humble goals of providing a decent and good government for the Venezuelans, and of seeing that, if it makes mistakes, it would assure that these would at least occur while trying to favor our country. My revolution would gladly welcome the foreign investor, but would be happy only when it manages to retain the Venezuelan investor. In my revolution—except for strengthening the OPEC by extending it to gas and inviting new members—achieving a pragmatic solidification of the Colombia-Venezuela relations, and working toward a rational environmental solidarity with the world, we would not have resources or time to spend on any other geopolitical considerations.

Even though I feel that selling Cuba some 53 thousand barrels of oil per day in too generous conditions is a venial sin compared to the not-so-long-ago proposals of selling 5 million barrels to the world at only 7 dollars a barrel, the fact is that as long as a Venezuelan dies of hunger, does not get a good education or a decent health service, my revolution would not give anything to anyone, except of course for what could be expected from human solidarity in emergencies like tsunamis and hurricanes.

Hugo has an amazing talent to communicate pedagogically Venezuelan messages to our nation and, in this respect, for those who believe that the future requires building many bridges of understanding he is an extremely valuable asset. Therefore, anyone who has access to Hugo, please beg of him not to waste his talent talking to his "Sovereign People" in Chinese with a Cuban accent.

From *El Universal*, Caracas, April 26, 2001

## April 11-13, 2002

On the 11th of April 2002, there was a big antigovernment rally that degenerated in a lot of confusion in which some Venezuelans died, and Chavez lost effective control of the government. After some of the most inept political handling ever seen in history by some who pretentiously took themselves to act in the name of the opposition, with equal confusion but luckily, I believe, with no additional deaths, Chavez returned to govern on April 13th. There is still a lot of discussion of what happened during these three days, but the following is what I published on April 16.

## Chavez's new opportunity

I have frequently been identified as a Chavista since I have written some opinions that sounded similar to some of the voices of the government. Quite the contrary, as I have also written many pieces against the government, others have frequently called me anti-Chavista. That is the risk which all of us nonpoliticians take who swim in the currents of the current turbulent waters, refusing the safety of any shore although we thereby risk drowning.

Even though on April 11th I felt somewhat nervous about being confounded with the darkest forces of opposition, tranquilized by so many known faces of friends and good persons, I participated in the march that asked for the resignation of Hugo Chavez. I did so out of inner conviction and not only to keep a watchful eye on my wife. My reasons for it are spelled out in an article which I wrote during the election campaign of 1998 when Chavez ran for the presidency, in which I said that one of the qualities I would like to see in my next president was the ability to evaluate his own performance, and, if it did not stand up to what he had promised, that he should have the courage and decency to resign, saving us from painful delays in the development of our country.

Chavez, however much blame he can with some justification assign the opposition, must know that at his first turn at the bat, he did not even see the ball and should be sent to the showers. Had he been a pupil of his father, he would certainly have flunked his school year. History, initially more severe, searched for his expulsion but then decided to give him another chance. Today it depends on him alone whether he wants to use this gift to go down as beneficial in our history books, or whether he will be satisfied with having his boots licked. As a Venezuelan, I cannot wish but that he bats a home run or graduates summa cum laude.

What advice could we give him? His parents, who surely must wish him the best, would probably tell him: "Son, beware of the bad company who drag you down and look for the good company that can pull you up!" Although it is clearly up to Chavez to pick his own company, as a concerned citizen I allow myself to give him some advice. Since there is nothing to be done if he is unable to identify those who are clearly just crooks, I will limit my advice to the more difficult case of the apparently capable government officials-to-be.

One of the first things that create affinity between persons is shared concerns and worries. In this respect, Venezuela, no doubt has a lot to be shared. Nonetheless, the fact that someone is perfectly able to identify how things should not be done, unfortunately does not imply at all that this person has any idea about how things should be done. In this respect, during Chavez's initial turn at governing, he hurt himself by appointing many well-intentioned officials who, although they might even have been able to do a great job auditing the expenses of a condominium, nonetheless plainly were not capable of planning the future of a country, much less of making such plans happen.

Hugo Chavez, be grateful for your second opportunity and give yourself the opportunity to do it well. If not God and your Nation will hold you responsible for it.

From *El Universal*, Caracas, April 16, 2002

### To the *opposition*

Having republished here some of my messages to President Chavez of Venezuela (they went unheeded, of course), the least I could do here is to recapitulate briefly some of my messages to the utterly frustrated and somewhat amorphous body known in Venezuela as the opposition. In fact, if there is any real victory that Chavez can show off to his followers until now, it is how he has the opposition confused and on the run. Truth be told, most of the time when the opposition have opened their mouths in the past, they have turned into the glue that holds Chavez' also amorphous body of followers together. I guess that Chavez' role in their defeat was that of assisting their political mass suicide. Well, here are some of my bullets to the current opposition.

- Every waking moment, pluck a daisy and count a good Chavez follower…a bad Chavez follower…a good…and so on. Otherwise, how will you be able to split Chavez' followers? Stop throwing them into the same sack where they unite.
- Don't worry an iota about unity that comes with time. For the time, worry about convincing the others. Do not choose the candidates you like the most, choose the candidates the other side dislikes the least.
- You don't have a chance to get power (or if it happens to hang onto it) unless you really know what to do with it. Do not attack Chavez for his intentions and declared purposes; attack him because his results are unacceptably bad, given the importance of those purposes.
- No matter what, accept that Chavez has turned into a mythological godlike figure for about 20% of the country. You do not build a future by deposing the god of 20% of your fellow countrymen. And so never attack him in person, since, if he is to be deposed, that should be for his followers to do, in due time.
- In all, stop worrying about your own unity and start worrying about the country's unity!

Finally perhaps the opposition would do well reading Steve Denning's books on the importance of storytelling, so as to learn how to communicate. In Denning's promotion of his last book, *The Leader's Guide to Storytelling*, April 2005, Jossey Bass, I heard him point out the importance of storytelling by mentioning that 14% of USA's GDP came from that source. To me, much more indisputable evidence is how an immense group of highly educated people do not stand a chance against a really good storyteller, like Chavez, who likes to tell stories on TV, for five hours, every Sunday, and also whenever else he gets a chance.

About three years ago, I saw on Venezuelan TV a colored girl describing how when she had met Chavez she had warned him not to embrace her since she was quite dirty and did not smell good. She went on to say that Chavez, on the contrary, had hugged her even more, saying "Negra, how could I not embrace you? You are the reason I am here." The girl concluded, "I would die for him." Most members of the opposition, blinded by their disgust with Chavez, have not yet even begun to understand how formidable their own opposition really is.

What will happen? Well sooner or later, the real concerns for the people that Chavez has expressed, and that are not for me to doubt, plus his very powerful storytelling, have to be backed up with real and concrete results. If these continue to be missing in action, well, as they say, something's gotta give.

## Synthesizing my current messages to my fellow countrymen

Finally and in addition to much of what is already included, the following brief messages synthesize most of my current views to my countrymen.

### Simón Bolívar

Like all Venezuelans, I do admire Simón Bolívar. He helped us get our independence in order to allow our Venezuela to be a great nation among the great and the included. That is why I am saddened to see how his name now is being misused to disconnect us from the world, just to capture some leadership among the small and excluded, for no reasonable purpose whatsoever.

### Venezuela's crime

Burning bridges instead of building them—and of this, all too many are guilty.

### Venezuela's role in the world

The world is turning very small, and humanity needs

urgently to find new ways how to live together. I think that Venezuela and its people could contribute very much to create those huge portals to the future through which even the currently excluded need and could go, and so it saddens me see them wasting their time painting small emergency doors of the past.

### What does it need most?

Since the only reasonable means to defend some of the value of the nonrenewable and finite resource of oil so as to avoid its falling to the marginal cost of extraction seems to be through OPEC, this implies that the industry needs to be state-owned. Unfortunately, having the oil income going directly to the state coffers only strengthens the stranglehold of politicians over the country. That in turn has, does, and always will result in imposingly omnipotent, incompetent, and impotent governments. In this respect, what Venezuela most needs is for a substantial part of that oil income to go directly to its citizens, perhaps through education and healthcare vouchers.

### Lack of alternatives

Well, you might know me by now. Listening to so many complaints from the opposition about their lack of candidates, I just could not resist suggesting the launch of a political version of a "Venezuelan Idol" to give some new faces the chance to break through the walls that traditional politicians have built up to keep them in place. Since politics anyhow seems mostly to be about media coverage, there should be nothing wrong with it.

But, at the end of the day, if we truly want leaders, they will appear, sooner or later, but, if we are willing to settle for "caudillos," well that's all we'll get.

## 167-to-0 — a postscript

On December 4, 2005, elections for congress were held in Venezuela. Although everyone is aware that it is a country where opinions are highly divided, the result was that 167 representatives who favor the government of Hugo Chávez were elected, and none, zero, zilch, of who differ with him. There are many explanations for these results, including the fact that most of the opposition withdrew their candidacies in protest a couple of days before the election but, at the end of the day, they are all irrelevant since a 167-to-0 ratio is plainly not acceptable. Just as Democrats would not stand for a United States Congress made up of 100% of Republicans, and just as Republicans would not stand for a Congress made up of 100% Democrats, this principle is just as true in Venezuela.

With these election results, and with the governments accepting them as legitimate and not doing anything about them, any of us who believe in liberty have no other choice now but to make our protests heard, even if this is with a tiny and only slightly noisy voice.

The following are the first two comments I wrote for the press outside Venezuela. I hope they will get published.

### What is the financial world to do with Venezuela?

Sir, In Venezuela, as in most other countries, Congress is supposed to exercise control over the executive branch. For instance, its Constitution establishes that 'No contract in the municipal, state or national public interest s determined shall be entered into with foreign states or official entities, or with companies not domiciled in Venezuela, or transferred to any of the same, without the approval of the National Assembly.'

Now, even though Venezuela is currently known as a very polarized nation, the fact is that after the elections of December 4, 2005, its Congress includes 167 members who are in favor of and obedient to him who wishes to be called 'Commander', and 0 representation for those many who are not in the least in agreement with Chávez's confused ramblings of his vision of a twenty-first-century socialism. This indeed poses some serious questions about its legitimacy and therefore some serious challenges for those who issue opinions.

For instance, what are legal counselors or credit-rating agencies to do after they might receive a letter from a Venezuelan citizen (or perhaps even read this letter in FT) informing them that sooner or later the debts now contracted by Venezuela might be questioned as 'odious debt', as they are not duly approved by a legitimate congress (167-0), nor are they needed, as can be evidenced by the many donations Venezuela, with its own so many very poor, has recently made, among them, to the relatively few somewhat poor of Massachusetts.

Sir, if a company like Nike has to worry about the labor conditions in the factories to which they outsource their production, why should the financial world be allowed to ignore civil representation issues in those countries it helps to finance?

## Massachusetts, please show some dignity!

Late in 1998, the price of a barrel of oil fell under 7 US$, but we never heard anyone volunteering to help out Venezuela's poor. In December 1999, Venezuela suffered some horrendous mudslides, but, when the US sent some well-equipped engineer corps to help out, Hugo Chávez, the president of Venezuela, refused them. Massachusetts has a yearly per capita income of US$ 41,801, while Venezuela has slightly less than a tenth of that, US$ 4.020

The ad in which Citgo, the oil company in the United States owned by PDVSA, the Venezuelan state owned oil company, announces the program shows a picture of a large, two-story, typical Massachusetts detached house, with a small garden and a big tree in front, beautifully decorated with what looks like Christmas ornaments, and a completely lit up porch. Please compare that house with our shanty towns in

Venezuela. Of course it is a wrongly chosen photo, and your Massachusetts poor do live in bad conditions, but, in fact, that they were not even able to choose the right picture just adds salt to our national injury.

The same ad, spelling out the partnership between PDVSA and the government of Hugo Chávez, ends with the statement: "The fuel assistance program isn't about politics. It's about offering humanitarian aid to those who need it. What could be more American than that?" The radical leftist Noam Chomsky recently described this as "one of the more ironic gestures ever in the North-South dialogue," but I, as a Venezuelan, can only classify it as a gesture of utmost cynical insolence.

Many Venezuelans are upset with Chávez giving away money all over the world, while our own country has so many very much poorer people but, currently at least, there is very little we can do about it and much less so after the elections for congress held on December 4, 2005. Although everyone knows that Venezuela is a country where opinions are highly divided, the result was that 167 representatives who favor the government of Hugo Chávez were elected, and none, zero, zilch, of who differ with him. There are many explanations for these results, but, at the end of the day, they are all irrelevant since a 167-to-0 ratio is plainly not acceptable. Hey, even Mugabe in Zimbabwe has a 107 to 43 to show for multiparty democracy there.

In these circumstances, I wonder, would it be too much to ask for some dignity in Massachusetts? Do you really take any gifts from anyone? Where is the limit?

## Colombia & Venezuela

Yes we are a true Knowledge Bank, but this does not mean that sometimes we are not completely lost. When two neighboring countries such as Colombia and Venezuela have their destinies and economies handled by two different regional areas, things are bound to go wrong. In one of the

Country Assistance Strategy sessions, there was no reference at all to the neighbor, except in the maps in the appendix, and, in the other CAS, the relations were explicitly described as insignificant. Goes to show...This reminded me of an English Merchant Bank, that symbol of global knowledge, which wanted to pull out its chaps from Buenos Aires, urgently, when their officials heard about some hostage taking in Bogotá.

That the Colombia-Venezuela nexus is so ignored is tragic to me. I believe that nowhere in the world could you ever find two countries that could benefit so much from total integration as Venezuela and Colombia. While together they could dream about greatness and actually find their path in this difficult world, separate they are lost and bewildered.

# My Farewell Speech on October 28, 2004

We frequently hear the World Bank being compared to a big oil tanker: slow to turn. And this might be a very appropriate imagery for management and most of staff. I also believe that some of our country officers do operate their units more as small flexible merchant vessels, something with which I myself identify a lot, since I was a sailor on a merchant boat, almost 40 years ago.

But, colleagues, for us the Board, let us confess that the Bank is just one extremely luxurious Cruise Ship, a real *Queen Elizabeth II* and who doesn't love a Cruise? I definitely do. An absolutely Great Captain (a Master and Commander, both technically and socially), extremely professional Officers, plus an extraordinary crew of thousands of dedicated Sailors, all working to make us feel good. The facilities are beautiful, the food is excellent, the support units are superb, the entertainment with so many interesting conferences and learn-how-to-do-it seminars is outstanding, and, even our shore visits—or ED's trips, as they are called in World Bank jargon—live up to the absolutely best industry standards. If we are forced to find fault, perhaps it would be about being a bit stingy on ballroom dancing.

And so, who would like to leave a Cruise Ship like this? I guess absolutely nobody, unless something tells him that he should go back to the real world, while he can and before it is too late.

Do not get me wrong. Although I in jest compare us to passengers on a Cruise Liner, we all are keenly aware that our mission is totally different from that of a joyful and relaxing trip. Nonetheless, given how the world operates—which might very well be how it always has and how it always will operate—I do not find any reasons to be ashamed about the contradiction between our noble mission of fighting poverty and the luxurious quality of the instruments at our disposal. However, I must admit that eating fish and chips with Christophle flatware might raise some eyebrows.

No, the reason I put forward the Cruise Line simile has more to do with the issue that being aboard, out there on the high seas, we might be talking too much to one another and, therefore, running the risk of losing perspective about the real world, and running out of creativity, power, and willingness to question.

Everyone, when the time has come to go ashore again, needs to think back a little about how he paid for his journey, and what he could have done better. I myself, thinking in retrospect, can say that I focused exaggeratedly though insufficiently, among other things, on the following:

1. Scaling-up IFC (by urging us and the shareholders we represent to put our money where our mouth is);

2. Abhorring "Debt Sustainability" frameworks (you should only award credits because they are going to be useful, never because they are just "sustainable");

3. Promoting the use of Country Systems (safeguards, procurement, operational procedures. Well, you already know my argument about learning how to ride a bike);

4. Preaching for transparency (information should be

timely and understandable), fighting corruption at all levels and supporting INT;

5. Fighting Basel (banking regulation should not solely focus on how to avoid crisis and bank failures, it also needs to promote credit and access to capital to foster growth);

6. Questioning MIGA (enough said);

7. Opening our eyes and those of our shareholders regarding the Bank's trade agenda: the fact is that there is much economic life beyond agriculture and manufacturing (for example, in services. You also know my ideas about bilingual training of people—nurses, for instance—or building senior citizen's retirement homes for the citizens of the developed countries in the emerging markets, and many more); and

8. The "Voice Issue", where I have fought not only for the developing countries, but for everyone's voice, by stressing the issue of the effectiveness of our Board and more work at the level of Committees. Even Plácido Domingo's voice would be heard neither in the desert nor in a Knick's NBA final minutes at Madison Square Garden.

I wish also to recall all the sessions of the Audit Committee, where under the able guidance of Mr. Pierre Duquesne and the interaction with my own colleagues, I hope we produced real advances in corporate well-behavior (like forcing our superb professionals in the Bank's financial complex to refrain from believing too much in their own extreme professional models).

Since most of you are outstanding professionals who come from the public sector, you make of the Board a very competitive environment when it comes to making special individual contributions. This is made even harder by the fact that you receive so many instructions directly from your capitals. However, in my case—since most of my professional experience comes from working in the private sector and, as a "radical of the middle" or an "extremist of the center," I am more or less free from political compromises—I have been extremely lucky in being cast as that innocent little boy who can shout out things like "the-emperor-is-naked" on so many issues.

Friends, I truly feel you have all been extremely generous and patient when interacting with me, and I sincerely thank you all for that, as I also thank my wife and daughters, and they also thank you, too.

I also want to thank our Home Port Authorities, the United States, represented by Carole Brookins and Bob Holland, for all the generosity and friendship extended to me and my family.

But NO Cruise could have been good if you had the wrong company in your private quarters. In this respect I have been blessed by the best company possible.

First, I would like to thank Liliana, Violeta ("Viole"), Carmen, and Teresa on how they managed me, and a special mention should go to Elisa Olmeda—our temporary research consultant—for all her support.

On Central American affairs, I had the incredible support of Roberto Simán, Jorge Wong-Valle, and Carmen María Madriz ("Cami").

With México—and also helping out as my in-house editor—I was assisted by my young and brilliant dear friend Francisco Castro-y-Ortíz (you all know him well, "Paco"). With Spain, through continuous discussions about who discovered whom—they insist on Columbus shouting out "Land Ahoy!" while I adhere to the hypothesis originated by Mr. Jose Ignacio Cabruja that it was in fact the wise Indian Guacaipuro who shouted out first "Ship arriving!"—I could not have been better assisted than by María Dolores Loureda ("Mariló"), María Teresa Tello ("Maité"), Galo Herrero, and, of course, my excellent Alternate, María Jesús Fernández, upon whom, with closed eyes, I entrusted 100% of our representation in the Personnel Committee.

A very special thanks should also go to my fellow Venezuelan, José Machillanda ("Pepe"), as I know that without his generous assistance in keeping my homeland Venezuela in the loop, this Cruise, independently of the ship's great stabilizers, could have rolled just a little bit too much, even for an old sailor like myself.

Finally, what could I have done better? As I am now thinking about writing a book—and you have already seen a big part of it in my informal e-mails and op-eds in Latin American newspapers—the only thing I regret is that I did not think to do it before, and so I could have informed you about it from the very beginning. I am sure that if you had in your mind something telling you "he is writing a book," I could have had a more powerful voice-strengthening instrument.

Dear Friends, see you on shore, but with due respect to our code of ethics, feel free to invite me on a weekend cruise.

God bless you all,

Per

# Did the Minister do right?

I recently ended my two years as an ED in The World Bank Group in representation of Venezuela and seven other countries. Even though it sounds strange, I was nominated for that job through a process that initiated in a chat box on the Web (Foro Nacional) where the then Minister of Planning, Mr. Felipe Pérez, asked for candidates.

I, as a born optimist, sent the Minister my curriculum vitae reminding him in clear terms that I had no experience in the public sector; that I was fiercely independent, "a radical of the middle or an extremist of the center," and that I had no interest at all in going to Washington if that meant silencing my own voice. But, if the government could live with all that, I felt myself both capable and honored to represent my country.

As I had met the Minister only briefly, once when he invited me to give a conference in IESA about the taxes charged on gasoline in the consuming countries, I did not harbor any major expectations, and, in fact, I forgot all about it. One month later, out of the blue, the minister calls me on my cell phone, and informs me I had been nominated.

The nomination of an Executive Director, politically independent, from the private sector, with no public-service trajectory, and picked on the Web, did also surprise the World Bank, and therefore the question posed by the article's title. Its answer is not easy.

First. Was my election simply an accident, a craze of the moment never to occur again, or was it just the tip of the iceberg of a new way. If an accident, I was just lucky, but, in fact, the new technological advances are pointing toward new forms of government. In the future, instead of governing by polling opinions, we could have daily referenda, with all citizens, at zero costs, for good or bad. In this sense, as Mr. Perez seems to be a person who believes a lot in the revolutionary power of transparency, my selection could have been a precursor, and the Minister a prophet. Even though I harbor many doubts about where so much transparency could take us, intuitively I support it as such advances seem to be an important evolution of our society.

Second. Of an ED in the World Bank it is expected that he represents, simultaneously, both the interests of his constituency and the interests of the Bank, as an institution. And that balancing act is not easy. In this respect, the question is whether someone with my characteristics could walk the rope. Though clearly someone from the public sector and appointed for political reasons should be much better positioned to represent the short-term interests of the current governments, a free agent like me, inasmuch as he can provide new perspectives on issues, could also turn out to be useful, both for the institutions as well as for the country.

Subjectively, I have no doubt that the Minister did splendidly. I have had an incredible experience and I believe that I have served well the interests of my beloved Venezuela, of the other brother countries I represented, of The World Bank Group and of that whole little planet earth where we are all stuck on. And so…Thank you, Felipe!

To be published at some future date in *El Universal*, Caracas

# And now what?

the reader should be able to imagine by now, I have many things I would like to do in many places. Of course I would like to go back to my Venezuela, where I still have my home, most of my family, many friends, and, I hope, still, some of my old clients, but, for many reasons, that might not be in the works yet.

Whether in Venezuela, Washington, or some other place, the fields in which I would most like to work are those new services that could be offered by poor, developing countries to the world—like retirement homes, health services (certified bilingual nurses), and environmental protection In fact it's all there in my brief chapter about cross-border services and emigration.

All these areas that present so many interesting challenges and that could create so many win-win opportunities for the world could benefit exactly from the help and assistance which the World Bank Group has to offer.

For instance, as the elderly seem to be especially exposed to frauds and there is a special need for developing projects that meet very high corporate-governance standards and can count on strong institutional support from governments, this situation opens up a world of possibilities to launch innovative Public Private Partnerships (PPPs) where IFC clearly could play a truly catalytic role.

Prison services might initially sound a bit farfetched, but they also represent some very concrete possibilities. Just think of a modern prison, built by private investors in a Central American country, managed by a private, qualified, and experienced prison operator from the United States, that would provide well-defined prison services at a much lower cost to many of the states in the United States, especially ones that already have a large number of inmates originally from Central America. It could provide good job opportunities as jailers for many poor Central Americans; it might perhaps shame their governments into providing more decent conditions for their own prisoners; and after forty years it would be handed over free to the host country. All this sounds to me like a very clear win-win cross-border PPP.

Another book? Forget it! Too much grinding! I'll stick to articles. You sweat a lot but at least you get them over fast. Now, nonetheless, if anyone would pay me handsomely to investigate and write a book about how on earth Argentina managed to negotiate its debt-restructuring deal, I could be tempted. I did not have time to follow that process too far, but I remember going to sleep with the *Financial Times* declaring the odds for Argentina to achieve its goals very low, and waking up to the fact that Argentina had surpassed those very goals, after all. What happened? What are the implications? Yes, it is a tempting topic!

And if all initial plans fall apart, and my spoken voice is not welcomed anywhere, I guess I could always do a career change and push my other voice, recording a "Much Noise and hopefully little Voice." I could tour among friends...of course with Mercedes as my full time sound engineer.

# The President's succession

## My thoughts on the issue

Having voiced so much opinion on so many issues, it would be strange to be silent on the question of who is going to replace Mr. Jim Wolfensohn as President of the World Bank Group. And so here I go again, with a short post script.

Mr. Wolfensohn is or was definitely a class act, if anything, perhaps a bit too classy. In the Board we saw fairly little of him, although I never doubted that he was using his time much more effectively than being with us. Come to think of it, at the Board we were kept so busy that in fact we did not have much time to be with him either. Therefore you should be warned that my following comment might not be based on as much insider knowledge as one could believe…and besides I could anyhow be totally wrong.

From what I saw, heard, and read of JW's years, he definitively proved to all of us that the World Bank Group needs a top-notch traveling ambassador. But while doing so, he also turned into a living proof that a generous soul, which you have to be if you are really going to stand a chance as an ambassador to convince the world of helping out, will get into trouble prioritizing, if he does not count with a tight and effective back-office manager.

Therefore, instead of asking just one person to replace Wolfensohn, poor soul, we should perhaps be thinking of splitting up the position in two. For instance into one Chairman of the Board and one Executive President.

But if we split it up, is it a north-north affair or is there room for south too? As the Ambassador will surely need to play the good cop, who would want to be the bad? And at the end of the day, who will really control the Bank, he who is chummy with the world, or he who controls the house? Will they get paid the same? Who plays the harmonica and who plays the cello? Oh Boy!

Nonetheless I am confident that the Executive Directors, my dear ex-colleagues, will know what to do about all that. Good luck!

### The OK Corral and the World Bank

Jeffrey Sachs in his Op-Ed "It is time to free the World Bank," *Financial Times*, March 22, 2005, calls for an OK Corral type of showdown to decide whether the guy in the black hat or the one in white should be managing the Bank after Jim Wolfensohn, a man of many hats, steps down. Sachs has four criteria to pick his hero.

The first is whether he (or she?) full-heartedly supports the Millennium Development Goals. If the answer is yes, ask him the next question, even though only a very small minority of the world's population has even an inkling of what these goals are.

Second, the Sachs candidate has to endorse actively the target that developed nations dedicate 0.7% of their GNP to official development assistance. Frankly, I cannot imagine even someone wearing the blackest of hats so evil as to refuse on paper this modest sum.

Third, the gunslinger has to make clear where he stands with respect to the market ideologies that want to privatize public health, infrastructure and education or, on the other hand, the acceptance that increased public finance is essential for these sectors. Here Sachs has lost me, as I believe that this is not a question of either-or, but that the world needs both. That is why there has been so much talk of public-private partnership lately.

Finally Sachs expects his candidate to support a bigger voice and vote for developing countries in the World Bank and the International Monetary Fund: very nicely said, no objection raised. However, at the end of the day, the real needs of the developing countries are development itself and a voice not just in the banks but in the World-at-Large...which is really where it counts.

I frequently agree with much of Jeffrey Sachs' thoughts, but, in this case, perhaps whom the world in general needs in the World Bank, is someone who wears a grey hat and is willing to speak and listen to everyone. Come to think of it, the developing world might be better of knowing that they are speaking with a guy in a black hat rather than kidding themselves about what might turn out to be an artificial white hat, or a white hat that will turn black from today's global dusty winds. Come to think of it, if the black hat wins the duel, the first thing he needs to do is to get the white hat.

And now that he's been elected, the following are the recommendations he would receive from this Ex-ED. (Come to think of it, should I perhaps change my name to Kurowolfski?)

## A letter to an another new American World Bank President
Dear Mr. Wolfowitz:

The world might soon come to face a serious energy and environmental crisis exactly when there could be severe financial constraints as the United States looks to regain fiscal and current-account equilibrium. At that moment, if the world is to avoid a conflict-trap, we need political decision making to escape its local confines and go global, before it runs out of money, resources, time and willingness.

From this perspective, maybe we have already missed the boat. Maybe it is too late to provide development through our traditional instruments and programs. Maybe now we just need to scramble for survival. To do so will as a minimum require identifying new sources of growth, since the reading of current development strategies of individual countries makes one think of the If It's Tuesday, This Must Be Belgium line: it is very hard to tell them apart.

Finding growth is not easy, but we might at least suggest two principles for those taking on the quest. The first is to look where there is a better chance of finding the source of growth. A review of global production over the last decades makes it clear that the importance of agriculture and manufacturing in the GNPs is going down while services go up. So, if development plans are developed without a priori shackling them to potential losers, some countries might stand a better chance of making it.

We already observe how the remittance flows from migrant workers in the service sector to the developing countries exceed foreign-aid flows and there are many other similar opportunities waiting to be mined, such as offering medical and old-age care at lower prices to the developed countries' otherwise financially unsustainable social-security systems.

Second, we must not worsen the emergency by panicking and setting up unreasonable timelines. As an example, perhaps the Millennium Development Goals (MDGs) help to focus attention on truly important issues, but by introducing a deadline, 2015, they could also be inducing everyone to run towards a final goal when in fact we cannot realistically even begin to dream of completion of development and poverty reduction.

The "brain drain" in the health sectors of sub-Saharan Africa illustrates the problem, as it is frequently presented as a major obstacle for reaching the MDG in 2015 while, without the distractions of a goal-line, it might instead be recognized as an opportunity to channel developing funds into schools for nurses and doctors. Educated nurses and doctors, even working abroad, might, if "heart drain" is avoided, return to their country, sooner or later, and provide it much more capacity and long-term sustainability than the continuance of foreign aid.

Also to find growth we need to make sure we are working with leaders who truly want to eradicate poverty in their country, no matter what it takes, and not with those leaders who somehow seem to thrive, financially or politically, just on accommodating poverty. No matter how much we should look for "sustainability," let us make certain that it is not poverty we sustain.

Finally, running out of money and time should hopefully inject a surge of adrenaline into our development institutions and that could foment the creativity needed now. Instead of advancing development, many of the current assistance programs seem designed only to make up for the lack of development...very virtuous, but not necessarily what the world needs or can afford.

# On some current books, a movie, and a future book

Venezuela had one of the best political and social and about anything writers ever, José Ignacio Cabrujas, and just the possibility of a comparison, might unconsciously have kept me from writing until two years after he had passed away. I still pray that a reprint of his does not appear the same day I publish one of my articles. In the same vein, while waiting for my editor to come back with the corrections and improvements for this book, I had the chance to read some splendid current books on the World Bank and other development issues, the ease and style of which might have very well have caused me to lose my courage had it not been for the continuously timely support of my editor. I wish to include some brief and clearly nonexhaustive remarks on some of these books.

### *The World's Banker* by **Sebastian Mallaby**

Subtitle: *A Story of Failed States, Financial Crises, and the Wealth and Poverty of Nations*, New York: The Penguin Press, 2004: This is a great book and I am truly glad that it did not appear before my two years as an Executive Director since Mallaby's very interesting and credible way of recounting history and his many convincing arguments could have quite seriously fogged my own lenses. By the way, I have heard some rumors to the effect that Jim Wolfensohn was not too pleased and, if true, I sincerely don't understand it. I sure wish someone would speak so nicely bad about me!

### *The End of Poverty* by Jeffrey Sachs

The Penguin Press, 2005. It's a great book where Sachs makes a compelling case for the need of much more development aid, and I liked it, although for some reasons I did not connect too much with it. Those reasons are probably my own. When that group of poor unnourished young boys in Africa did not even react when I threw them a ball, they made me understand that there was a basic horrendous kind of poverty that I was personally not able to deal with, even comprehend much less to help out with. That poverty requires much aid, many Mother Teresas, and plenty of dedication by development professionals, perhaps not to end poverty but at least to make it more bearable.

Really to end poverty for me has nothing to do with just getting people over the two-dollar-per-day trap. Rather, we need to rethink the whole strategy just as we need to do if we are ever going to have a chance to face our global challenges like those of the environment. To me poverty is not going to be ended through good-heartedness but through realizing the fact that this is a truly small planet where we all depend on each other and that there is no way we can isolate ourselves. I come from a country where when the public-education system started to fall into pieces, those who could afford it took refuge in private schools and now they are wondering why their well-educated kids are having difficulties getting along with the neighbors.

In his list of what things to do, Sachs includes the rescuing of the World Bank and strengthening the United Nations. Having seen how efficiently the WBG is managed given its size I would suggest that the UN could become much stronger on its own if it adapted some of the checks and balances of the WBG.

But yes, perhaps WBG needs to be reformed, perhaps by splitting it up into three parts. The first, to do the most basic development work that Sachs describes. A second part that is to work towards generating best practices for the ever more global issues and public goods in need of it…to have a chance of ending poverty. And, the third part, to be thrown out because, frankly, after 60 years, you are bound to accumulate a lot of what you don't need, but that is so hard getting rid of.

### *The Elusive Quest for Growth* by **William Russell Easterly**

Subtitle: An Economists' Adventures and Misadventures in the Tropics, Cambridge, Massachusetts: MIT Press, 2002: The Roman philosopher Seneca defined luck as the moment when preparation meets opportunity, and in this excellent book Easterly analyses some big-bang moments of development luck, and even extends the concept to include the possibility of unpreparedness meeting opportunity—for instance when not being held down by merely recent technology allows for a better use of the very latest.

The book makes a great case for PPPs Private Public Partnerships or, as one famous president of Venezuela would have put it, "It is not the private sector or the public sector but just the opposite." The book explains very well the need for developing the right incentives for development, although in doing so it might not emphasize sufficiently those other variables that help the sustainability of development, such as a reasonably equitable income distribution. Also, a book that discusses the benefits which development receives from "knowledge leakage" but also promotes strong intellectual-property rights as incentives must, obviously, enter into some contradictions. But, then again, with no contradictions, what would be the role of luck? The book is crystal clear about the destructive role of bad governments. When Easterly calls for banning the concept of a financial gap, I feel much at home with my arguments against debt-sustainability analysis. When the author writes, "Thinking about luck is good for the soul. It reminds us self-important analysts that we might just be totally witless about what's going on," I know that William Easterly is one of those rare Ph.D.s whom I could gladly consider inviting to my "Guaranteed Ph.D.-Free University."

### *The World Is Flat* by **Thomas L. Friedman**

Subtitle: A Brief History of the Twenty-First Century, New York: Farrar, Straus and Giroux, 2005. This is in all senses a great book, and perhaps its only weakness is that its fabulous title might perhaps be just a bit too clever for it, since, when reading it, I just felt that it proved that the world kept going round and round, faster and faster. As it is written from the perspective of a citizen of a developed country and with the clarity and objectivity that perhaps comes from having a return ticket home, it describes very accurately the growth potential that lies in having the developed and the undeveloped world complement each other. Unfortunately, when you, like me, come from a sandwich country where you need to think not only about how to become competitive with the developed world, but also how to survive in competition with the successful developing world, things are never that simple, and the future never seems to shine as bright.

### *The Pentagon's New Map* by **Thomas P. M. Barnett**

Subtitle: War and Peace in the Twenty-First Century, New York: G. P. Putnam's Sons, Berkley Books, 2004. It has been a long time since I made so many handwritten (oops) comments in a book that I almost needed to buy a new copy. Though on paper we should have little in common and though I do not agree with many of his conclusions, when Barnett writes that the world needs to go from describing "horrible futures to be prevented" to "a future worth creating," I just know that here is a brother-in-peaceful-arms. Barnett's world map separating a "Functioning Core" from a "Nonintegrating Gap" and his brainstorm ideas on how to go forward are extremely helpful to open up spaces for the constructive dialogues the world so urgently needs.

Since Barnett's book contains so many extremely important wake up calls directed to his fellow countrymen about how the USA is best to face their own and also very varied challenges of globalization, there is little one as a foreigner would like to comment, being it somewhat like overhearing a family debating their issues in intimacy. That said on some specifics related to this book, Barnett's chapter about the "Flow of People" evidences an open mind that were it to become part of the mainstream of USA thinking it would bode very well for the future and for the world.

On the other hand when commenting about energy Barnett, of course, does not seem to be able to shake himself loose from the prevailing status quo visions. Just as an example he repeats that "Developing economies use energy less efficiently than advanced ones, and truly poor societies are the most wasteful" and puts forward as evidence that an "economy like the United States can achieve one percent of growth in GDP while increasing its energy use less than one percent" while…"China, will—on average—grow its economy and energy use at roughly a one-to-one rate." This when talking about finite oil reserves is somewhat like totally ignoring in the desert the per capita consumption of water, allocating it to those who sweat the least when running, without even asking of why on earth they are running. Nonetheless, as I said before, Barnett will be at the forefront of looking out for just and livable solutions…as he clearly realizes it is in his own and in his descendants' best self interest.

Barnett's eye opening description of the Cold War nostalgia that lingers on in many Pentagon hearts caused me to react fast, and send out the following message: Friends, On July 13th 2005 the House Armed Services Committee held a hearing on the potential national-security implications in the possible merger of the China National Offshore Oil Corporation with Unocal Corporation. It is not my wish to qualify what was discussed. However, hearing so many arguments about the United States' own survival in terms of energy, rumors of cadres of spies, and fears of bad and conspiratorial intentions—all so eagerly and emotionally juggled around—I wish to advance the possibility that, as of this date, the Cold War is back in town. Take due note!

Finally a comment on the *Map* itself. In it, my Venezuela appears in the "gap" and although I couple of years ago I would have fought like crazy for a redefinition of its borders, unfortunately, recent events, oblige me to shut up, for a while at least.

### *And the Money kept Rolling In (and Out)* by Paul Blustein

Subtitle: Wall Street, the IMF, and the Bankrupting of Argentina, New York: Public Affairs, 2005. A must read for any blind believer in the possibilities of Debt Sustainability and of anyone interested in Argentina's recent rollercoaster, where it went from villain to golden poster boy and back to villain again—and all this in a few years. I find the book also quite relevant in terms of what it leaves out. First, there is very little analysis of how politicians can get a country indebted without anyone really being able to stop them, and, second, there is not a word related to the public foreign indebtedness that occurs when public services are privatized. On July 20, 2005, I read in the Financial Times that "The Argentine government this week made a triumphant return to the dollar denominated debt market only three and a half years after staging the largest default in world history...investors, led by foreign investment banks, oversubscribed the $500m offer by more than three times." I hummed, "when will they ever learn, when will they ever learn."

And so of course;

***Confessions of an Economic Hit Man* by John Perkins**
San Francisco: Berrett-Koehler Publishers, 2004. This book made it to The New York Times Bestseller List and after that anyone who has ever worked for WBG and other similar development institutions is now exposed to hear: "Daddy/Mommy, were you ever an Economic Hit Man? And, when you answer NO!, hear them ask: "Daddy/Mommy where've you been?

I found the lack of general protest to the book absolutely astonishing, and so I feel compelled to include the following note I have posted on some Web sites. The last thing I heard about the book was that it has been nominated for a book-of-the-year award…in the category of Business! Holy mackerel!

## Perkins' Confessions…The mother of all mid-life crises

I just read the *Confessions of an Economic Hit Man* by John Perkins. It is a repulsive autobiography, I guess about the mother of all mid-life crises, as the author describes his remorse with the active role he played in a conspiracy aimed at inducing developing countries to incur excessive debts so as to subjugate them and control their natural resources. That individuals could on purpose miscalculate in order to gain benefits is a fact of life, but that this would be happening with malice on a worldwide scale and as part of an American conspiracy is just too much to fathom—and then just sit back.

I haven't the faintest clue whether the book is true or not and in fact I don't care because, in either case, Mr. Perkins needs to be prosecuted. Either by American or international courts for committing fraud and crimes against humanity, or, by the same courts, for seeding that kind of distrust that makes it so much harder for good people to trust good people—a basic requisite if the world is to stand a chance.

Something should be done, soon, before it gains more credibility. The book is already a *New York Times Bestseller* and even though it states that the "World Bank doesn't help them [the poor countries] to defend themselves. In fact, it forces them into this position," on the back cover we read a former lead economist of The World Bank saying that it "succeeds as a wake up call because the reader cannot help but assess his or her role on a personal level, thus providing impetus for change." Pearson ends his book with, "Like all confessions, it is the first step toward redemption." Good for you! But, pal, a rough book tour is not punishment enough!

I have been vociferously arguing against the Debt Sustainability Analysis of poor developing countries which is currently so much in vogue, basically because I feel that debt should always be contracted because it is productive, not because it might be sustainable. Nonetheless, against Perkins' Confessions my arguments do sound hollow and naïve though, come to think of it, I much prefer to live out my life with this kind of naïveté than to live with the cynicism otherwise obligatory. Perkins says he wrote so that his daughter could have a future. So do I—for my daughters and for his.

### *The Constant Gardener* and the UN

Whether the big international medical laboratories are able do their job right or not is clearly an element of that puzzle that will determine whether we are going to live in a livable or an unlivable world. As I see it, we have two choices: we either treat them with much mistrust, bordering on contempt, or we give them some slack and put some trust in their people. That pair of polar opposites explains why I did not feel totally satisfied after seeing, while I was wrapping up this book, that splendid movie The Constant Gardener.

I believe that trusting people to do their best and creating social rewards for good behavior will always, in the long run, produce better results than the constant show of mistrust of an organization that, like a self-fulfilling prophecy, will only result in attracting to it the kind of people of whom we truly need to be suspicious. Boy, does Kurowski sound naïve! Perhaps, but if we can't find the way to bring in more of the spirit of working shoulder-to-shoulder for a good common cause into all our vital organizations, then the world stands little chance of solving its problems, at least as human beings. The United Nations is an example. Don't push it down with controls, lift its spirit instead, and, if you want more control, don't spend too much on the internals but instead open the UN more to the world. For instance, any position in the UN that is filled should leave a record on the Web naming who were the selection commission members, and giving a copy of the résumé of who was finally chosen. We do need to avoid the outright crooks but without falling also into the hands of the smooth operators.

Clearly, if naïveté expels common sense then we are in trouble, but, if it expels absolute cynicism, then we at least are on the right track

### The future very last book about *Harry Potter*

As the books about Harry Potter have meant so much for the upcoming generation and sometimes they even represent the only books it has read, there can be no doubt that the last Potter installment can actually seal this world's fate for a long time to come. J. K. Rowlings, or Jo as we are instructed to call her in her Web page, is someone to watch, very closely. Not that I distrust her, but we should perhaps think about censoring her (discreetly). What will be the lessons she will imprint on her young and not so young and even quite old (like me) readers' minds with her final book? What if she goes haywire? I guess I'll manage it, I hope, but will the young ones?

# My book, Amazon's profits and the value of its shares

I am including below "Virtual Tulipomania in New York City," an article that I wrote in April 1999 for the following reasons:

When I started to write this book in 2004, I fretted over having to invest tremendous efforts in getting a publisher interested and, if successful, then having to negotiate lengthily in order to defend my copyright interests. Then I discovered the existence of some new publishing facilities that allow a rookie book writer like me to outsource. As these new facilities print the book "on demand," there is no need to invest piles of money in printing too many copies that would reflect the author's general sense of optimism and that could only later end up as tombstones in memory of shattered dreams. Well, it so happens that the new-wave publisher I chose was recently acquired by Amazon and as the article has to do with that company, I also found the perfect excuse to include it in the book...for a very worthy reason...that of shameless self-promotion.

As a financial analyst (which is what an economist frequently does for a living) I am especially proud of this article since it evidences how I managed and dared to question the whole dot.com boom, at its peak, just by doing some thinking on my own. Of course, now, with the profits Amazon should expect from its new investment...and my book, I guess that once again the sky should be the limit for them.

One brief note though about these new "on demand" one-at-a-time printing methods. With them it seems that what we know as "editions" first, second, third, will in fact disappear and this might negatively impact book collectors and rare-book stores. Will they disappear?

Not necessarily, since this method could make collection even more challenging as you could view each individual book as an individual edition and therefore be able to improve your collection by moving up few slots at the time, perhaps from the 12.834th to the 235th edition. Whatever, just in case, you better hedge your bets and rush out and buy yourself a second copy of an early edition of this book.

Given that it is so easy and inexpensive to make changes to the book by using this publishing system, we could also have an incredible amount of different editions which might make debates about the book much more interesting—in one, I would write in yellow, and in another, in blue, and so I might finally reach the green I am looking for—by seeding confusion. Then rare-book stores would have unlimited access to rarities.

## VIRTUAL TULIPOMANIA IN New York City

The tulips planted all along Park Avenue were in full bloom in a kaleidoscope of colors as I read that the share price of one particular firm reached the skies in New York. Both things conspired to remind me of a book by John Kenneth Galbraith, *A Short History of Financial Euphoria*.

In the chapter "Tulipomania," we read: "Speculation, it has been noted, comes when popular imagination settles on something seemingly new in the field of commerce or finance." "...by 1636, a bulb of no previously apparent worth might be exchanged for 'a new carriage, two grey horses and a complete harness.'" The value of one particular bulb, the Semper Augustus, would be the equivalent of US$ 50,000 at today's prices! Everyone, from nobles to servants, speculated, cashing in their property and investing in flowers. Capital inflow inundated Holland. "In 1637, came the end."

Now, April 1999, in New York, the share price of a company which initiated operations in 1995, has never registered a profit, has (according to management itself) no short-term possibility of doing so either, does not possess any major tangible assets, and has issued a management report in accordance to SEC rules and regulations in which it makes known a series of risks that would make any investor's hair stand on end, trades at US$ 200 per share, up from US$ 10, only a year ago.

Evidently, the company that I believe has joined the rank and files of the "tulipomanias" sells books through Internet and to conclude as much it should suffice to analyze some of the risks the firm itself has enumerated in various reports.

The Internet is above all else a medium for the transfer of information and in this context, developing technology known as "shopping agents" will permit clients to quickly compare one company's prices to those of its competition. This would seem to presage an eventual but fierce price war, an environment that is not exactly the breeding ground for profits that back the market valuation we are observing. The low cost of entry and the probability that sooner or later some efforts will be aimed at prohibiting any monopolistic controls of the Web are also factors which can make the advantages created by an early incursion disappear in a flash.

All this has nothing to do with the company itself and all that I've read about it makes me believe it is well managed and that it most probably has a brilliant future. The problem lies solely in the market's irrational expectations. The company reported in 1998 total sales of US$ 610 million, a net loss of

US$ 124 million and a book value (assets less liabilities) as of the 31st of December 1998 of only US$ 139 million. Today's market value of the firm, equivalent to the share price times the amount of the shares issued surpasses US$ 33 billion.

Let us now have a look at its potential. Total book sales in the United States during 1998 were worth close to US$ 23 billion. If we assume that a profit margin of 8% would be reasonable, this would mean that there would be US$ 1.8 billion available to reimburse capital invested, both equity as well as debt financing. If we then, for the sake of simplicity assume an overall return of 10%, we can estimate the global value of companies that sell books in the United States in the order of US$ 18 billion. If our company that today commands less than 3% of market share eventually attains a whooping 20%, its value could then reach US$ 3.6 billion. Now double that to take into account the rest of the world and then double that again to take into account of its declared intention of adding other products to its line of products, and we will still reach only about a third of its current value.

As this Financial Euphoria seems to have infected many firms associated with the Internet, I conclude that this must be a modern version of the speculative Dutch tulips. I also conclude that both these and the real tulips thrive in New York in spring.

From *The Daily Journal*, Caracas, April 30, 1999

# The last items in my outgoing tray

**Pray for us, Karol**

The world is running out of the oil necessary to meet the increased demand from growing economies such as those of China and India. Its main economic locomotive, the United States of America, is running out of steam with its huge fiscal and current-account deficits. We are all running into catastrophic environmental problems. Many developing countries are running out of patience with respect to many clear injustices and are looking for radical ways out. Africa's desolation just makes us want to run—anywhere—in shame. No one knows where to run when discoveries of the human race such as the mapping of the human genome generates intellectual-property rights to be exploited by a few. Morally we are all running loose and wild.

What a frightening time to lose one of the very few lampposts that could help light the way out of our current predicaments and teach us how to share. Some of us are panicking, so, Karol, please pray for us.

Your most admiring Protestant

## We must aim higher!

The first of *The Millennium Goals* has us trying to reduce in half by 2015 the proportion of people living on less than one dollar a day and of their suffering hunger. The intentions of that goal are good, and the world needs to support it by reaching a high economic growth, much more equitably distributed around the world. When will we hear more, not only of the individual country's Gini coefficient, but also about the world's? (The Gini coefficient is one of the statistical formulas used to try to measure inequality.) Obviously achieving those goals by just eliminating the poor (genocide), or just splitting up what is currently available, has nothing to do with that goal.

Nonetheless, I feel that we should always remind ourselves to consider that goal an absolute minimum—not only because of humane and civilized motivations, but also because a person earning a dollar a day and not having hunger, does really have very little to do in making a world that is increasingly more interconnected become more sustainable or politically viable.

No! As, instructed by a Chinese proverb, we need to aim to the stars since even if we don't reach them we will at least reach much higher than if we aim at something on our level. In this sense, I believe we need to review all our current efforts, as if the income goal was at least 10 dollars a day or, if it makes you feel better...9.99.

## Afterthought

Globalization is not about how to ascertain the dominance of some tribes, but about finding solutions for all humankind. As globalization contains so many of the elements needed to take the human race forward, we absolutely have to make certain it is not exploited for less worthy short-term causes.

### Might I have gone bananas?
"We don't see things as they are, we see them as we are."
Anaïs Nin (1903—1977)

### Book interruption
I've got to stop here or else the book will never be printed. A book of this nature is never finished; it is only interrupted. That's it...the perfect moment to fade away has to be after putting one idea down on paper and before a new one hits you.

God bless!

Bethesda, Maryland, December 2005

# List of my fellow passengers who also dined at the captains table

AGHA, Tanwir Ali—Pakistan (Afghanistan, Algeria, Ghana, Islamic Republic of Iran, Iraq, Morocco, Tunisia)

ALJAZZAF, Mahdy Ismai—, Kuwait (Bahrain, Arab Republic of Egypt, Jordan, Kuwait, Lebanon, Libya, Maldives, Oman, Qatar, Syrian Arab Republic, United Arab Emirates, Republic of Yemen)

ALYAHYA, Yahya Abdullah M., Saudi Arabia

ASUMPINPONG, Rapee—Thailand (Brunei, Darussalam, Fiji, Indonesia, Lao PDR, Malaysia, Myanmar, Nepal, Singapore, Thailand, Tonga, Vietnam

AUSTIN, Thomas John—New Zealand (Australia, Cambodia, Kiribati, Republic of Korea, Marshall Islands, Federated States of Micronesia, Mongolia, Palau, Papua New Guinea, Samoa, Solomon Islands, Vanuatu)

BAYER, Kurt—Austria (Belarus, Belgium Czech Republic, Hungary, Kazakhstan, Luxembourg, Slovak Republic, Slovenia, Turkey)

BIER, Amaury—Brazil (Colombia, Dominican Republic, Ecuador, Haiti, Panama, Philippines, Suriname, Trinidad & Tobago)

BOSSONE, Biagio—Italy (Albania, Greece, Malta, Portugal, San Marino, Timor-Leste)

BROOKINS, Carole—United States

CANUTO, Otaviano—Brazil (Colombia, Dominican Republic, Ecuador, Haiti, Panama, Philippines, Suriname, Trinidad and Tobago)

DEUTSCHER, Eckhard—Germany

DUQUESNE, Pierre—France

GOMES, Paulo Fernando—Guinea-Bissau (Benin, Burkina Faso, Cameroon, Cape Verde, Central African Republic, Chad, Comoros, Cote d'Ivoire, Democratic Republic of Congo, Djibouti, Equatorial Guinea, Gabon, Guinea, Madagascar, Mali, Mauritania, Mauritius, Niger, Republic of Congo, Rwanda, Sao Tome and Principe, Senegal, Somalia,Togo)

GUADAGNI, Alieto—Argentina (Bolivia, Chile, Paraguay, Perú, Uruguay)

HARADA, Yuzo—Japan

HYDEN, Neil Francis—Australia (Cambodia, Kiribati, Republic of Korea, Marshall Islands, Federated States of Micronesia, Mongolia, New Zealand, Papua New Guinea, Republic of Palau, Samoa, Solomon Islands, Vanuatu)

INGOLFSSON, Thorsteinn—Iceland (Denmark, Estonia, Finland, Latvia, Lithuania, Norway, Sweden)

JONCK, Finn—Denmark (Estonia, Finland, Iceland, Latvia, Lithuania, Norway, Sweden)

KASEKENDE, Louis A., Uganda (Angola, Botswana, Burundi, Eritrea, Ethiopia The Gambia, Kenya, Lesotho, Liberia, Malawi, Mozambique, Namibia, Nigeria, Seychelles, Sierra Leone, South Africa, Sudan, Swaziland, Tanzania, Uganda, Zambia, Zimbabwe)

KVASOV, Alexey—Russian Federation

MASSÉ, Marcel—Canada (Antigua and Barbuda, the Bahamas, Barbados, Belize, Dominica, Grenada, Guyana, Ireland, Jamaica, St. Kitts and Nevis, St. Lucia, St. Vincent and the Grenadines)

MELKERT, Ad—Netherlands (Armenia, Bosnia & Herzegovina, Bulgaria, Croatia, Cyprus, Georgia, Israel, former Yugoslav Republic of Macedonia, Moldova, Netherlands, Romania, Ukraine)

OKUBO, Yoshio—Japan

PASSACANTANDO, Franco—Italy (Albania, Greece, Malta, Portugal, San Marino, Timor-Leste)

SCHOLAR, Tom—United Kingdom

VASUDEV, Chander—India (Bangladesh, Bhutan, India, Sri Lanka)

VEGLIO, Pietro, Switzerland (Azerbaijan Kyrgyz Republic, Poland, Serbia & Montenegro", Tajikistan, Turkmenistan, Uzbekistan)

ZHU, Guangyao—China

# A too long C.V. or a too short memoir, and acknowledgements

My mother Ingrid is from Sweden and my father Tady was from Poland, and I was born in 1950, in San Cristóbal, Venezuela, close to the Colombian border. By the way, if you would end up thinking I am having an adventurous life let me assure you it's nothing when compared to that of my parents.

Sweden: After Venezuela, Sweden is undoubtedly the country that has had the most influence on my life, and I will always harbor an immense gratitude to it. It is a truly amazing country, and I pray its future generations really get to understand and appreciate what it has been able to achieve and why they need and should defend their way of doing it over and over again. I am certain that our best chances for the ongoing globalization of the world to end in something good lies completely in the hands of being able to use Sweden (and their neighbors) as shining examples of roads worthy to follow.

Poland: Even though I do not know it (yet), and I do not speak a word of Polish, I have always felt very much identified with my father's homeland. My third name is Stanislaw, and through it I feel connected to the rebellious spirit and freedom urge of my ancestors. It was indeed one of my proudest moments when I and my daughters received our Polish passports.

The United States of America and I: In a world where everything is radicalizing and so many believe that if you are not 100% for, you have to be 100% against, I need to make a very personal comment about the United States, because I refer to it frequently in this book, given its importance in the world.

My father, as a Polish soldier taken prisoner of war by the Germans, spent five years in concentration camps, from the last of which he was liberated by American soldiers. I was brought up on a pro-American diet and for many years counted To Hell and Back, the 1955 movie that recounted the life of Audie Murphy, America's most-decorated soldier in the Second World War, among my favorites. There is no way on earth that I could suffer from any sort of real anti—United States of America phobia. If I criticize, make recommendations, or observe some things that I believe could be improved in the United States, I always do so as a sincere friend who truly wishes for that much-admired country to live up to those very high standards of which I feel it is capable. And when it doesn't, I am just a much-saddened friend, but never a foe. The United States should not ignore the fact that out there it has many true friends who truly wish it well. It should never confuse them with all those who are plain bootlickers.

Also, if the ongoing globalization is to stand a chance to end in something good for the world, this will also very much depend on the willingness of the USA to do the right things right.

But please, do not let the previous comments confuse you...I am foremost and above all a Venezuelan.

### Young

My studies started in Venezuela, in a kinder at a catholic nun school, with a 3-boys-to-100 girl ratio, unfortunately at a time when I had yet to grasp the significance of this numerical advantage. My primary school happened in a very small—really tiny—Evangelical school in San Cristóbal. Television had not yet arrived to the region and neither had telephones to Palmira, where we lived. My contacts with the outer world occurred, therefore, through radio and books... but so intensively that CNN never really surprised me.

### Youth

From there, at the age of 12, I took off to Sweden to a boarding school in Sigtuna. The school was quite renowned (in Sweden) as their future king of Sweden was studying there. Also, in the closet of my room, Olof Palme, the illustrious and later assassinated Prime Minister of Sweden, had also scribbled his name.

### My Andean Pact Trip

In 1966 at age 16 and a week, I took a summer job on a Swedish merchant boat for four months mostly scrubbing dishes and rust. This trip took me from Europe to South America where I visited ports in Venezuela, Colombia, Ecuador, Peru and Chile. Bolivia did not have a port but luckily for me, as the vessel's name was MS Bolivia, I was able to later argue that it was a full Andean Pact trip. I need not say that this type of summer jobs was not that frequent in my boarding school.

### Academics

Between 1969 and 1971, very fast, two years plus many—many summer courses, urging to get back to Venezuela before the tranquility of Sweden got a final grip on me, I graduated as an economist in the University of Lund.

Back to Caracas, between 1972 and 1974, fulltime immersion at the Instituto de Estudios Superiores de Administración, IESA, and where I earned my MBA, with distinction. Thereafter I started my professional life, with two initial brief and surrealistic experiences:

### Diversifying into the blue

The first, in a local important commercial bank had me going, after just one week, to Panama, to participate in a workshop arranged by their associate, a big international big bank, to discuss the latter's worldwide diversification strategy…Fortunately, it took us less than an hour to agree that no one of us had the slightest idea of what we were supposed to be doing, so we gave up on the intent, and had a good time over the weekend. (I still remember with much fondness a great show, in a very dingy place, by Daniel Santos, one of the long gone icons of boleros, that beautiful lamenting bluesy tropical musical that had everyone cutting their veins…normally because of non-answered love).

### Some weeks of public…disservice?

Back in the bank, after just another two weeks, and I guess because of my Panama experience, my name was put forward as a candidate for the post of Diversification Manager in the Venezuela Investment Fund that was being created to handle the oil income surpluses of the nation. I entered the Fund its very first day, and I left a couple of weeks later the same day my desk arrived, utterly frustrated when the Fund was requested to analyze, and obviously endorse, the economic feasibility studies of a 4 billion dollar investment known as the Fourth Plan of SIDOR, the big Venezuelan iron and steel complex. With an "if something goes wrong with this project the Venezuelans might have the right to hang us in Plaza

Bolívar, and I'm much too young for that" I slammed the door on the public sector...for the following 28 years.

### Riding harvest combines

Urgently back to the real world...although I must say a bit too real for my taste. During the following year I traveled around Venezuela harvesting rice and sorghum, with a fleet of ten beautiful big light-blue combines, all perfectly inadequate for Venezuelan conditions. I got trapped into this when one of the partners in what seemed a viable agribusiness proposal, the agronomical engineer of the group, on the spur of a moment, decided to buy 10 totally untested combines, arguing that by doing so we had won the right for an exclusive representation of that brand in Venezuela. As we were never able to reduce the droppings of the combine to less than 20%, I guess it was pure beginner's luck that we did not combine our problems by using these rights and selling these combines to others. Being that the concept of an MBA was quite new in Venezuela and no one really knew what they were for, least I, the group deemed me to be the right universal tool to get it out of its serious predicament...and so they sent me out as their line manager, all over Venezuela.

### Back to harbor...or new frontiers

A year later, tired of being pursued by angry farmers, I cut my losses, not by far short enough, and with a substantial negative balance (zero assets and a lot of debt) I went to do what an MBA is suppose to do, manage, for big bucks, other peoples companies. In a few years I managed to turn into an eminent financial leasing company expert and even the manager of one. In this I was greatly assisted by the fact that few in Venezuela really knew what leasing was all about... which gave me a lot of leeway.

## Personal blessings

I did well. Not only did I manage to repay my debts but also, most importantly, I married Mercedes. Besides being a wonderful wife and mother, Mercedes is an excellent lawyer with 20 years of corporate experience in Venezuela, recently overhauled with an LLM from Georgetown University. Besides, she also moonlights, for free, as my Spanish editor. To round up this personal paragraph let me say that Mercedes and I have been blessed with three beautiful and most talented daughters, Mercedes, Alexandra and Adriana, and who also, when push comes to shove, stand in as great friends. As the only man in the house, I have been staged in the role of the gentle and good World Bank, while Mercedes, poor her, has to play...and be...the strict IMF.

## Learning how not to bike

I made some splash with my statement of learning how to bike during the debates about using Country Systems. Therefore I believe I should confess here (in an appendix) that my youngest daughter, Adriana, set out to bike with her roller skates on—and crashed (The biking skates on part turned out to be all wrong but this is what I always had believed until I wrote this book). We had to look in the dark for her two front teeth and, instructed through cell phone by my favorite dentist, my brother Sven, I reinserted them. I got it wrong the first time, so I had to take them out and do it again. But, don't worry, Adriana's fine. Her confidence did not take a beating; she stills bikes, but does not rollerblade, at least not simultaneously. As for me, I had the type of experience you just don't really need as a father.

## An intermezzo

From mid 1979 until mid 1980, before the girls were born my wife and I also took a year out in London. There I practiced at Kleinwort and Benson, one of the truly old English Merchant Banks that has since then, as so many others, gone down, disappeared or been diluted, in the oceans of globalization. During this year I also had the chance to attend London School of Economics, as a listener to International Commerce and take the Corporate Finance Evening Course at London Business School. I made some money investing in currency futures...but I got out of it...as I did not see a real win-win opportunity in it...more the contrary.

### Financial brewer

Back in Venezuela, by mid 1980, I signed up as Finance Director for a brewery that was facing serious troubles as their market share was dropping from 30% to 8%, over few months, so fast that it finally could not service, even the first quarterly installment of a huge international bank syndicated loan. The scandal, not of my doing, resulted in the first real Chapter 11 type of proceedings ever initiated in Venezuela for a public listed company, and helped me (and some others) build a small reputation in work-outs.

### At last my niche

In 1983, I had had enough doing just one thing all the time, and so I entered into private consultancy, that allowed me to suggest other people what to do...all of their time.

From then until 2002, I enjoyed 19 years of great and varied experience. In areas of hotels, resorts, industries, hospitals, aluminum, oranges, chemicals, real estate, paper, printing...and so on. Mostly for local clients, but also for some multinationals, some which even led me to negotiate a deal with IFC during the early nineties. I worked mostly in traditional corporate financial and strategic planning and marketing, but I also got seriously into some exotic products such as debt equity conversions. I worked mostly in Venezuela, but also managed to get some interesting assignments in Colombia.

## Mangoes

With the aid of friends, I dappled in some ventures and one of them was exporting mangoes. We actually managed to get into Harrods' delicacy department with our beautiful multicolored and individually wrapped mangoes and we were doing great...until. Our largest individual cost was the airfreight to London, that we had to pay in advance and so when a finance minister woke up in Venezuela and announced, that according to him, the Bolivar was undervalued and then he executivized it from 36 to 24 to the dollar (something perfectly feasible in the short term in an oil country) the day before we were to convert into Bolivars all our British Pounds, he bombed our cash flow. Having to fight against the mosquito in the mangoes or the flight schedules of British Airways was one thing, having also to fight against the ego of a finance minister, was just too much.

## Teaching

For a very brief moment, 1974-75 I taught corporate finance at Universidad Metropolitana in Caracas. Also at IESA, I shared for a couple of years the responsibility of lecturing in International Finance. Teaching has always attracted me but somehow no one ever baited me irresistibly enough. Even nowadays, I still toy with the idea of going back to get my PHD, not because I am truly convinced about it, but because it seems to have turned into an obligatory requirement for allowing you to either teach or research. (Might there be a market opportunity for a University principled on No Ph.D.s allowed?)

## Bank representative

For about 10 years I acted as the representative in Venezuela for the O'Higgins Bank of Chile, later Banco the Santiago... until the Banco Santander of Spain purchased the Chilean bank and globalized me out of a nice and cozy relation. During those years I had the chance of frequently going to Chile and study their real and their not so real progress. While doing so, I had to hear so much hoopla about their social security system that I guess I developed some antibodies that might currently affect how I look on this whole issue. Nonetheless, I do admire many of their other efforts and I wish them all of the best as they are really great people.

### Almost banking

As the Chile representation was almost a sideline, and as the name correctly indicates, mainly a representation, I never actually worked in real banking. That said, I had a lot to do with many banks, developing for some great strategic plans that were never executed, and holding the hand of others in difficult times such as interventions. These close but afar relationships with the banks and their clients, is what inspired me later to set out on my Get-Basel-Under-Control mini crusade.

### Honduras & Guatemala

A friend, Christopher Jennings whom I had met when the company he worked for was trying to get the mandate to operate the Caracas water system and I initially handled this quest, made it to the Inter-American Development Bank. From there he called out for assistance in setting up the financial mechanism of some water projects plus some other tidbits and I will always be very grateful for these opportunities, as they became the looking glasses with which a private sector man like me could peek into the public...and opine. Many of my Central American experiences were made much more enjoyable through the great support I always received from Ian Walker and all his associates in ESA Consultores.

### Writing

In July 1997 I suddenly got the chance to write some articles...and have them published. This turned out to be a blessing. Not only was the writing an escape valve that released the pressure I felt as an unsatisfied citizen in a country with very unsatisfactory showings, but also a very energizing tool as it forced me to get close to what was going on in the world as large. Soon I will have written four hundred articles and I might have a loyal following that, unfortunately, does not always guarantee the inclusion of my three daughters...Daddy what have you been writing about lately?

### Music

I cannot come close to describing my life without including some lines about music. I play the guitar and harmonica...as a totally self-taught amateur...who is at his best when there is no real musician close by as a reference...and I love it. In fact there was a time when my sound engineer (Mercedes, my wife) and I escaped to the Island of Margarita over weekends so that I could play incognito for foreign tourists at a small hotel where I as a small shareholder could exercise some influence. Once after my concert (concert...no understatement there), I was tipped by a German tourist, and I still remember that as a very proud moment...by the way, my sound engineer was also once approached in terms of what she would be doing after she got off her duties. During three consecutive years, I participated in a choir at my alma mater IESA, twice a week, from 6 to 8 p.m....what a lovely way to catch up with life. At the World Bank, to help show that we EDs could also be "somewhat" human, I could not resist Tara Sharafudeen's very insistent invitation to participate in the Celebration of Cultures show with my guitar and my harmonica. Because of logistical considerations, it had to be during an Asian show where I, among a lot of participants from India, sang about Venezuela...I defended the whole mix up by advancing the thesis that India was quite naturally doing a little bit of musical outsourcing to South America.

### And that was when...

In August 2002, the Planning Minister of Venezuela,

Dr. Felipe Perez, a man who, I feel, deeply believes in transparency, local participation…and open systems (Linux), communicated, on the Web, about Venezuela's turn to nominate an ED in the World Bank, asking for candidates. With probably unwarranted but still unchecked optimism, I went for it.

### CV Acknowledgements

There is no way I could write this type of CV memoir without also including my thanks to the rest of my family and some very special friends. First of all Fredrik, my younger brother, who by relieving me of many of the older-brother-duties, helps me to travel lighter in life and also Sven and Karin, my still younger siblings, without whom family would not remotely be family. From my Sweden of so many years ago, I still feel next to me Klas Gierow, Otto Ramel, Lars Henriksson, and Anders Hedborg. Of course there are others from the opposite sex, whom I have not forgotten, but here I am perhaps better off by cryptically referring to a Willie Nelson and Julio Iglesias song. From my professional years in Venezuela there's no way I can get by without mentioning Jose Manuel Egui and Antonio Iszak. And through my years as consultant, what would I have done without my partners in crime, Daniel Boersner and Rafael Lorenzo. Let me also give some special thanks to all of Mercedes' family. Her father, Jose Antonio Cordido-Freytes, a young judge in Venezuela, officially married my parents soon sixty years ago…talk about conspiracy theories…and her mother, Eva Mercedes stands out as a model for the mother in law you all would have killed for.

\*\*\*

Finally I must acknowledge the great help received in putting together this book from my editor in chief, James T. McDonough, Jr., and his personal editor, his wife Zaida. As he wrote his Ph.D. dissertation on The Structural Metrics of the Iliad and among his many editorial credits lists a World Dictionary of Foreign Expressions and a couple of medical dictionaries, I found him perfectly suited to guide me through a globalization book without taking any of my uttering for granted. I let many of his comments be a part of the book without even talking about copyright issues with him. I guess that if we run into some problems, we can both count on Zaida and Mercedes to bail us out.

# Some more blurring details about the MDGs

### The operative targets

**Goal 1—Eradicate extreme poverty and hunger.**
Target 1: Halve, between 1990 and 2015, the proportion of people whose income is less than $1 a day.
Target 2: Halve, between 1990 and 2015, the proportion of people who suffer from hunger.

**Goal 2—Achieve universal primary education.**
Target 3: Ensure that, by 2015, children everywhere, boys and girls alike, will be able to complete a full course of primary schooling.

**Goal 3—Promote gender equality and empower women.**
Target 4: Eliminate gender disparity in primary and secondary education, preferably by 2005, and in all levels of education, no later than 2015.

**Goal 4—Reduce child mortality.**

Target 5: Reduce by two-thirds, between 1990 and 2015, the under-five mortality

**Goal 5—Improve maternal health.**
Target 6: Reduce by three-quarters, between 1990 and 2015, the maternal mortality ratio

**Goal 6—Combat HIV/AIDS, malaria, and other diseases.**
Target 7: Have halted by 2015 and begun to reverse the spread of HIV/AIDS.
Target 8: Have halted by 2015 and begun to reverse the incidence of malaria and other major diseases.

**Goal 7—Ensure environmental sustainability.**
Target 9: Integrate the principles of sustainable development into country policies and program and reverse the loss of environmental resources.
Target 10: Halve, by 2015, the proportion of people without sustainable access to safe drinking water and basic sanitation.
Target 11: Have achieved, by 2020, a significant improvement in the lives of at least 100 million slum dwellers.

**Goal 8—Develop a global partnership for development.**
Target 12: Develop further an open, rule-based, predictable, nondiscriminatory trading and financial system (including a commitment to good governance, development, and poverty-reduction—both nationally and internationally).
Target 13: Address the special needs of the least developed countries (this policy would include tariff—and quota-free access for exports, an enhanced program of debt relief for highly indebted poor countries (HIPC), cancellation of official bilateral debt, and more generous official development assistance (ODA) for countries committed to poverty reduction).
Target 14: Address the special needs of landlocked

countries and small island developing states (through the Program of Action for the Sustainable Development of Small-Island Developing States and 22nd General Assembly provisions).

Target 15: Deal comprehensively with the debt problems of developing countries through national and international measures in order to make debt sustainable in the long term.

Target 16: In cooperation with developing countries, develop and implement strategies for decent and productive work for youth.

Target 17: In cooperation with pharmaceutical companies, provide access to affordable, essential drugs in developing countries.

Target 18: In cooperation with the private sector, make available the benefits of new technologies, especially information and communications.

## The official MDGs' Partners:
Food and Agriculture Organization (FAO)
International Energy Agency (IEA)
International Labor Organization (ILO)
International Monetary Fund (IMF)
Inter-Parliamentary Union (IPU)
International Telecommunication Union (ITU)
Organization for Economic Cooperation and Development (OECD)
Partnership in Statistics for Development in the 21st Century (PARIS21)
United Nations
United Nations Center for Human Settlements (Habitat)
United Nations Children's Fund (UNICEF)
United Nations Development Fund for Women (UNIFEM)
United Nations Development Group (DevLink)
United Nations Development Program (UNDP)
United Nations Environment Program (UNEP)

United Nations Framework Convention on Climate Change (UNFCCC)
United Nations Millennium Declaration
United Nations Millennium Project
United Nations Population Division
United Nations Fund for Population Activities Fund (UNFPA)
United Nations Statistics Division (UNSD)
The World Bank Group's Data and Statistics
International Union for Conservation of Nature and Natural Resources (IUCN)
World Health Organization (WHO)
World Trade Organization (WTO)
United Nations Educational Scientific and Cultural Organization (UNESCO)
United Nations Program on HIV/AIDS (UNAIDS)

# Shutting down

### Keep in touch

Friends, if you've read until here or you just skipped pages and landed here, I must say that I would not like to lose contact with you and so please keep in touch, through kurowski@telcel.net.ve, my www.voiceandnoice.blogspot.com, or whatever other media the future has in store for us. I promise to answer as many e-mails as soon as I can, but please remember that this will not always be overnight.

Absolutely final words!
Accepting full responsibility
(Its fashionable...but I am not really sure what it implies)
### The Buck Stops Here
One final word though. I have, with typical Latin machismo, asserted my fierce independence by making some unauthorized changes to the text, and daring to introduce some paragraphs that my editor Jim is not even aware of. Therefore, to get Jim off the hook, I need to take full responsibility for all remaining mistakes. By the way Jim should

carry his own warning label, since having a really good editor is something extremely addictive. I am now back writing on my own (typing with two fingers)…and I am suffering severe withdrawal symptoms.

# Endnotes

[1] The Organization for Economic Cooperation and Development and that represents a group of thirty countries, most of them developed and rich.

[2] List, F. 1885. *The National System of Political Economy*, translated by Sampson S. Lloyd from the original German published in 1841. London: Longmans, Green, and Company.

[3] Attributed to Johanna, the grandmother of Vilhem Moberg (1898–1973), the author of a famous four-novel series about the emigration from Sweden to the United States.

[4] Mahmood Iqbal, "Are we losing our minds?" in Policy Options, Sep. 1999, pp.34–38.

[5] Tobin tax refers to a very low tax proposed by James Tobin, Nobel Prize in Economics, 1981, of between 0.05 and 0.1 per cent, to be applied on all trade of currency across borders, in an effort to put a penalty on short-term speculation in currencies.

Made in the USA
San Bernardino, CA
26 March 2016